Word 2000
fast&easy™

Send Us Your Comments

To comment on this book or any other PRIMA TECH title, visit our reader response page on the Web at **www.prima-tech.com/comments**.

How to Order

For information on quantity discounts, contact the publisher: Prima Publishing, P.O. Box 1260BK, Rocklin, CA 95677-1260; (916) 632-4400. On your letterhead, include information concerning the intended use of the books and the number of books you wish to purchase. For individual orders, visit PRIMA TECH's Web site at **www.prima-tech.com**.

Word 2000
fast&easy™

Diane Koers

A DIVISION OF PRIMA PUBLISHING

A Division of Prima Publishing

Prima Publishing and colophon are registered trademarks of Prima Communications, Inc. PRIMA TECH and Fast & Easy are trademarks of Prima Communications, Inc., Rocklin, California 95677.

Publisher: Stacy L. Hiquet

Associate Publisher: Nancy Stevenson

Managing Editor: Dan J. Foster

Senior Acquisitions Editor: Deborah F. Abshier

Project Editor: Kevin Harreld

Technical Reviewer: Jim Terry

Copy Editor: Sydney Jones

Interior Layout: Marian Hartsough

Cover Design: Prima Design Team

Indexer: Katherine Stimson

Microsoft, Windows, Windows NT, Outlook, PowerPoint, PhotoDraw, MSN, and FrontPage are trademarks or registered trademarks of Microsoft Corporation.

Important: If you have problems installing or running Microsoft Word, go to Microsoft's Web site at **www.microsoft.com**. Prima Publishing cannot provide software support.

Prima Publishing and the author have attempted throughout this book to distinguish proprietary trademarks from descriptive terms by following the capitalization style used by the manufacturer.

Information contained in this book has been obtained by Prima Publishing from sources believed to be reliable. However, because of the possibility of human or mechanical error by our sources, Prima Publishing, or others, the Publisher does not guarantee the accuracy, adequacy, or completeness of any information and is not responsible for any errors or omissions or the results obtained from the use of such information. Readers should be particularly aware of the fact that the Internet is an ever-changing entity. Some facts may have changed since this book went to press.

ISBN: 0-7615-1402-3
Library of Congress Catalog Card Number: 98-68247
Printed in the United States of America

99 00 01 02 03 DD 10 9 8 7 6 5 4 3 2 1

To Christopher

You'll always be my sunshine.
I love you and I'm very proud of you.

Acknowledgments

I am deeply appreciative to the many people at Prima Publishing who worked on this book. Thank you for all the time you gave and for your assistance.

To Debbie Abshier for the opportunity to write this book and her confidence in me. To Sydney Jones for her assistance in making this book grammatically correct, to Jim Terry for his honesty in reviewing, and to Kevin Harreld for all his patience and guidance.

Lastly, a big thank you to my husband, Vern, for his never-ending support and big shoulders for me to cry on.

About the Author

DIANE KOERS owns and operates All Business Service, a software training and consulting business formed in 1988 that services the central Indiana area. Her area of expertise has long been in the word processing, spreadsheet, and graphics area of computing as well as providing training and support for Peachtree Accounting software. Diane's authoring experience includes Prima's *Lotus 1-2-3 97 Fast & Easy, WordPerfect 8 Fast & Easy, Windows 98 Fast & Easy, SmartSuite Millenium Fast & Easy* and *Works 4.5 Fast & Easy* and has co-authored Prima's *Essential Windows 98*. She has also developed and written software training manuals for her clients' use.

Active in church and civic activities, Diane enjoys spending her free time traveling and playing with her grandson and her three Yorkshire Terriers.

Contents at a Glance

Contents

PART IV
USING TABLES, CHARTS, AND COLUMNS 165

Introduction

This new Fast & Easy book from Prima Publishing will help you use the many and varied features of one of Microsoft's most popular products—Microsoft Word.

Microsoft Word is a powerful word processing program that will take your documents far beyond what you can produce with a typewriter. Whether you want to create a simple letter to a friend, produce a newsletter for a professional organization, or even write a complicated, multi-page report containing graphics and tables with numerical data, you will find the information that you need to quickly and easily get the job done in the *Word 2000 Fast & Easy* guide.

This book uses a step-by-step approach with illustrations of what you will see on your screen, linked with instructions for the next mouse movements or keyboard operations to complete your task. Computer terms and phrases are clearly explained in non-technical language, and expert tips and shortcuts help you produce professional-quality documents.

Word 2000 Fast & Easy provides the tools you need to successfully tackle the potentially overwhelming challenge of learning to use Microsoft Word. Whether you are a novice user or an experienced professional, you will be able to quickly tap into the program's user-friendly integrated design and feature-rich environment.

Who Should Read This Book?

The easy-to-follow, highly visual nature of this book makes it the perfect learning tool for a beginning computer user. However, it is also ideal for those who are new to this version of Microsoft Word, or those who feel comfortable with computers and software, but have never used a word processing program before.

In addition, anyone using a software application always needs an occasional reminder about the steps required to perform a particular task. By using *Word 2000 Fast & Easy*, any level of user can look up steps for a task quickly without having to plow through pages of descriptions.

In short, this book can be used by the beginning-to-intermediate computer user as a learning tool or as a step-by-step task reference.

Added Advice to Make You a Pro

You'll notice that this book uses steps and keeps explanations to a minimum to help you learn faster. Included in the book are a few elements that provide some additional comments to help you master the program, without encumbering your progress through the steps:

- **Tips** often offer shortcuts when performing an action, or a hint about a feature that might make your work in Word quicker and easier.
- **Notes** give you a bit of background or additional information about a feature, or advice about how to use the feature in your day-to-day activities.

In addition, two helpful appendixes will give you additional tips on installing Microsoft Word and working with shortcut key combinations.

Read and enjoy this Fast & Easy book. It certainly is the fastest and easiest way to learn Microsoft Word 2000.

PART I

Creating Your First Document

1

Getting Started with Word 2000

If this is your first opportunity to use Word, you may be a little intimidated by the vast array of buttons and icons on the opening screen. Just remember that although Word is a powerful program, it's also easy to use, which is why many businesses have adopted it. Don't worry! You'll be creating your first document after just a couple of mouse clicks. In this chapter, you'll learn how to:

- Start Word 2000
- Use toolbars and menus
- Make selections in dialog boxes
- Enter text and move around the screen

Starting Word

Microsoft Word appears as an icon on the Programs menu of the Start button.

1. **Click** on the **Start button**. A pop-up menu will appear.

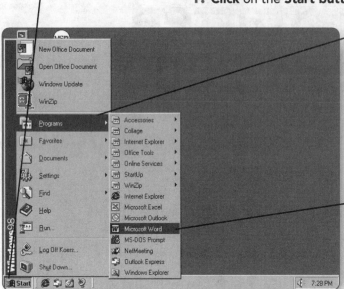

2. **Move** your **mouse pointer** up to **Programs**. Another pop-up menu will appear.

3. **Move** your **mouse pointer** to the right and down **to Microsoft Word**. Microsoft Word will be highlighted.

4. **Click** on **Microsoft Word**. The Welcome to Word screen will appear briefly before the main Word window appears.

Discovering the Word Screen

The Word screen includes a variety of items:

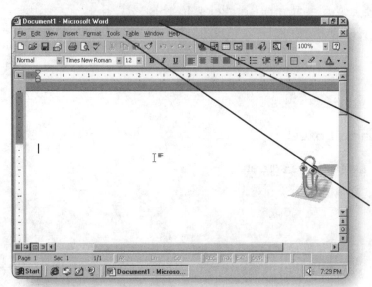

- **Title bar**—A bar displayed at the top of a document that displays the name of the current document.

- **Menu bar**—A grouping of all available features in the Microsoft Word program.

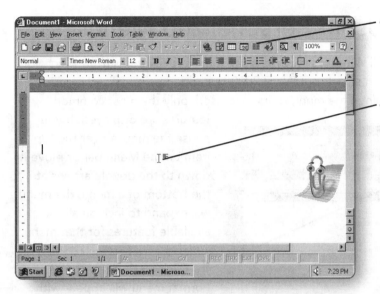

- **Toolbars**—A selection of commonly used features. A single click on a toolbar item activates the feature.

- **Mouse pointer**—The mouse pointer, which will change as it moves to different locations on the screen.

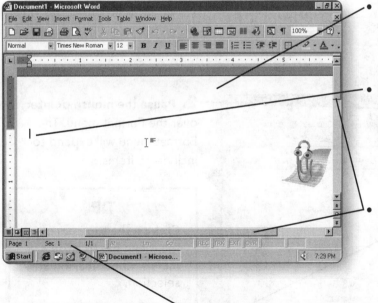

- **Document screen**—The white area of the screen where the actual text will appear.

- **Insertion point**—The blinking vertical line in the document screen that indicates where text will appear when you begin typing.

- **Scroll bars**—Horizontal and vertical bars on the bottom and right side of the screen that allow you to see more of a document.

- **Status bar**—A bar at the bottom of the screen indicating document information such as the current page or the location of the insertion point.

Using Personalized Menus

All Windows programs use menus to list items from which you can select, but Word 2000 has added personalized menus. When the menu is first accessed, only the most common features are displayed. If you pause the mouse over the top item on the Menu bar or move it down to the double arrows at the bottom of a menu, the menu will expand to include all available features for that menu.

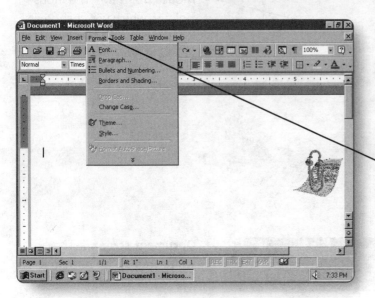

1. Click on **Format**. The Format menu will appear with nine options.

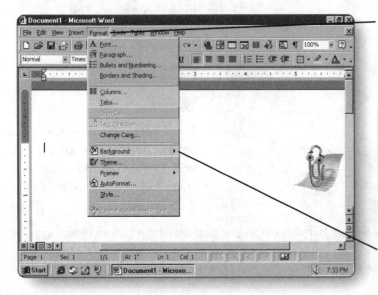

2. Pause the **mouse pointer** over the Format menu. The Format menu will expand to include 15 items.

TIP

Click on the top item of the Menu Bar to close a menu without making any selection.

When you see a right-pointing arrowhead in a menu, it means another menu is available.

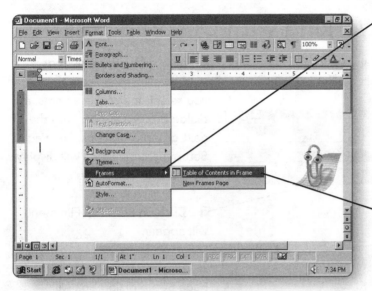

3. Move the **mouse pointer** down the first menu until the item with the arrow is highlighted. A second menu will appear.

4. Move the **mouse pointer** to the right of your selection. The selection will be highlighted.

5. Click on the **selection**. The feature associated with that menu item will be activated.

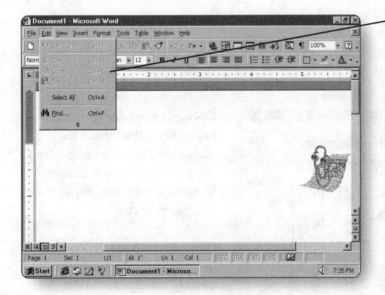

Some options in the menu may appear dimmed, meaning that they are not available at this time. You probably need to open a document or select text before you can use items that are dimmed.

Working with Dialog Boxes

Many selections in the menu are followed by three periods, called ellipses. Selections followed by ellipses indicate that, if you select one of these items, a dialog box will appear with the next group of options. The Page Setup menu selection will display an example of a dialog box.

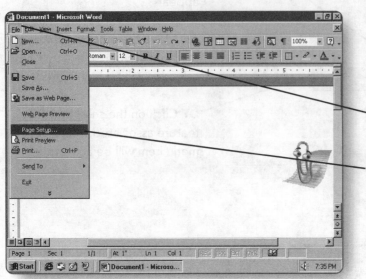

1. Click on **File**. The File menu will appear.

2. Click on **Page Setup**. The Page Setup dialog box will open.

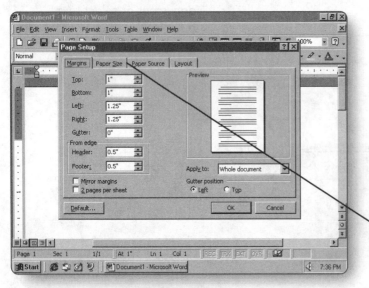

Options have been grouped together by the tabs in the dialog box. In this example, you can select from these groups: Margins, Paper Size, Paper Source, or Layout.

Depending on the dialog box, several types of selections will display.

3. Click on **Paper Size**. The Paper Size tab will come to the front.

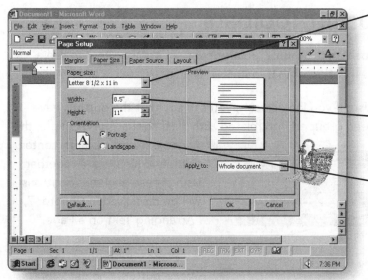

- **Drop-Down lists**—You can select from drop-down lists by clicking on the down arrow and then clicking on a desired choice.

- **Spin boxes**—Adjust numbers by clicking on the up arrow and down arrow.

- **Option buttons**—Select one of the available options by clicking on the small circle (or the words next to it). The selected option will display a small back dot in the circle.

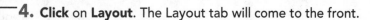

4. Click on **Layout**. The Layout tab will come to the front.

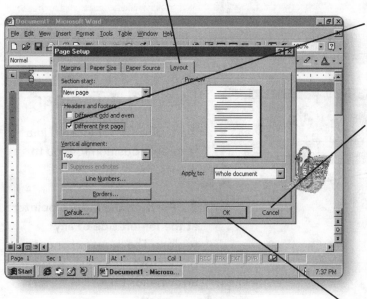

- **Check boxes**—Turn features on or off by clicking on a box to insert or delete a check mark. Multiple check box options may be selected.

- **Command buttons**—Usually indicated with an OK or Cancel button. Selecting OK tells Word to accept the choices you have made and close the dialog box. Selecting Cancel tells Word to ignore any changes you have made and close the dialog box.

5. Click on **OK**. The dialog box will close.

Using Toolbars

Position the mouse pointer over any toolbar item to see a description of that feature.

Also, if you look closely, you can see that the buttons have been grouped into related activities, so that, for example, the Alignment buttons (left, center, right, and justify) are together. Using these alignment buttons will be discussed in Chapter 7, "Arranging Text on a Page."

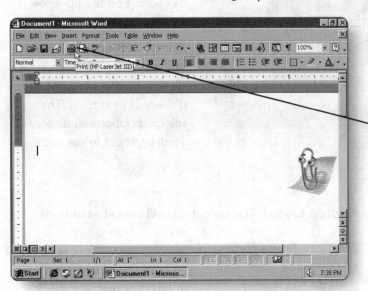

1. Place your **mouse pointer** over a button. The name of the button will appear.

2. Click on the **button**. The requested action will occur.

Moving a Toolbar

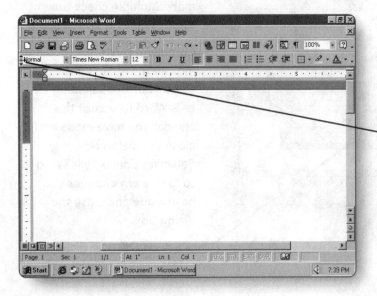

If a toolbar is not located in a favorable position for you to access, move it!

1. Position the **mouse pointer** at the far-left side of any toolbar. The mouse changes to a black cross with four arrowheads on it.

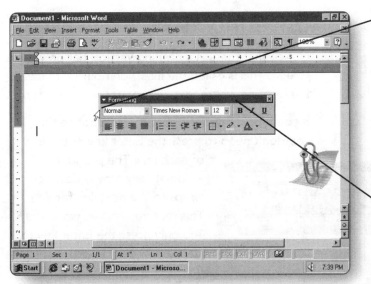

2. Hold down the **mouse button** and **drag** the **mouse** into the document area. The toolbar will change shape.

3. Release the **mouse button**. The toolbar will be moved.

TIP

To put a toolbar back in its original position, press and hold the mouse button over toolbar title bar and drag it back up to the top of the screen.

Turning Off Toolbars

If you find you don't use the toolbars and they are taking up valuable screen space, you can easily turn the display of the toolbars off.

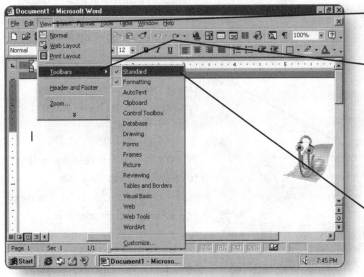

1. Click on **View**. The View menu will appear.

2. Move the **mouse pointer** down to **Toolbars**. The Toolbars submenu will appear displaying a list of available toolbars. Toolbars that are currently displayed have a check mark beside them.

3. Click on a **toolbar** with a check mark beside it. The display of the toolbar will be turned off.

TIP

Click on View, then Toolbars, and then click on any unchecked toolbar to turn on the display of that toolbar.

Entering Text

Notice that there is a flashing vertical bar on your screen. This is called the insertion point. It marks the location where text will appear when you type.

If you type a few lines of text, you'll notice that you don't need to press the Enter key at the end of each line. The program automatically moves down or wraps to the next line for you. This feature is called *word wrap*. You only press the Enter key to start a new paragraph.

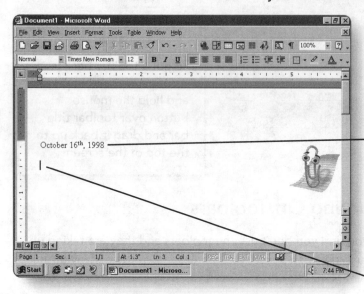

1. Type a small amount of **text,** such as today's date. The text will display on the screen.

2. Press the **Enter key**. The insertion point will move down to the next line.

3. Press Enter again. The insertion point will move down another line creating a blank line between your paragraphs.

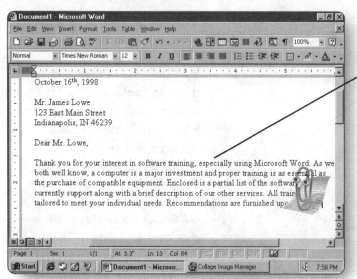

4. Type a **paragraph** of **text**. Don't press Enter; just keep typing until you have several lines of text.

Word's text wrap feature will take care of moving the insertion point down to the next line when necessary.

5. Continue typing text until your document is complete.

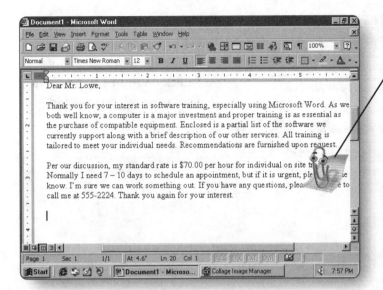

NOTE

Don't be concerned about the entertaining paper clip that appears on your screen. That's the Office Assistant, which I'll discuss in Chapter 2, "Getting Help."

Moving Around the Screen

To work with your document, you'll need to place the insertion point. You can use several methods to move around the Word screen, and Word 2000 includes a new feature called Click and Type.

Using Click and Type

If you prefer using the mouse rather than the keyboard to move around the screen, you can position the insertion point with the mouse and double-click where you would like to enter text.

You'll need to make sure you're using Word's Print Layout View or Web View before you can use Click and Type. Views are covered in Chapter 6, "Working with Pages."

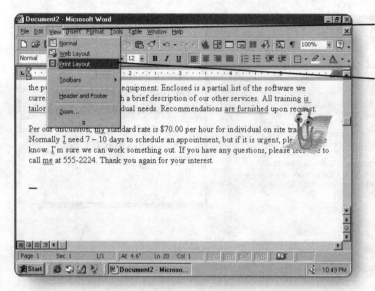

1. Click on **View**. The View menu will appear.

2. Click on **Print Layout**. Print Layout view will be selected.

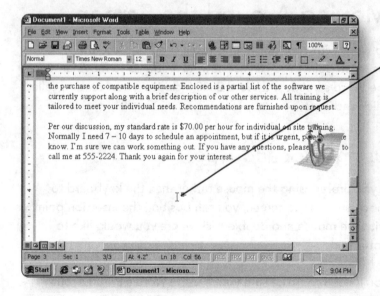

TIP

Before double-clicking the mouse, pay close attention to the position of the lines surrounding the pointer. If the lines are to the right of the I-beam, the text you type will flow to the right of the insertion point. If the lines are to the left, the text will flow to the left of the insertion point. If the lines are under the I-beam, the text will be centered at the insertion point.

NOTE

If the Click and Type feature isn't available, click on Options from the Tools menu. On the Edit tab check the Enable click and type box.

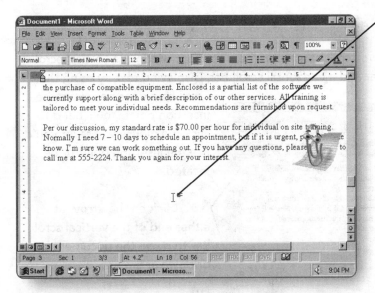

3. Double-click the **mouse** anywhere on the white text area of the screen. A blinking insertion point will appear.

4. Type some **text**. The text will appear at the insertion point where you clicked.

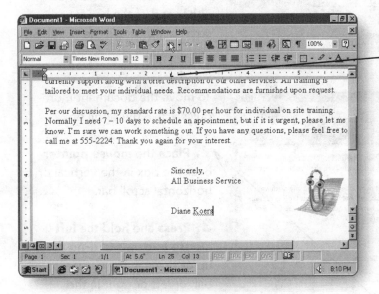

NOTE

Word is actually placing a tab stop at the position of the double-click. Tabs are covered in Chapter 7, "Arranging Text on a Page."

5. Double-click the **mouse** at a different location in the white text area. The insertion point will move to that location.

Using the Scroll Bars

Two scroll bars are in the document window; a vertical scroll bar and a horizontal scroll bar. Displaying text by using the scroll bars does not move the insertion point. You'll need to click the mouse wherever you'd like the insertion point to be located.

1a. Click on the **arrow** at either end of the vertical scroll bar to move the document up or down in the window.

OR

1b. Click on the **arrow** at either end of the horizontal scroll bar to move the document left or right.

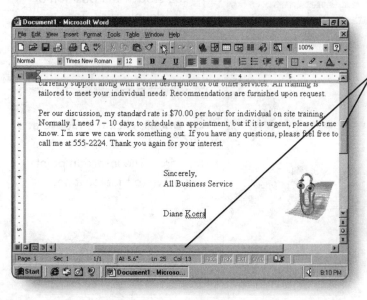

To move the document more quickly, use the scroll box.

2. Place the **mouse pointer** over the box in the vertical or horizontal scroll bar.

3. Press and **hold** the **left mouse button** and **drag** the box up or down in the vertical scroll bar, or left or right in the horizontal scroll bar.

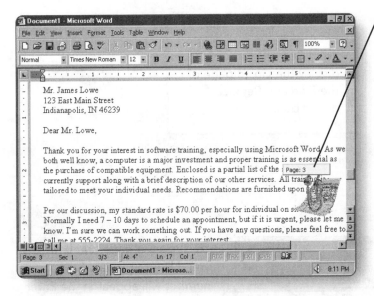

Notice that when you move the scroll box in the vertical scroll bar, if you have more than one page, an indicator box will appear telling you which page you're on.

4. Release the **mouse button** at your desired location. The screen will move to that location.

5. Click the **mouse pointer** in the body of the document. The insertion point will be moved.

Using the Go To Command

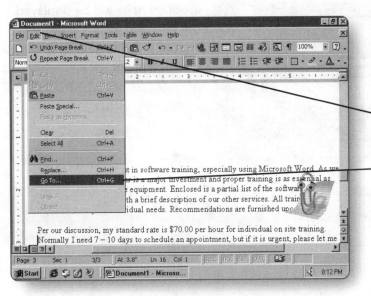

If you have a rather lengthy document, use the Go To command to jump to a specific location in the document.

1. Click on **Edit**. The Edit menu will appear.

2. Click on **Go To**. The Go To page of the Find and Replace dialog box will appear.

NOTE

The Go To command is one of those commands that may not display immediately upon choosing the Edit menu. Hold the mouse over the Edit menu for a few seconds to display the full Edit menu.

TIP

Press Ctrl + G to quickly display the Go To page of the Find and Replace dialog box.

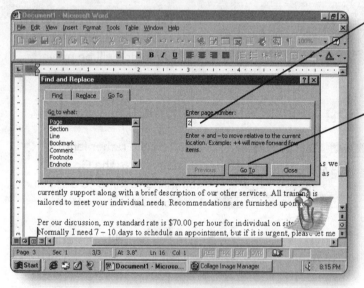

3. **Type** the **page number** you'd like to display. The number will appear in the Enter Page Number text box.

4. **Click** on **Go To**. The specified page will be displayed. The insertion point will be located at the beginning of the specified page.

2

Getting Help

Although you'll find many answers to your questions in this book, sometimes you need additional information. Microsoft supplies you with several types of assistance. In this chapter, you'll learn how to:

- Work with the Office Assistant
- Use the Help menu
- Get help on the Web

Using the Office Assistant

When you opened Word 2000 for the first time, you probably noticed that little paper clip trying to get your attention. That's Clippit, the Office Assistant, Word's new Help feature.

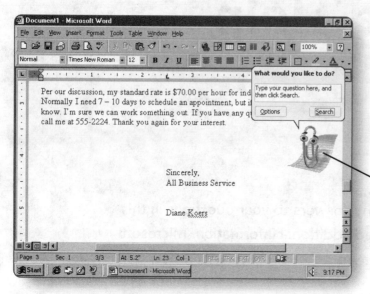

Asking the Assistant for Help

What sets Office Assistant apart from other Word help is that you can use simple, everyday language to ask for help.

1. **Click** anywhere **on the Office Assistant**. A balloon will appear asking, "What would you like to do?"

TIP
Pressing F1 also brings up the Assistant query window.

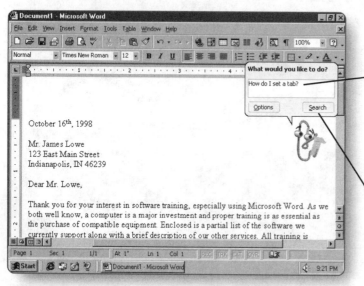

2. **Type** in a **question** or a word or two. An example might be, "How do I create a table?" The text will appear in the white text box.

3. **Click** on **Search**. A new window will appear with more choices related to your topic.

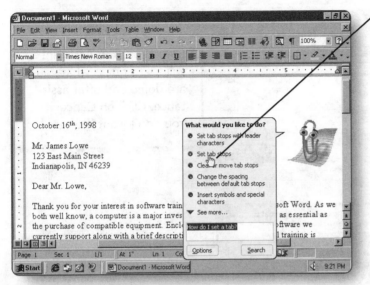

4. Click on the **topic** in which you need help. The help information window will appear on your screen.

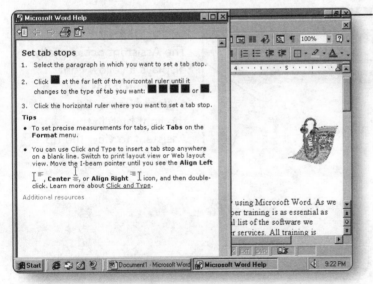

5. Click on the help **Close button** when you are finished reading the help topic. The help window will close and the Word window will return to full size.

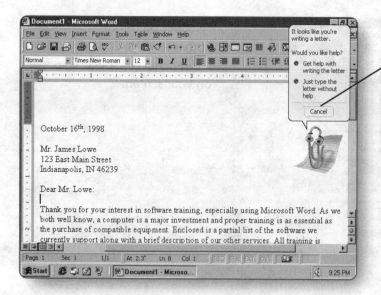

NOTE

Sometimes the Assistant will try to guess what you are doing and offer assistance. Click on Cancel if you don't want the help.

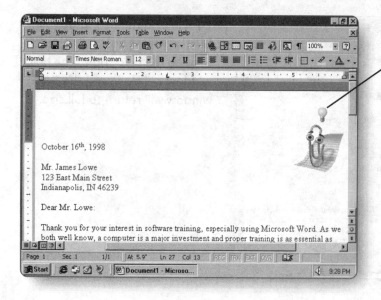

NOTE

The Assistant occasionally displays a yellow light bulb when it has a tip on a Word feature. Click on the light bulb in the Assistant to view the tip.

Having Fun with Office Assistant

Want to see Clippit do some tricks? He may not sit or roll over on command, but he can be quite entertaining!

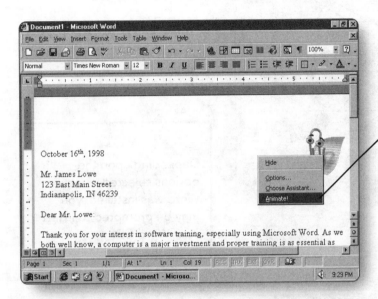

1. Click the **right mouse button** (called right-clicking) while the mouse is positioned on top of the Assistant. A shortcut menu will appear.

2. Click on **Animate**. Clippit will perform some small trick on your screen.

Each time you choose animate, Clippit picks a trick from its library.

Choosing a Different Assistant

Is Clippit, the helpful little piece of metal, getting a little dull or just not you're style? You may be able to select a different icon for Office Assistant.

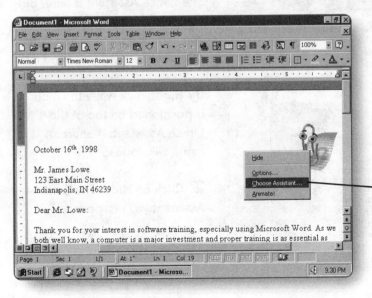

1. Right-click on the **Assistant**. A shortcut menu will appear.

2. Click on **Choose Assistant**. The Office Assistant dialog box will open with the Gallery tab on top.

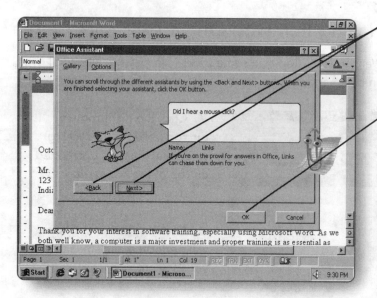

3. **Click** on **Back** or **Next** to view other Assistants. A picture and description of the available assistants will appear.

4. **Click** on **OK** when you see the one you want. The Office Assistant dialog box will close and you'll have a new helper!

NOTE
Depending upon the options selected when Word was installed, you may be prompted to insert your Word CD.

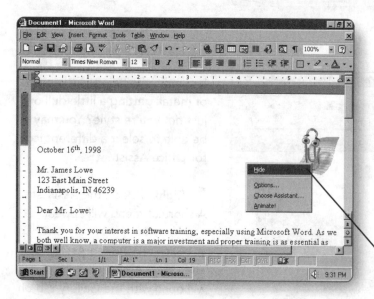

Hiding the Assistant

The Office Assistant is cute, but sometimes it's just in your way. You can hide the Assistant and recall it whenever you need it.

1. **Right-click** while the mouse is positioned on top of the Office Assistant. A shortcut menu will appear.

2. **Click** on **Hide**. The Office Assistant will disappear.

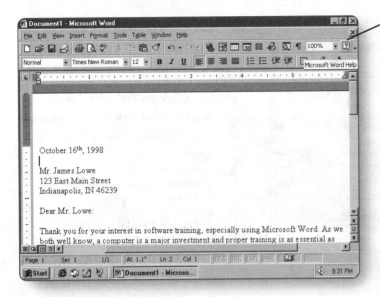

3. Click on the **Microsoft Word Help button**. The Office Assistant will reappear ready to answer your next query.

NOTE

If the Office Assistant is in the way when you are typing text in your document, it will automatically move as your insertion point gets close to it. You can also move it manually by clicking on top of it and dragging it to a new location.

Turning Off the Assistant

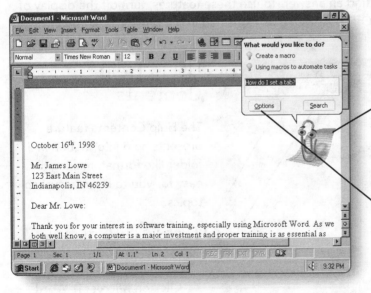

If you find you don't use the Office Assistant and don't want to see it, you can choose not to display it at all.

1. Click anywhere on **the Office Assistant**. The "What would you like to do?" balloon will appear.

2. Click on **Options**. The Office Assistant dialog box will open.

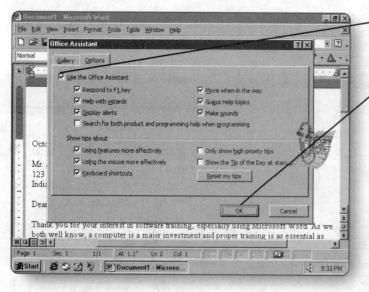

3. **Click** on **Use the Office Assistant**. The check mark from the box will be removed.

4. **Click** on **OK**. The Office Assistant will be turned off until you manually choose to use it again.

TIP

Click on Help and then click on Use Office Assistant to return the Assistant to an active status.

Using Help Without the Assistant

Word Help includes Table of Contents and Index features to help you find an answer. To use these features, turn off the display of the Office Assistant as explained in the previous section.

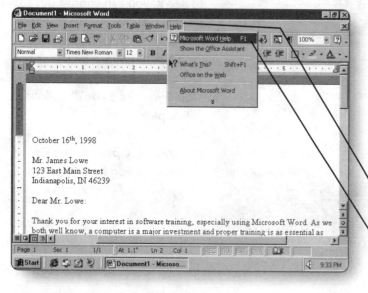

Using Help Contents

The Help Contents feature presents help information in a folder-like format, making it easy for you to browse available topics.

1. **Click** on **Help**. The Help menu will open.

2. **Click** on **Microsoft Word Help**. The Microsoft Word Help window will open.

3. Click on **Contents.** The Help Topics dialog box will open with the Contents tab on top.

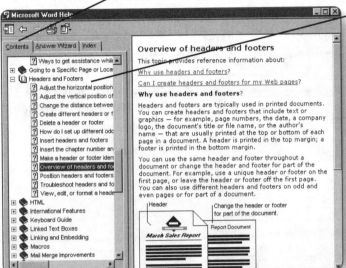

4. Double-click on a **general topic.** The topic folder will open.

NOTE

A *general topic* has *specific topics* and is signified by a red book, whereas a specific topic is indicated by a yellow paper with a question mark on it. Some general topics may have other general topics listed under them.

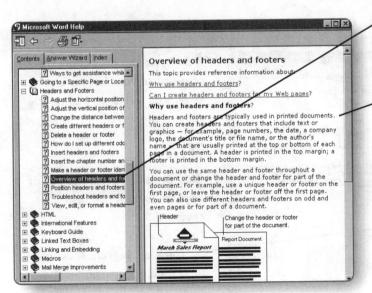

5. Click on the **specific topic** you want to view. The specific topic will be highlighted.

The information on that topic will be displayed in the Help window.

6. Click on the **Close button.** The Help window will close.

Using the Help Index

Word's help features also include an extensive index of topics.

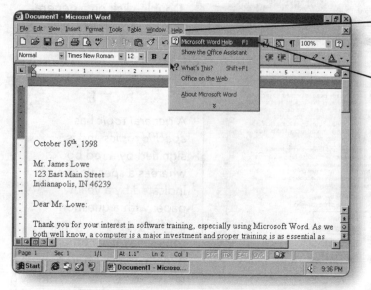

1. Click on **Help**. The Help menu will open.

2. Click on **Microsoft Word Help**. The Microsoft Word Help window will open.

3. Click on **Index**. The Help Index window will appear.

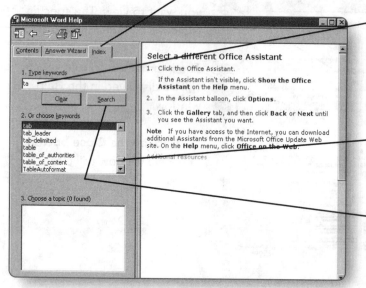

4a. Type the **first characters** or **word** of your keyword. The keywords will jump alphabetically to the word that you typed.

OR

4b. Scroll through the **list of keywords** until you find your keyword.

5. Click on **Search**. A list of topics will appear under the keyword list.

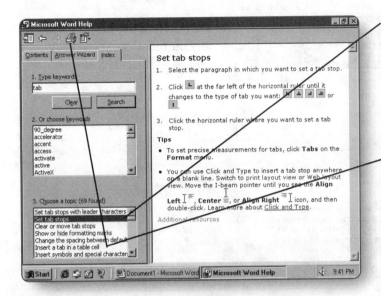

6. Click on the **topic** you're interested in. The information will be displayed in the Help window.

7. Click on the **Close button.** The Help window will close.

Using What's This?

There are so many items on a Word screen, it's hard to remember what each item is or does. Use the What's This? feature to identify the various buttons and components.

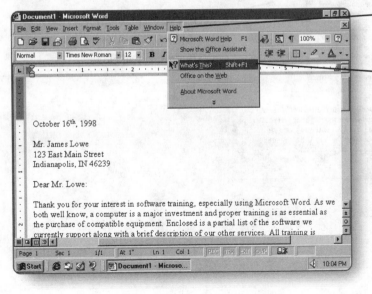

1. Click on **Help**. The Help menu will appear.

2. Click on **What's This?** The mouse pointer will change to a black pointer with a question mark.

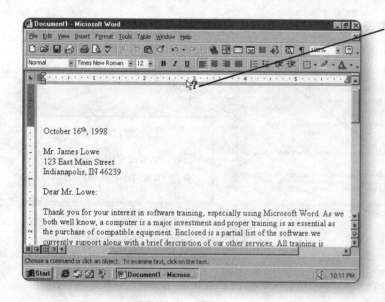

3. Position the **pointer** over any button or item on the screen.

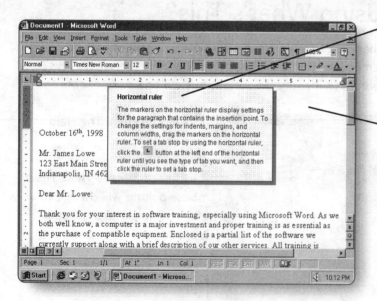

4. Click the **mouse**. A detailed information screen tip will appear explaining the function of the item you clicked on.

5. Click anywhere on the **Word window**. The What's This? screen tip will close.

Searching the Web for Help

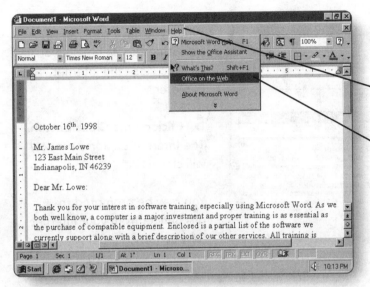

If you have access to the Internet, Microsoft includes some assistance on its Web site.

1. **Click** on **Help**. The Help menu will appear.

2. **Click** on **Office on the Web**. Your Web browser program will launch.

If you are not already connected to the Internet, you will be prompted to connect.

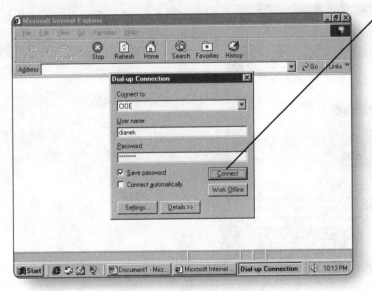

3. **Click** on **Connect**. Your Internet connection will be established and the Microsoft Office home page will be displayed.

NOTE

Web pages change frequently. The Web page you see may not be the same one displayed in this book.

4. Follow the **instructions** on the screen. You'll have access to various help topics.

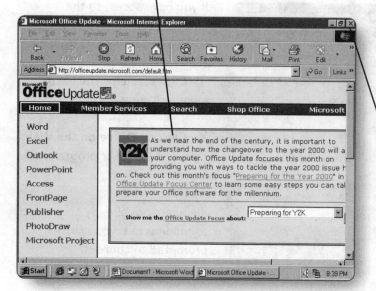

When you have completed accessing the Web help, you'll want to close the Internet Explorer.

5. Click on the **Close button**. The Internet Explorer window will close.

You may be prompted to disconnect from your Internet Service Provider (ISP).

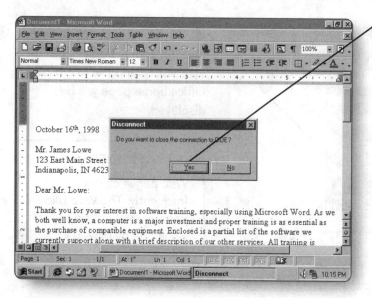

6. Click on **Yes**. The connection to the ISP will close.

3

Saving, Opening, Closing, and Printing

With the adoption of e-mail within corporations and extensive use of the Internet, many documents today might never be printed on paper; they might only exist electronically. However, before you can send these documents into cyberspace, you need to save them. There always will be times when you need a paper copy. In this chapter, you'll learn how to:

- Save a document
- Use AutoRecover
- Print a document
- Create a new document and open an existing one
- Work with windows and close Word

Saving Your Document

Anyone who uses a computer has probably lost data at one time or another. If you haven't been saving to disk regularly, it only takes a few seconds to lose hours of work. Word has built-in features to help protect you against this eventuality. However, you still need to save.

Saving a Document the First Time

When you first create a document, it has no name. If you want to use that document later, it must have a name so Word can find it. Word asks for a name the first time you save the document, and after that, the name you give it will appear in the title bar at the top of the screen.

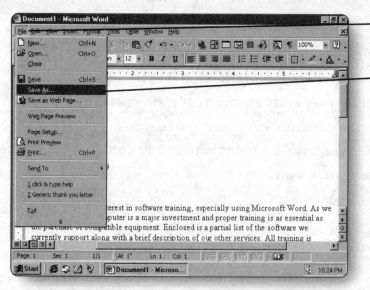

1. Click on **File**. The File menu will appear.

2. Click on **Save As.** The Save As dialog box will open.

NOTE

The Save in drop-down list box lists folder options where you can save the document. The default folder that appears is "Documents." If you don't want to save it to this folder, or if you want to save your document to another disk, you can select another one. Click on the down arrow to browse.

3. Type a **name** for your file in the File name text box. The file name will be displayed.

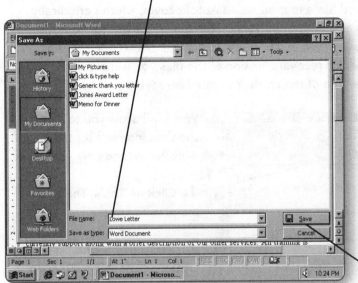

TIP

If you want to save the document with a different name or in a different folder, click on File, then click on Save As. The Save As dialog box will prompt you for the new name or folder. The original document will remain as well as the new one.

4. Click on **Save**. Your document will be saved and the name you specified will appear in the title bar.

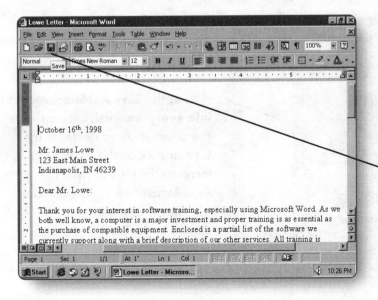

Resaving a Document

As you work on your document, you should resave it every 10 minutes or so to help ensure that you do not lose any changes.

1. Click on the **Save button**. The document will be resaved with any changes. No dialog box will open because the document is resaved with the same name and in the same folder as previously specified.

Enabling AutoRecover

Word has a feature called AutoRecover, which periodically saves a temporary version of your document for you. After a crash, when you boot up and reopen Word, the program opens a recovery version of the files you were working on at the time of the crash. You can then save them.

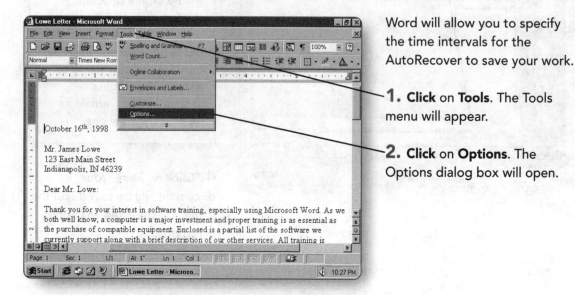

Word will allow you to specify the time intervals for the AutoRecover to save your work.

1. Click on **Tools**. The Tools menu will appear.

2. Click on **Options**. The Options dialog box will open.

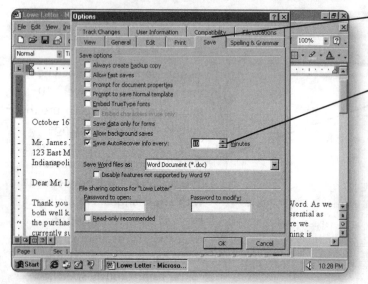

3. Click on the **Save** tab. The Save tab will come to the top of the stack.

4. Set the **Save AutoRecover info every: interval.** Click on the down arrow to decrease the time or click on the up arrow to increase the time between AutoRecover saves. The number of minutes you select will appear in the box.

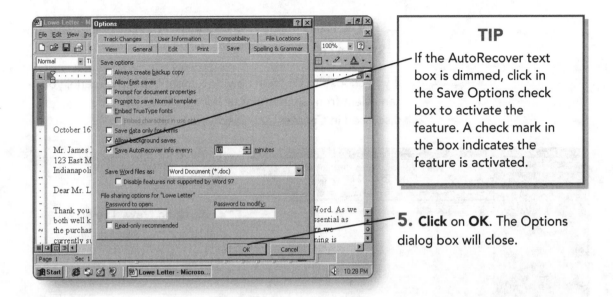

5. Click on **OK**. The Options dialog box will close.

Creating a New Document

When a Word session is first started, a blank document appears ready for you to use. However, during the course of using Word, you may need another blank document. Word includes several methods to access a new document.

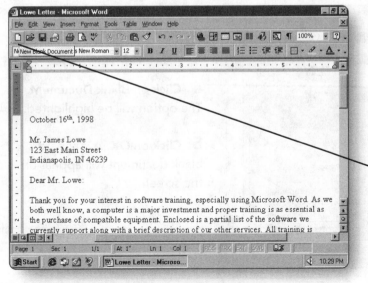

Creating a New Document Using the Toolbar

Creating a new document using the standard Word template is only a mouse click away!

1. Click on the **New Blank Document button**. A new screen will appear with the title Document 2, 3, 4, and so on, depending on how many documents you've created during this session.

Creating a New Document Using the Menu

If you choose to create a new document using the menu, you can select from a variety of templates. Templates are discussed in Chapter 22, "Discovering Templates."

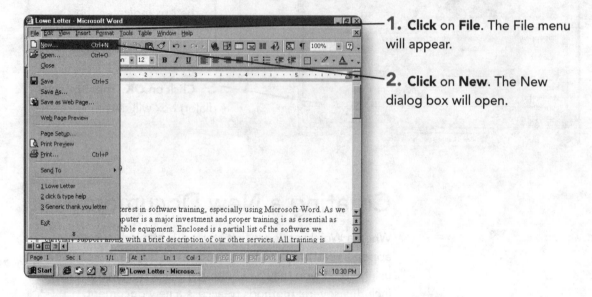

1. Click on **File**. The File menu will appear.

2. Click on **New**. The New dialog box will open.

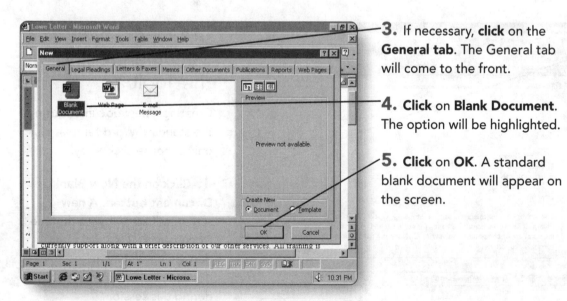

3. If necessary, **click** on the **General tab**. The General tab will come to the front.

4. Click on **Blank Document**. The option will be highlighted.

5. Click on **OK**. A standard blank document will appear on the screen.

Closing a Document

When you are finished working on a document, you should close it. Closing is the equivalent of putting it away for later use. When you close a document, you are only putting the document away—not the program. Word is still active and ready to work for you.

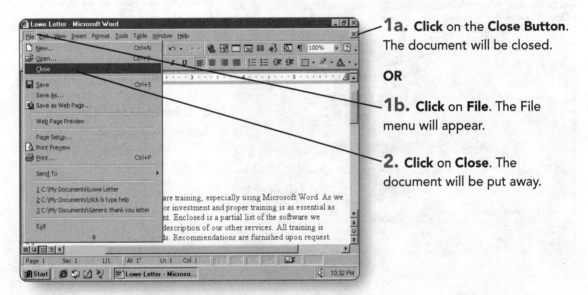

1a. Click on the **Close Button**. The document will be closed.

OR

1b. Click on **File**. The File menu will appear.

2. Click on **Close**. The document will be put away.

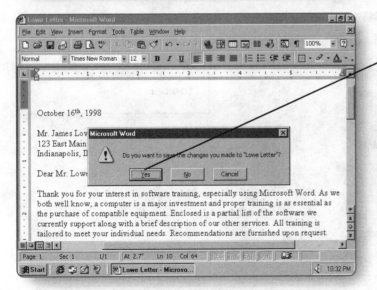

NOTE

If you close a document with changes that have not been saved, Word will prompt you with a dialog box. Choose Yes to save the changes or No to close the file without saving the changes.

Opening an Existing Document

Opening a document is putting a copy of that file into the computer's memory and onto your screen so that you can work on it. If you make any changes, be sure to save the file again.

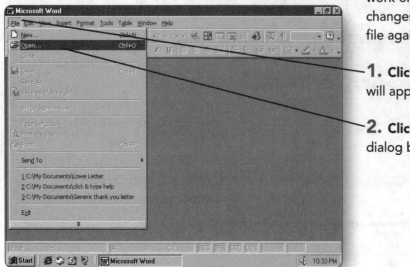

1. **Click** on **File**. The File menu will appear.

2. **Click** on **Open**. The Open dialog box will open.

TIP

Optionally, click on the Open button on the toolbar.

3. **Click** on the **file name** you want to open. The file name will be highlighted.

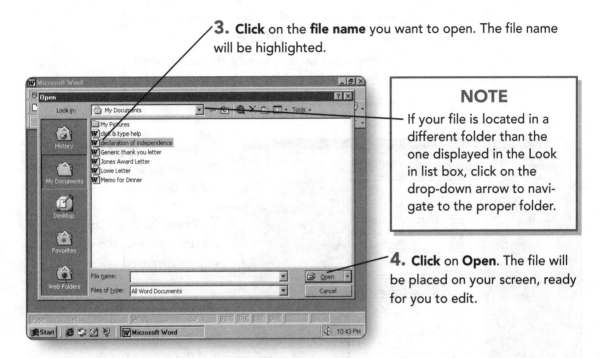

4. **Click** on **Open**. The file will be placed on your screen, ready for you to edit.

Printing a Document

When your document is complete, it is time to print it. You can send it to your printer for a hard copy of the document.

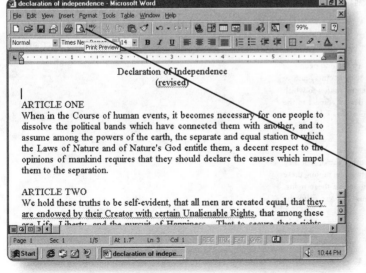

Using Print Preview

Before you print your document, you should preview it full-screen. Previewing a document allows you to see how document layout settings, such as margins, will look in the printed document.

1. **Click** on the **Print Preview button**. The document will be sized so that an entire page is visible on the screen. The mouse pointer will become a magnifying glass with a plus sign in it.

NOTE
You won't be able to edit the document
from the Print Preview screen.

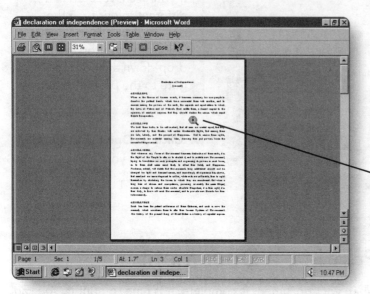

2. Press the **Page Down key.**
The next page of the document
will be displayed.

3. Press the **Page Up key.** The
previous page of the document
will be displayed.

4. Click anywhere on the **body**
of the document. The text will
become larger on the screen
and the mouse pointer will
become a magnifying glass with
a minus sign in it.

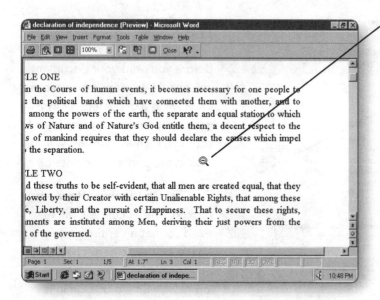

5. Click anywhere on the **body**
of the document. The text will
become smaller on the screen.

6. Click on the **Multiple Pages button**. A selection of available views will appear.

7. Click on the **number of pages** you'd like to display at the same time. The number of pages you selected will display on the screen.

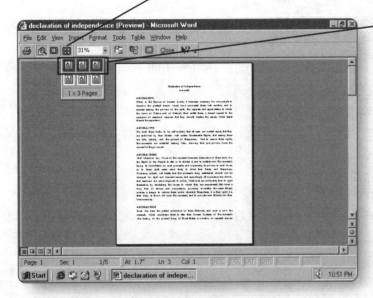

8. Click on the **One Page button**. The view will return to a single page.

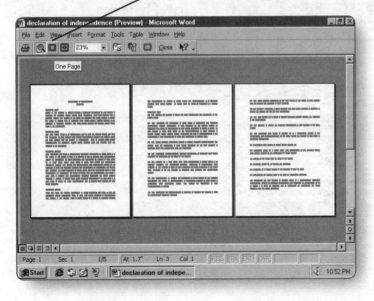

9. Optionally, **click** on the **Print button**. The document will automatically print with standard options.

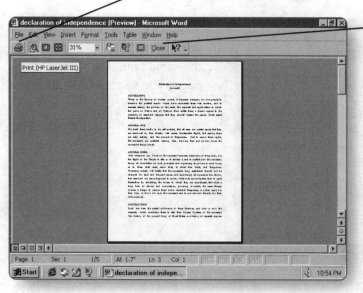

10. **Click** on **Close**. The document will be returned to the normal editing view.

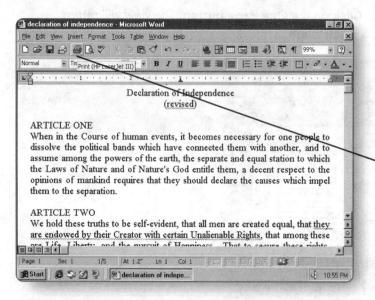

Printing with the Print Button

The fastest and easiest way to print is to use the Print button included on the Word toolbar.

1. **Click** on the **Print button**. The document will print with standard options.

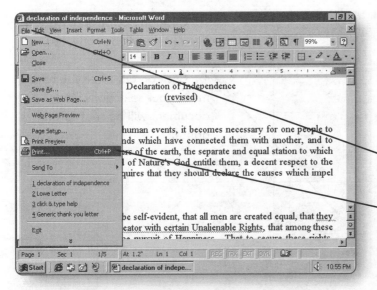

Printing from the Menu

If you'd like more control over the printing of your document, use the Print dialog box.

1. Click on **File**. The File menu will appear.

2. Click on **Print**. The Print dialog box will open.

Many options are available from the Print dialog box, including the following:

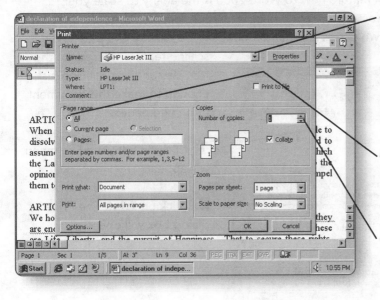

• **Name**. If you are connected to more than one printer, you can choose which one to use for this print job. Click on the down arrow in the Name drop-down list box and make a selection.

• **Print range**. You can choose which pages of your document to print with the Print range options.

• **Number of copies**. Choose the number of copies to be printed by clicking on the up or down arrows at the right of the Number of copies list box.

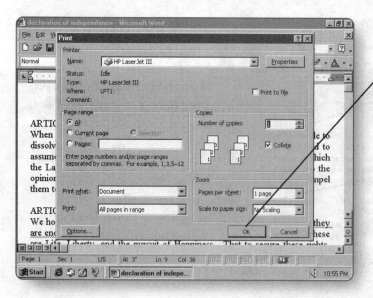

3. Click on any desired **option**. The option will be activated.

4. Click on **OK** after you have made your selections. The document will be sent to the printer.

Scaling Your Document for Printing

A feature new to Word 2000 is the ability to scale your documents. For example, if your document is just a little over two pages long, and it needs to be exactly two pages, the scaling feature will reduce the font size and line spacing just enough to make the document fit on two pages.

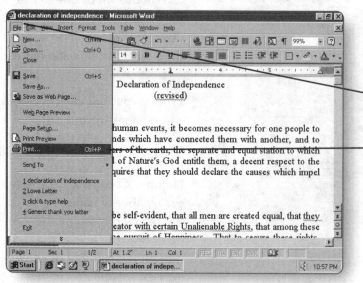

1. Click on **File**. The File menu will appear.

2. Click on **Print**. The Print dialog box will open.

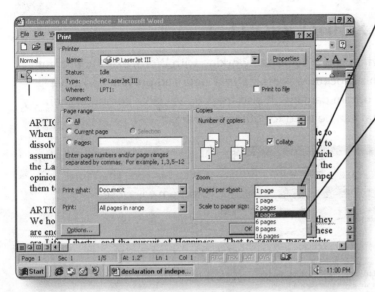

3. **Click** on the **down arrow** in the Pages per sheet drop-down list box. A list of numbers will appear.

4. **Click** on the **number of pages** you want your document to be. The number will appear in the box. In this example, we are scaling a five-page document down to a four-page document.

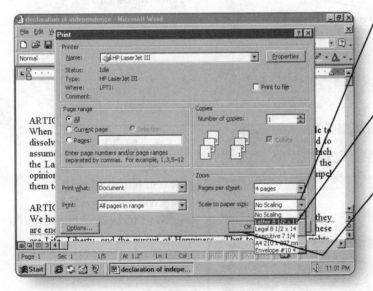

5. **Click** on the **down arrow** in the Scale to paper size drop-down list box. A list of paper sizes will appear.

6. **Click** on the **paper size** for your document. The paper size will appear in the box.

7. **Click** on **OK**. The document will print the number of pages you specified.

Exiting Word

When you are finished working with Word, exit the program. This procedure protects your data and prevents possible program damage. It also frees up valuable computer memory that can be used for other programs.

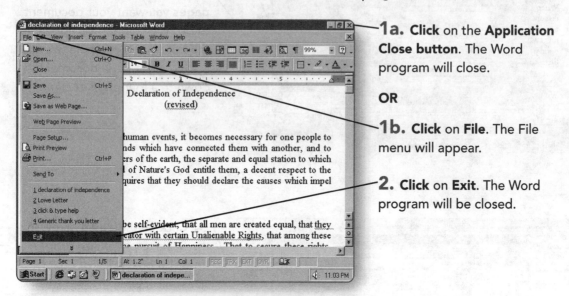

1a. Click on the **Application Close button**. The Word program will close.

OR

1b. Click on **File**. The File menu will appear.

2. Click on **Exit**. The Word program will be closed.

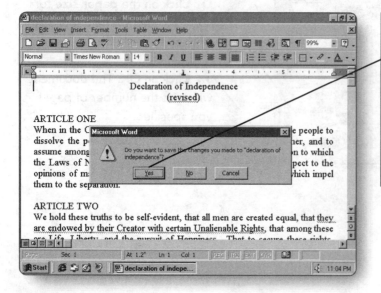

NOTE

If any documents are open that you haven't saved, Word will ask you whether you want to save changes to those files. Choose Yes to save the file or No to discard any changes.

4

Working with Multiple Windows

Word gives you the ability to work with multiple documents at the same time. When multiple windows are active, you'll need a way to manage them. In this chapter, you'll learn how to:

- Split a document window
- Move between open documents
- Tile document windows
- Maximize a document window

Arranging Windows

Word allows multiple documents to be open simultaneously.

Splitting a Window

If you want to see two parts of a document but you can't get them to fit on the screen at the same time, you can split a window. This enables you to view the opening paragraph of a long document in one window while you view the closing paragraph in the lower window.

1. Click on **Window**. The Window menu will appear.

2. Click on **Split**. A gray horizontal line with a double-headed arrow will appear.

3. Click the **mouse** where you want the window to be divided. The gray horizontal line will remain at the location you clicked.

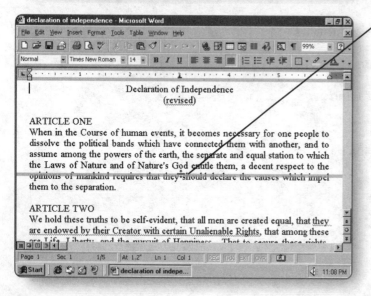

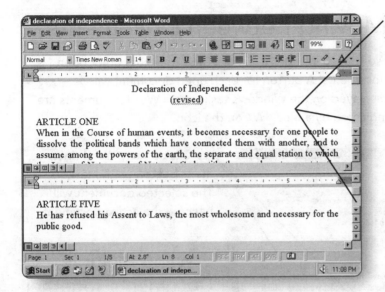

The window will be divided in two—each section having its own scroll bar.

Removing the Split

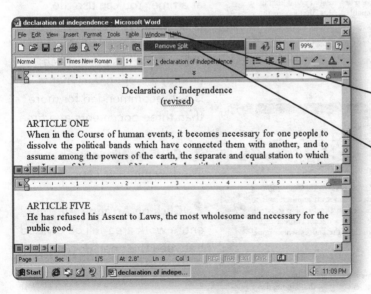

When you close the split, your document will appear all on a single screen.

1. Click on **Window**. The Window menu will appear.

2. Click on **Remove Split**. The split between the windows will disappear.

Moving Between Documents

Word 2000 includes a new method to access other open documents. A button for each open document will be displayed on the Windows taskbar. All Word documents are indicated by a blue "W" on the icon.

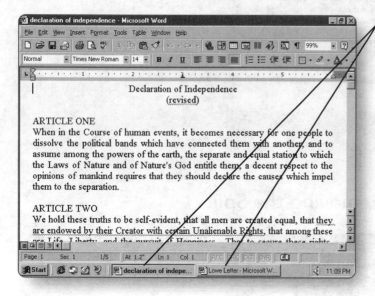

1. Click on any **Word document button** on the taskbar. The selected document will become the active document.

Viewing Multiple Documents Together

Occasionally, you may need to view more than one document at a time. You can use the Arrange All feature to accomplish this. Arranging All will divide the screen space among the open documents. It is not recommended for more than three documents at a time.

1. Click on **Window**. The Window menu will appear.

2. Click on **Arrange All.** The entire work area will be divided between the open documents.

TIP
If the Arrange All command does not appear on your menu, pause the mouse over the Window menu or over the double arrows at the bottom of the menu.

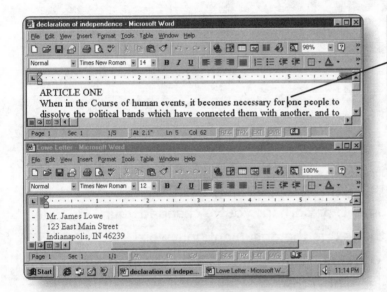

TIP
To edit a document, click anywhere on the window for that document.

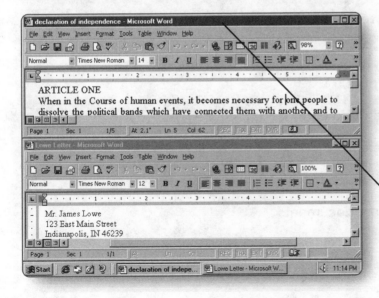

Restoring a Window to Maximized Size

After a window has been tiled, Word tends to leave the window at the smaller size. Use the Windows Maximize feature to fill your screen size.

1. Double-click on the **title bar** of the current document. The window will be maximized.

5

Editing Text

Unless you're a perfect typist, you probably have a few mistakes in your document, or perhaps you've changed your mind about some of the text in the document. In a word processing program, corrections and changes are easy to make. In this chapter, you'll learn how to:

- Insert and delete text
- Select text
- Change the case of text
- Use the Undo and Redo commands
- Move and copy text
- Discover Word's Collect and Paste feature
- Display symbols in a document

Inserting, Selecting, and Deleting Text

Editing text with Word is a breeze. Need extra words? Just type them in. Need to delete words? Just highlight them and press the Delete key.

Inserting Text

Word begins in *insert* mode. This means that when you want to add new text to a document, simply place the insertion point where you want the new text to be and start typing.

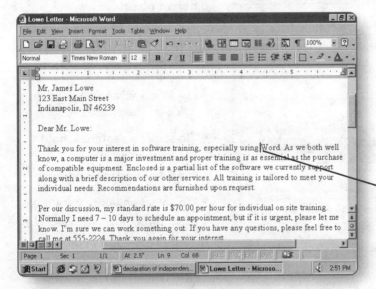

1. Click the **mouse** directly in front of the word in the body of the document where you want new text to appear. The blinking insertion point will appear.

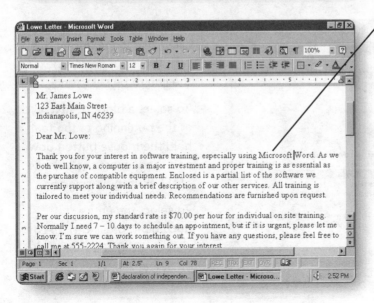

2. Type any new **word or phrase**, adding a space before or after as necessary. The new text will be inserted into the document.

Word will push the existing text to the right and keep moving it over or down to make room for the new text.

Selecting Text

To move, copy, delete, or change the formatting of text, select the text you want to edit. When text is selected, it will appear as light type on a dark background on your screen, the reverse of unselected text. You can only select a sequential block of text at a time, not bits of text in different places.

The following list shows different selection techniques:

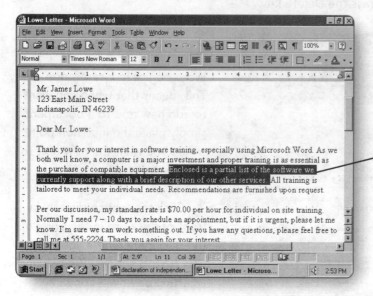

- To select one word, double-click on the word.

- To select a sentence, hold down the Ctrl key and click anywhere on the sentence.

- To select an entire paragraph, click three times (triple-click) anywhere in the paragraph.

- To select a single line of text, click once in the left margin with the mouse arrow next to the line to be selected.

- To select a block of text, click at the beginning of the text, hold the mouse button down, and drag across the balance of the text to be selected.

- To select the entire document, press Ctrl + A or click on Edit, and then click on Select All.

Deleting Text

You can delete unwanted text one character, one word, one paragraph at a time, or any combination of the above.

Two common keys used to delete text are the Backspace and the Delete key. Pressing the Backspace key will delete one character at a time to the left of the insertion point; pressing the Delete key will delete one character at a time to the right of the insertion point.

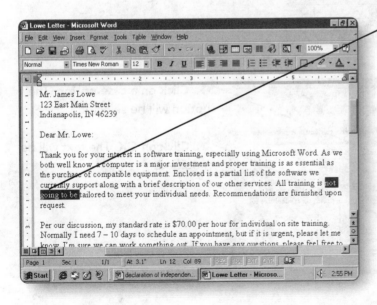

1. Select the **text** to be deleted. The text will be highlighted.

2. Press the **Delete key**. The text will be deleted.

Changing Text Case

When you need to change the capitalization case of text, Word provides an easy way to change it without retyping.

1. Select the **text** to be changed. The text will be highlighted.

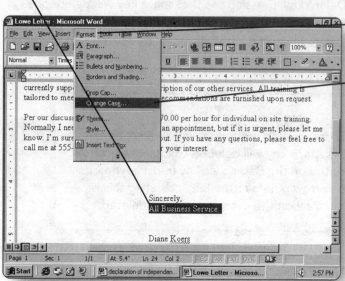

2. Click on **Format**. The Format menu will appear.

3. Click on **Change Case**. The Change Case dialog box will open.

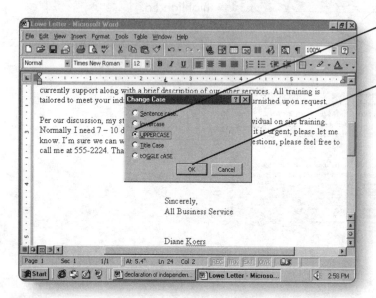

4. Click on a **case option**. The option will be selected.

5. Click on **OK**. The text will be modified.

Using Undo and Redo

If you want to restore text you deleted, or reverse an action recently taken, use the Undo feature of Word.

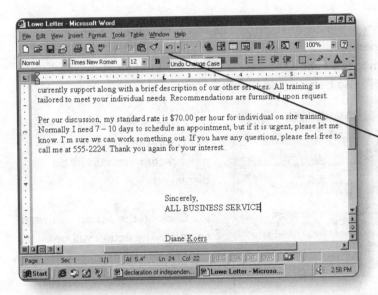

Undoing the Previous Step

You're one click away from reversing your previous action.

1. Click on the **Undo button**. The last action taken will be reversed.

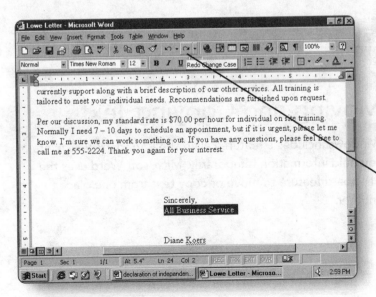

Redoing the Previous Step

If you undo an action and then decide you liked it better the way you had it, choose the Redo feature.

1. Click on the **Redo button**. The Undo action will be reversed.

Undoing a Series of Actions

Word keeps track of several steps you have recently taken. When you undo a previous step, you'll also undo any actions taken after that step.

For example, imagine you changed the case of some text, then bolded the text, and then underlined the text. If you choose to undo the case change, the bolding and underlining will also be reversed.

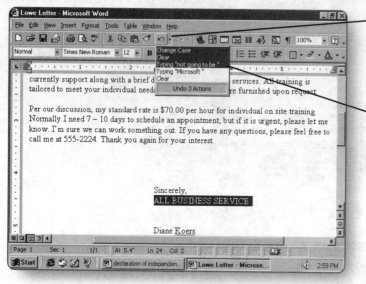

1. Click on the **arrow** next to the Undo button. A list of the most recent actions will be displayed.

2. Click on the **action** you want to undo. The action will be undone as well as all actions above it on the list.

Moving and Copying Text

Windows includes a feature called the *Clipboard*, which lets you hold information temporarily. Microsoft Word uses the Clipboard feature to move or copy text from one place to another.

Moving Text

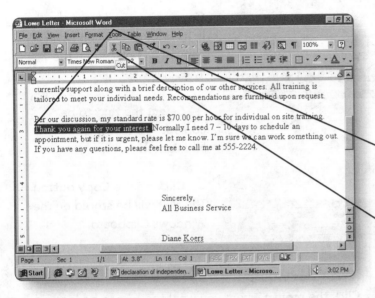

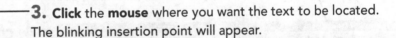

The features used to move text from one place to another are called *Cut and Paste*. With Cut and Paste, the original text is deleted and placed in the new location.

1. Select the **text** to be moved. The text will be highlighted.

2. Click on the **Cut button**. The text will be removed from the document and stored on the Windows Clipboard.

3. Click the **mouse** where you want the text to be located. The blinking insertion point will appear.

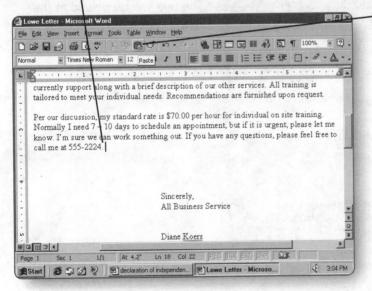

4. Click on the **Paste button**. The text will be placed at the new location.

NOTE

Text or objects placed on the Windows Clipboard remain on the Clipboard even after it's been pasted into a new location. It will remain on the Clipboard until other text or objects are placed on the Clipboard, or until the computer is restarted.

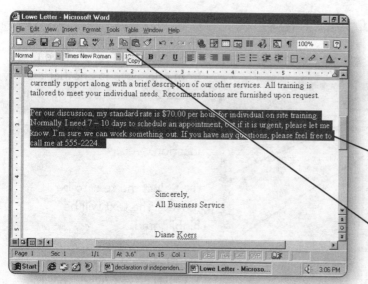

Copying Text

Copying text will leave the text in its original location while a copy of it is placed on the Windows Clipboard.

1. **Select** the **text** to be copied. The text will be highlighted.

2. **Click** on the **Copy button**. The text will be stored on the Windows Clipboard.

3. **Click** the **mouse** where you want the text to be located. The blinking insertion point will appear.

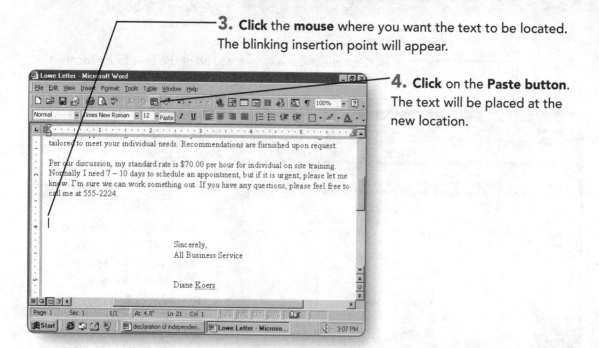

4. **Click** on the **Paste button**. The text will be placed at the new location.

Using Drag and Drop

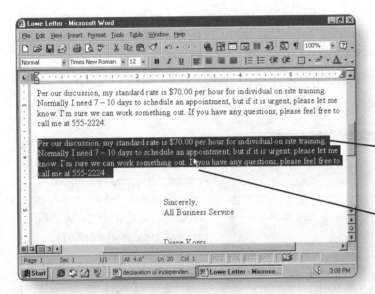

Another method of moving text from one location to another is to use Drag and Drop. The Drag and Drop method works best for moving a small amount of text a short distance.

1. Select the **text** to be moved. The text will be highlighted.

2. Position the **mouse pointer** on top of the highlighted text. The white mouse arrow will point to the left.

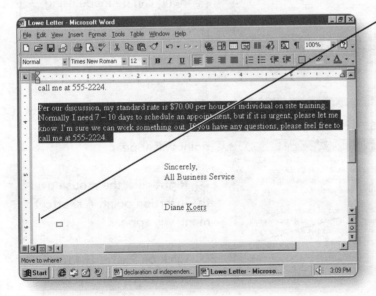

3. Hold the **mouse button** down and **drag** the text to the desired location. A small box will appear at the bottom of the mouse arrow and a gray line will indicate the position of the text.

4. Release the **mouse button**. The text will be moved.

TIP

To copy text with Drag and Drop, hold down the Ctrl key before dragging the selected text. Release the mouse button before releasing the Ctrl key.

Using the Shortcut Menu

A very quick way to use Cut, Copy, and Paste is to access it from Word's shortcut menu. A shortcut menu is one that appears when you right-click.

1. Select the **text** to be cut or copied. The text will be highlighted.

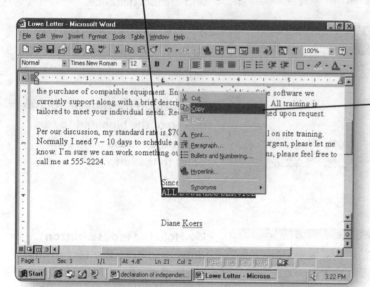

2. Position the **mouse** over the highlighted text and **right-click**. A shortcut menu will appear.

3. Click on **Cut** or **Copy**. The text will be cut or copied.

NOTE
Choices from a shortcut menu can be made using the left or right mouse button.

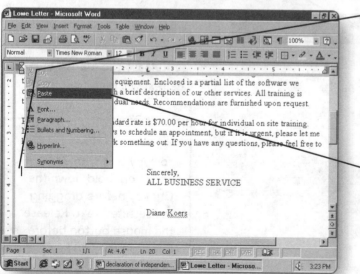

4. Click the **mouse** at the new location. The blinking insertion point will appear.

5. Right-click the **mouse** over the insertion point. A shortcut menu will appear.

6. Click on **Paste**. The text will be pasted into the new location.

Using Collect and Paste

If you want to copy nonadjacent items from one or more documents and place them together on the Clipboard, Word has a new feature called *Collect and Paste* to help you do this quickly and easily. To use the Collect and Paste feature, each item is appended to the Clipboard contents and then inserted as a group in a new location or document.

To use the Collect and Paste feature, you'll need to display the Clipboard toolbar.

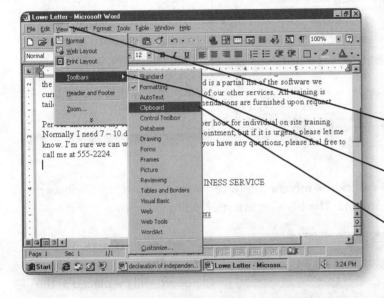

1. Click on **View**. The View menu will appear.

2. Click on **Toolbars**. The Toolbars submenu will appear.

3. Click on **Clipboard**. The Clipboard toolbar will be displayed.

4. Select the first block of **text** to be copied to the Clipboard. The text will be highlighted.

5. Click on the **Copy button**. The selection will be copied to the Clipboard.

NOTE

It doesn't matter which method you use to copy: the Standard or Clipboard toolbars, the Ctrl + C shortcut, the Edit menu, or the shortcut menu.

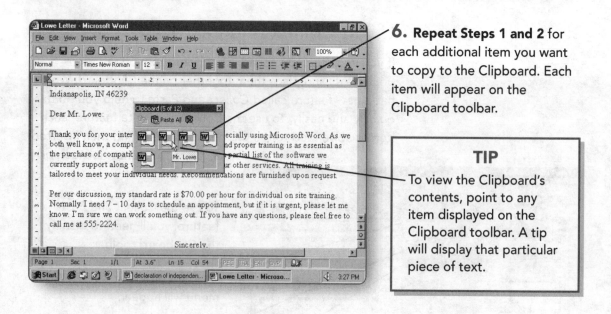

6. Repeat Steps 1 and 2 for each additional item you want to copy to the Clipboard. Each item will appear on the Clipboard toolbar.

TIP

To view the Clipboard's contents, point to any item displayed on the Clipboard toolbar. A tip will display that particular piece of text.

7. Click the **mouse** where you want to insert the Clipboard contents. The blinking insertion point will appear.

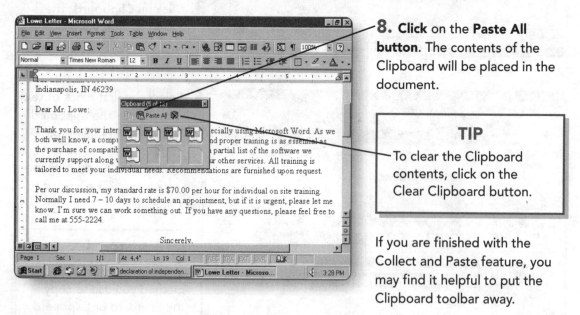

8. Click on the **Paste All button**. The contents of the Clipboard will be placed in the document.

TIP

To clear the Clipboard contents, click on the Clear Clipboard button.

If you are finished with the Collect and Paste feature, you may find it helpful to put the Clipboard toolbar away.

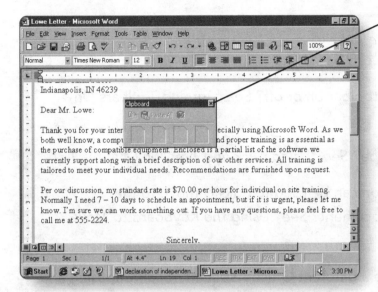

9. Click on the **Close Button.** The Clipboard toolbar will disappear.

Displaying Nonprinting Symbols

To assist you in editing a document, Word can display hidden symbols it uses to indicate spaces, tabs, and hard returns, which are created when you press the Enter key. These symbols do not print, but they can be displayed on your screen.

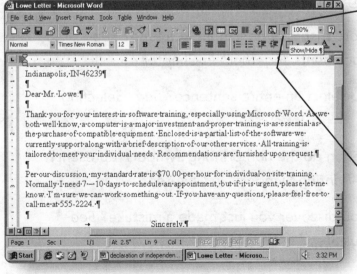

1. Click on the **Show/Hide ¶ button.** The hidden characters will be displayed.

Spaces are indicated with a dot: paragraph hard returns are displayed with the paragraph symbol—¶.

2. Click on the **Show/Hide ¶ button.** The displayed special characters will be hidden.

Part I Review Questions

1. How can you turn a toolbar on or off? *See "Turning Toolbars On and Off" in Chapter 1*

2. What is Click and Type? *See "Using Click and Type" in Chapter 1*

3. What key combination can be used to quickly move to the beginning of your document? *See "Using the Keyboard to Move Around" in Chapter 1*

4. How can you choose a different Office Assistant? *See "Choosing a Different Assistant" in Chapter 2*

5. What is AutoRecover? *See "Enabling AutoRecover" in Chapter 3*

6. Name one reason you might want to scale your document before printing? *See "Scaling Your Document for Printing" in Chapter 3*

7. How can you view more than one document at a time? *See "Viewing Multiple Documents Together" in Chapter 4*

8. What's a quick way to select an entire sentence? *See "Selecting Text" in Chapter 5*

9. What type of information do the non-printing symbols represent? *See "Displaying Non-Printing Symbols" in Chapter 5*

10. What can you do if you discover you just made a mistake? *See "Undoing the Previous Step" in Chapter 5*

PART II

Making Your Document Look Good

6

Working with Pages

Balancing *white space*—the amount of blank space compared to print on a page—is an important aspect of designing professional-looking pages. You can tune white space by adjusting margins and the amount of text you place on a page. In this chapter, you'll learn how to:

- Set and adjust margins
- Change the document orientation
- Select a document paper size
- Insert and remove a page break
- View a document from different perspectives

Setting Margins

Margins are the space between the edges of the paper and where the text actually begins to appear. Word will allow you to set margins for any of the four sides of the document and will also allow you to mix and match margins for different pages.

The default margins are 1 inch on the top and bottom and 1.25 inches for the left and right margins.

Setting Margins for the Entire Document

You can set the document margins before you begin entering text into a document, after you've completed the entire document, or at any time in between.

1. **Click** on **File**. The File menu will appear.

2. **Click** on **Page Setup**. The Page Setup dialog box will open.

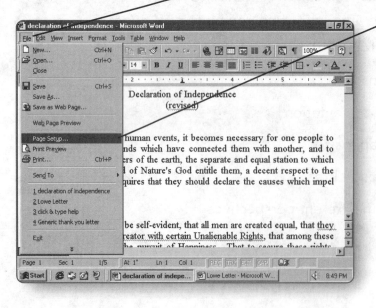

3. If necessary, **click** on the **Margins tab**. The Margins tab will be displayed.

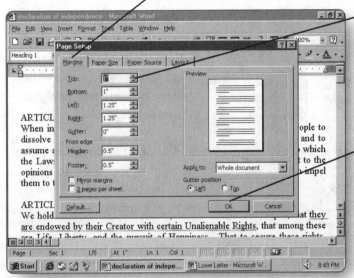

4. Click on the **up or down arrows** to the right of the Top, Bottom, Left, and Right text boxes to increase or decrease the top, bottom, left or right margin settings.

5. Click on **OK**. The new settings will be applied to the entire document.

Adjusting Margins for Part of a Document

Word can apply different margin settings to selected sections of a document.

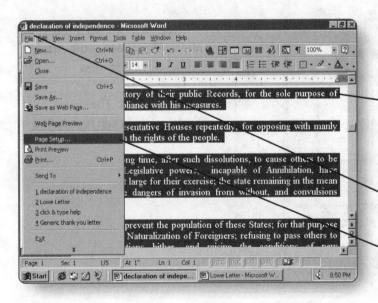

1. **Select** the **text** in the document that you want to adjust. The text will be highlighted.

2. Click on **File**. The File menu will appear.

3. Click on **Page Setup**. The Page Setup dialog box will open.

4. If necessary, **click** on the **Margins tab**. The Margins tab will be displayed.

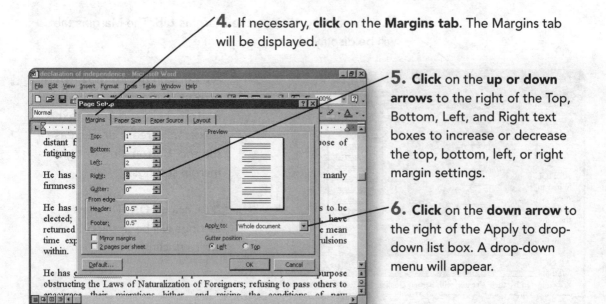

5. Click on the **up or down arrows** to the right of the Top, Bottom, Left, and Right text boxes to increase or decrease the top, bottom, left, or right margin settings.

6. Click on the **down arrow** to the right of the Apply to drop-down list box. A drop-down menu will appear.

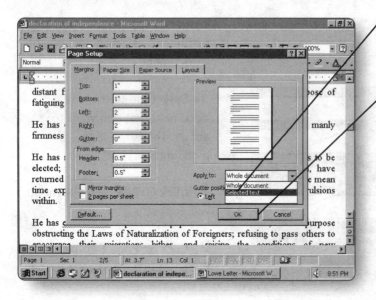

7. Click on **Selected Text**. The option will appear in the Apply to drop-down list box.

8. Click on **OK**. The new margin settings will be applied.

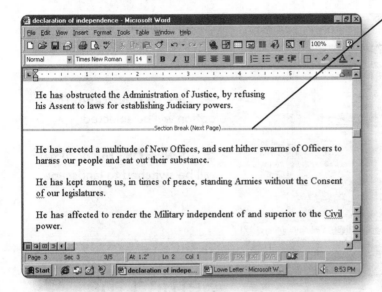

Word will insert section breaks before and after the selected text and will apply the new margin settings.

Changing Document Orientation

Use the Page Setup dialog box to change your document to be printed in landscape (along the long edge of the paper).

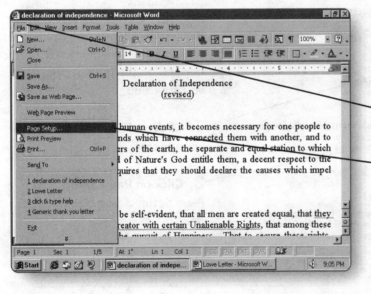

1. Click on **File**. The File menu will appear.

2. Click on **Page Setup**. The Page Setup dialog box will open.

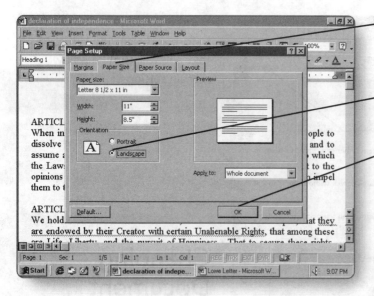

3. Click on the **Paper Size tab**. The Paper Size tab will come to the top.

4. Click on **Landscape**. The option will be selected.

5. Click on **OK**. The document will be switched to landscape.

Setting the Paper Size

Although Word can work with many different sizes of paper, the available selections will depend on the type of printer you are using.

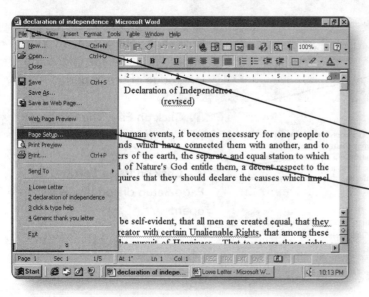

1. Click on **File**. The File menu will appear.

2. Click on **Page Setup**. The Page Setup dialog box will open.

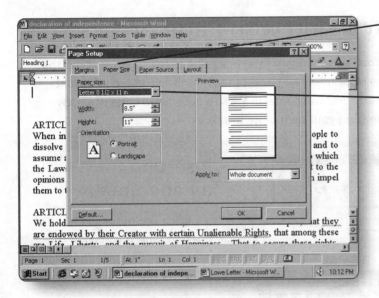

3. Click on the **Paper Size tab**. The Paper Size tab will come to the top.

4. Click on the **Paper size down arrow**. A list of available paper sizes will appear.

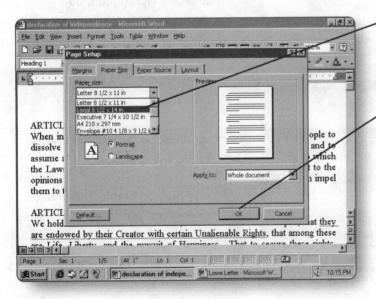

5. Click on a **paper size**. The selected paper size will appear in the Paper size dorp-down list box.

6. Click on **OK**. The Page Setup dialog box will close.

Working with Page Breaks

Word automatically inserts a page break when text fills the page. Sometimes page breaks don't fall where you want them. You can override Word's automatic page break by creating your own page break.

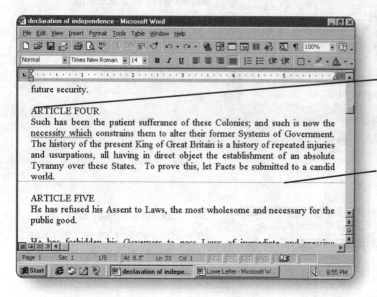

Inserting a Page Break

1. Click the **mouse** in front of the text where you want the new page to begin. The blinking insertion point will appear.

Notice the normal page break location Word would be applying.

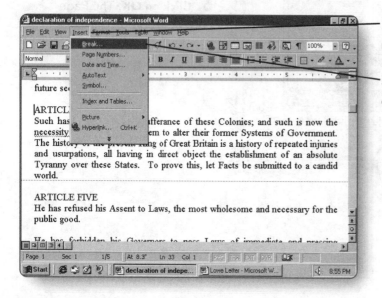

2. Click on **Insert**. The Insert menu will appear.

3. Click on **Break**. The Break dialog box will open.

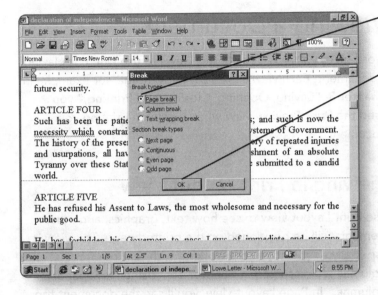

4. Click on **Page break**. The option will be selected.

5. Click on **OK**. The page break will be inserted.

TIP

A faster way to insert a page break is to follow Step 1 and then press Ctrl + Enter.

Depending on which document view you are using, you may see the words "Page Break" along with a dotted line where the new page begins. Document views are discussed later in this chapter.

NOTE

This page break is called a *hard page break* because unlike the page breaks that Word inserts, this one will not move if you delete text above it, adjust the margins, or otherwise change the amount of text on the page.

Deleting a Page Break

Word's automatic page breaks cannot be deleted, but the hard page breaks that you have inserted manually can be deleted at any time.

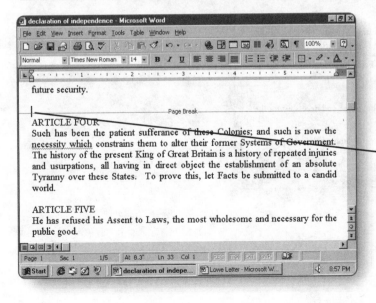

1. Click the **mouse pointer** on the page break indication. The blinking insertion point will appear.

2. Press the **Delete key**. The page break will be deleted.

Viewing a Document

Word gives you several different views to use when displaying a document. Each view has its own advantage; for example, in Chapter 3, "Saving, Opening, Closing, and Printing," you used the Print Preview view when you were printing your document.

Viewing in Print Layout View

Use Print Layout view to see how text, graphics, and other elements will be positioned on the printed page. This view is especially helpful if you are working with text columns. Columns are discussed in Chapter 16, "Using Newspaper Columns." In Page Layout view, you'll see the document top and bottom margins as well as headers and footers.

1. Click on **View**. The View menu will appear.

2. Click on **Print Layout**. The document view will change to print layout.

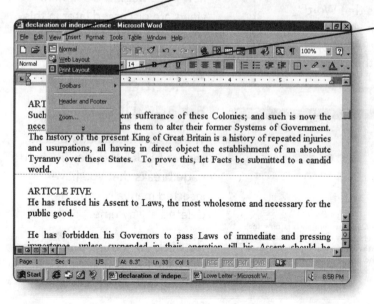

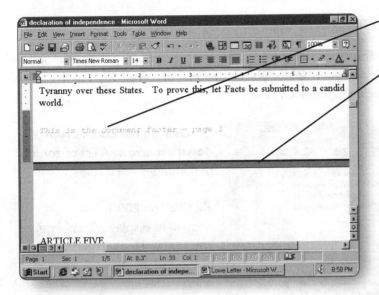

The footer is displayed in a light gray type.

Breaks between pages are indicated by a thick dark gray area.

Viewing in Normal View

Normal view is the default view for Word and is used for typing, editing, and formatting text. It simplifies the layout of the page so you can type and edit quickly. Headers, footers, page margins, backgrounds, and some other objects do not appear in Normal view.

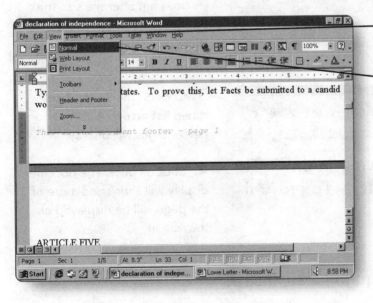

1. Click on **View**. The View menu will appear.

2. Click on **Normal**. The document view will change to normal.

NOTE

Another view, Web Layout view will be used when creating a Web page. You'll be able to see backgrounds and objects as they might be seen in a Web browser. Chapter 25, "Using Word to Create Web Pages," will show you how to create a Web page using Microsoft Word.

Using the Zoom Feature

Using Word's ability to zoom in allows you to get a close-up view of your text or you can zoom out to see more of the page at a reduced rate.

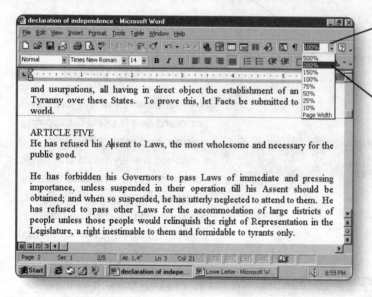

1. **Click** on the **Zoom drop-down list arrow.** A list of zoom percentages will display.

2. **Click** on **200%.** The document display will enlarge. The text will look larger, but less of the overall page will appear on the screen.

NOTE

Using the Zoom feature does not alter the size the document will print.

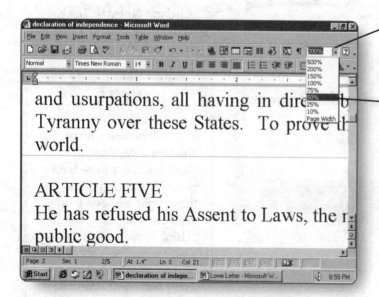

3. **Click** on the **Zoom drop-down list arrow.** A list of zoom percentages will display.

4. **Click** on **50%.** The document display will shrink and more of the page will be displayed on the screen.

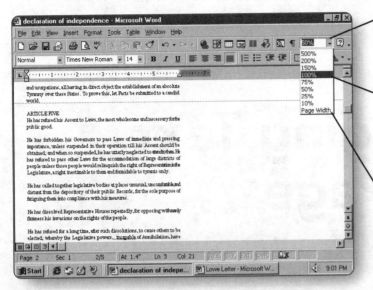

5. Click on the **Zoom drop-down list arrow**. A list of zoom percentages will display.

6. Click on **100%**. The document display will return to normal.

TIP

Setting the Zoom to Page Width can be very helpful if your document page is set to landscape.

7

Arranging Text on a Page

Word includes several features to assist you in placing text on the page just the way you want it. You can align text left to right with tabs or alignment options, or you can adjust your text vertically using the line spacing options. In this chapter, you'll learn how to:

- Set, move, and delete tabs
- Select line spacing
- Center, justify, left-align, and right-align text

Working with Tabs

If you press the Tab key to move across the page, you'll notice that Word has default stops set every 1/2 inch.

Setting Tabs

You can set tabs at particular points along the ruler so that when you press the Tab key, the cursor moves to that point automatically, instead of stopping every five spaces.

1. **Place** the **mouse pointer** on the Tab button at the left end of the ruler to select from the following alignments:

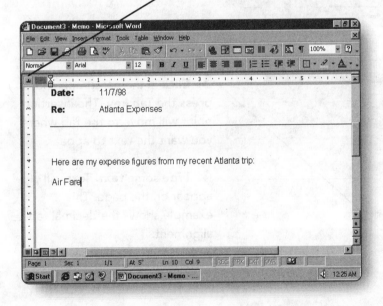

- **Left**. The Tab button is already set to the left tab symbol, an "L." Text will appear with the left edge of the text at the tab.

- **Center**. Click one time to display the center tab symbol. An upside-down "T" will appear. Text will center around a center tab.

- **Right**. Click two times to display the right tab symbol. A backward "L" will appear. Text will appear with the right edge of the text at the tab.

- **Decimal**. Click three times to display the decimal tab symbol. An upside-down "T" with a dot on the right will appear. Decimal points, such as dollars and cents, align to the tab. The decimal tab is selected in this example.

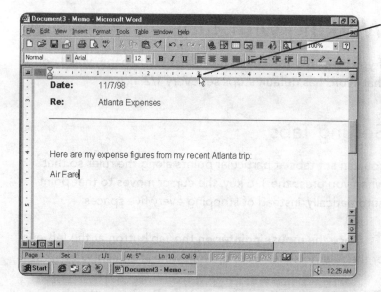

2. Click on the **ruler** to set the tab for the current paragraph or any currently selected text. A left, right, center, or decimal tab symbol will appear in the ruler at the spot you selected.

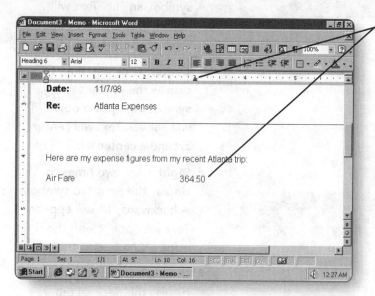

3. Click in the paragraph and **press** the **Tab key**. The insertion point will move to the tab where you want the text to appear.

4. Type some **text**. Text will appear on the page. This example shows the decimal tab alignment.

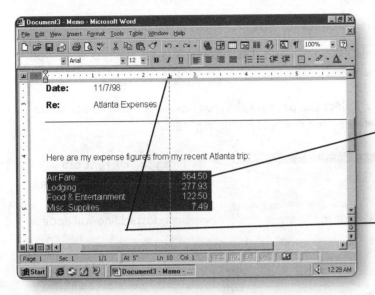

Moving a Tab

If you don't like the position where you placed the tab stop you can easily move it!

1. Select the **paragraphs** that have a tab that needs to be moved. The text will be highlighted.

2. Drag the **current tab setting** to the new desired location on the ruler bar. A vertical dotted line indicates the new tab position.

3. Release the **mouse button**. The tab will be reset and any text will be moved.

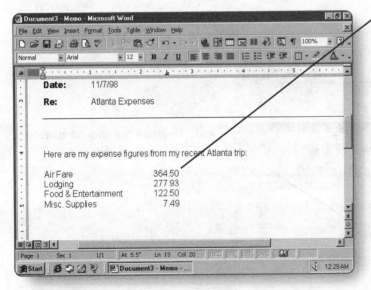

Deleting a Tab

Deleting an unwanted tab stop is an easy process when you use Word's ruler.

1. Select the **paragraphs** that have a tab that needs to be deleted. The text will be highlighted.

2. Drag the **current tab setting** off the ruler, into the body of the document. A vertical dotted line will appear.

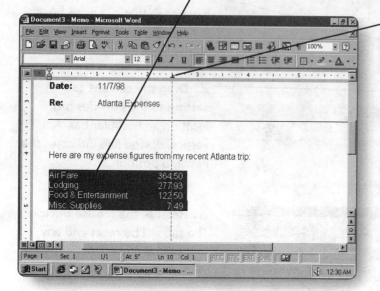

3. Release the **mouse button**. The tab will be deleted.

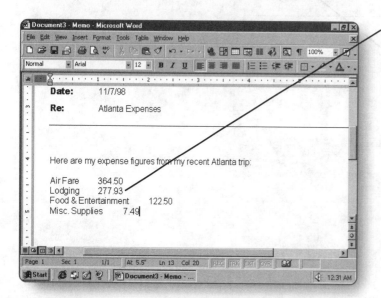

Changing Line Spacing

Line spacing is the amount of vertical space between each line of text. You might want to change line spacing when you want to make a document easier to read, for example, or for a draft so that the reader has room to make changes.

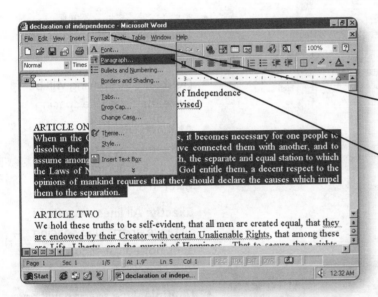

1. Select the **text** in which you want to change the line spacing. The text will be highlighted.

2. Click on **Format**. The Format menu will appear.

3. Click on **Paragraph**. The Paragraph dialog box will open.

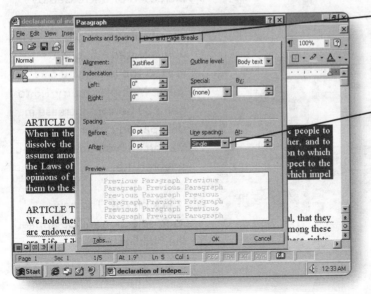

4. If necessary, **click** on the **Indents and Spacing tab**. The Indents and Spacing tab will come to the front.

5. Click on the **down arrow** to the right of the Line spacing text box. A list of options will display.

6. **Click** on one of the following **options**:

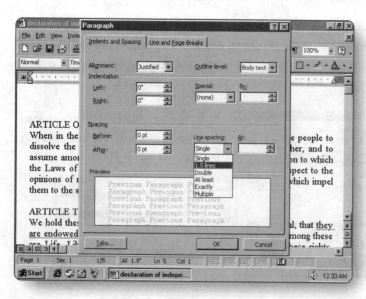

- **Single**: Line spacing will adjust to accommodate the largest font in the line and a little extra.

- **1.5**: Line spacing will be set one-and-a-half times that of single spacing.

- **Double**: Line spacing will be twice that of single spacing.

- **At least**: Line spacing adjusts to the minimum required to include a graphic or large letter in a line.

- **Exactly**: All lines are a fixed distance apart. Line spacing does not adjust according to font size.

- **Multiple**: Line spacing will be increased or decreased by the percentage that you specify. For example, if earlier you selected 1.5, but it looked too large, you can select Multiple and try 1.3 to get a 30 percent increase in the spacing rather than the 50 percent you got when you selected 1.5.

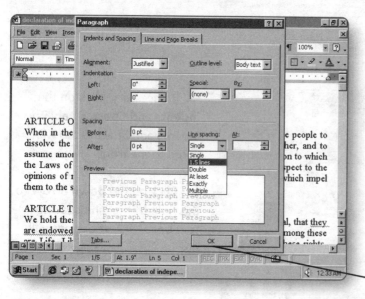

7. **Click** on **OK**. The new spacing selection will be applied to the highlighted text.

> **TIP**
>
> Shortcut keys to set line spacing are Ctrl + 1 for single spacing, Ctrl + 2 for double spacing, and Ctrl + 5 for 1.5 line spacing. You must use the numeric keys at the top of the keyboard. These shortcuts do not work with the numeric keypad.

Aligning Text

Alignment arranges the text to line up at one or both margins, or centers it across the page. Like line spacing, alignment is usually applied to an entire paragraph or document.

You can align paragraphs of text to the left, right, or center. You can also justify your text, which means that the text will be evenly spaced across the page from the left edge to the right edge.

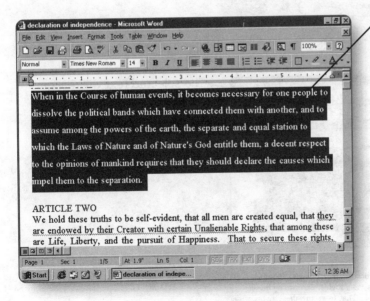

1. Select the **text** that you want to align. The text will be highlighted.

2. Click on the appropriate **alignment button**:

- **Align Left**: The text will be aligned at the left margin. This is the default choice in Word.

- **Center**: The text will be centered.

- **Align Right**: The text will be aligned at the right margin.

- **Justify**: The text will be spaced evenly across the page.

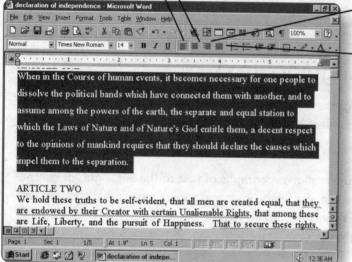

The selected text will realign according to the option you selected.

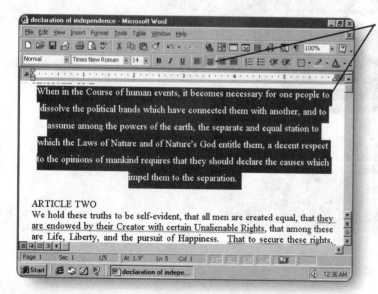

8

Using Fonts Effectively

When you speak, the tone of your voice conveys how you feel about what you're saying. You can convey your enthusiasm (or lack of it), be friendly, or be sarcastic. In a similar way, *fonts*, which are families of design styles for the numbers, letters, and symbols that make up text, can provide additional information to the reader. Fonts can, for example, make a document appear mature and businesslike or young and casual. In this chapter, you'll learn how to:

- Choose and apply an appropriate font
- Change the default font
- Add Bold, Underline, and Italic
- Use special effects, such as outlining, embossing, subscripts, or animation
- Copy formatting from one selection to another

Selecting a Font and Font Size

In addition to the fonts you already have on your machine, Word 2000 comes with extra fonts. The name of the currently selected font and font size for selected text is displayed on the Font and Font Size drop-down lists on the toolbar.

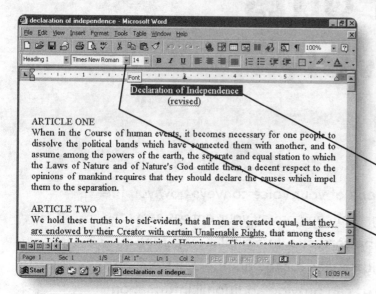

Choosing a Font

Choose a font such as Times New Roman if you want the text to be modern and businesslike, or choose a font like Monotype Corsiva for a handwritten style!

1. Select the **text** to be formatted. The text will be highlighted.

2. Click on the **down arrow** to the right of the Font drop down list. A list of fonts will appear.

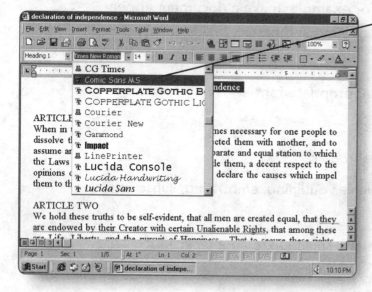

3. Click on a **font**. The new font will be applied to your text.

Choosing a Font Size

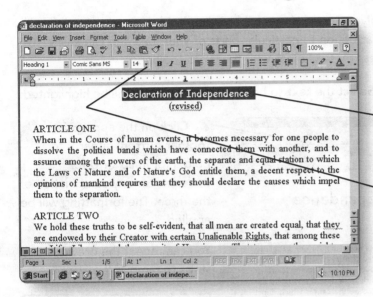

Each font can be used in different sizes. Font sizes are measured in *points*, and a point is actually 1/72 of an inch.

1. Select the **text** to be formatted. The text will be highlighted.

2. Click on the **down arrow** to the right of the Font Size drop-down box. A list of available sizes will appear.

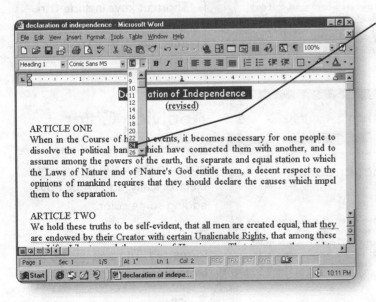

3. Click on a **size**. The new size will be applied to your text.

Applying Bold, Italic, or Underline

Applying formatting attributes like **bold**, *italic*, or underline will call attention to particular parts of your text. You can easily access these choices with the Word toolbar.

1. Select the **text** to be formatted. The text will be highlighted.

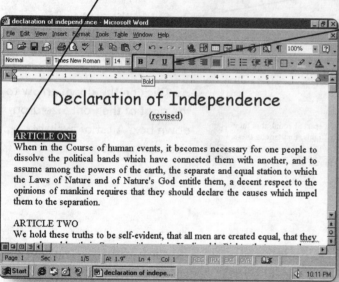

2. Click on the appropriate **toolbar button**: either **B** for bold, *I* for italic, or U for underline, or any combination of the three. The formatting will be applied.

You can repeat the previous steps to remove the attribute.

> **TIP**
>
> Shortcut keys include Ctrl + B for bold, Ctrl + I for italic, and Ctrl + U for underline.

Applying Color

If you have a color printer or are going to share the document electronically, add impact by adding some color.

1. Select the **text** to be formatted. The text will be highlighted.

2. Click on the **down arrow** to the right of the Font Color button. A list of available colors will appear.

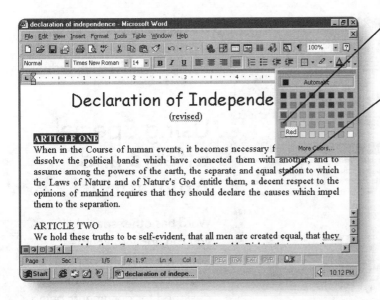

3. **Click** on a **color** in the palette. The Color Palette box will close.

4. **Click** anywhere **in the document** to deselect the text. The text will appear in the selected color.

Highlighting Text

You can highlight text in your document in the same manner that you highlight text in a book with a marker. You can even choose the color of highlighter your want to use. On a black and white printer, highlighting appears with gray shading over the text.

1. **Select** the **text** to be formatted with highlighting. The text will be highlighted.

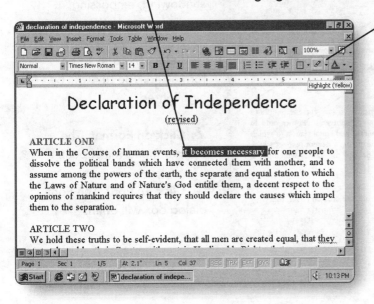

2. **Click** on the **down arrow** to the right of the Highlight button. A list of available colors will appear. The default color is yellow.

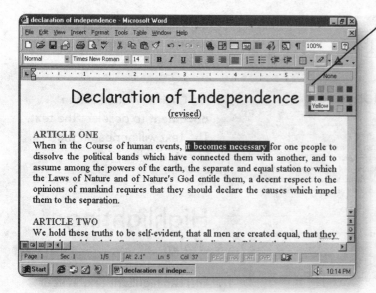

3. **Click** on a **color**. The text will become deselected and highlighting will be applied.

Using Special Effects and Animation

Word has other special effects you can apply to your text. Some are great for printed documents, whereas others are designed for documents being shared electronically.

Applying a Font Special Effect

Font effects can include shadowing, embossing, engraving, and others.

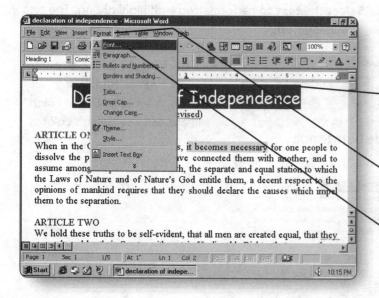

1. **Select** the **text** to be formatted. The text will be highlighted.

2. **Click** on **Format**. The Format menu will appear.

3. **Click** on **Font**. The Font dialog box will open.

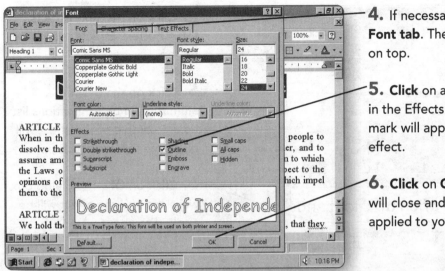

4. If necessary, **click** on the **Font tab**. The Font tab will be on top.

5. Click on any desired **options** in the Effects boxes. A check mark will appear in any selected effect.

6. Click on **OK**. The dialog box will close and the effect will be applied to your text.

Adding Animation to Text

Word includes six animation effects that can be added to a document. These effects will only display on a document being viewed electronically.

1. Select the **text** to be formatted. The text will be highlighted.

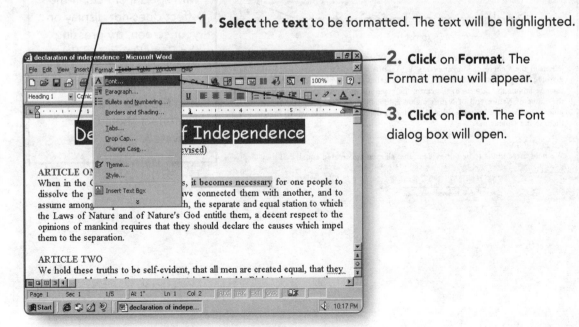

2. Click on **Format**. The Format menu will appear.

3. Click on **Font**. The Font dialog box will open.

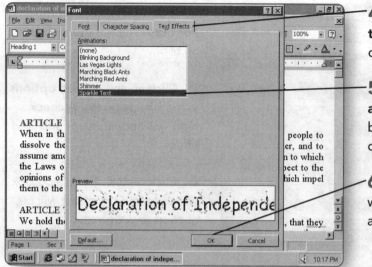

4. **Click** on the **Text Effects tab**. The Text Effects tab will be on top.

5. **Click** on the desired **animation** in the Animations list box. A sample of the effect will display in the preview box.

6. **Click** on **OK**. The dialog box will close and the effect will be applied to your text.

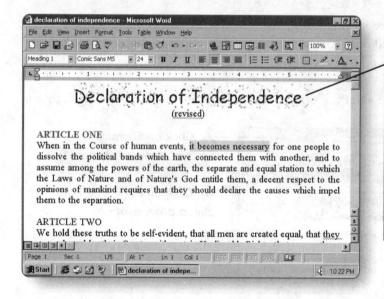

NOTE

Word is quirky sometimes with special effects. If the effect does not display on your screen, try pressing the Page Down and Page Up keys a few times and then returning to the text with the special effect. The effect should be activated.

Copying Formatting to Another Selection

If you spend several minutes setting up just the right formatting for a heading that will appear multiple times in a long document, you don't want to have to try and remember your selections and repeat them. Instead, you can use the Format Painter tool.

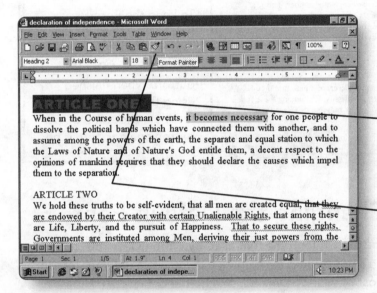

1. Select the **text** that has the formatting you want to use elsewhere. The text will be highlighted.

2. Click on the **Format Painter button**. The mouse pointer will change to a paintbrush.

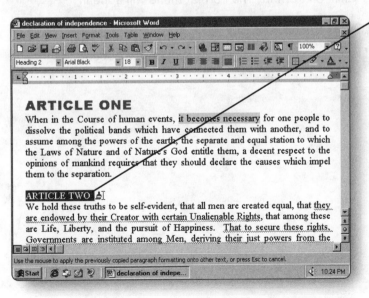

3. Press and **hold** the **mouse button** and **drag** over the text to be formatted. The new text will become highlighted.

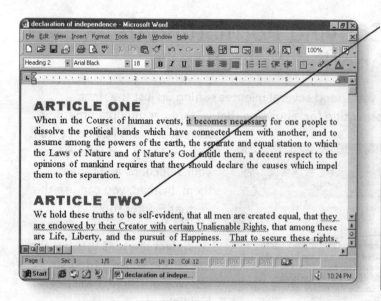

4. Release the **mouse button**. The new text will have the attributes of the original text.

TIP

To keep the Format Painter function on for repeated use, click twice on the Format Painter button. When finished using the Format Painter function, click on the button again to turn it off.

Changing the Default Font

The default font, the font used by Word unless you change it, is 12-point Times New Roman. If you use a different font for most of your documents, change the default.

1. Click on **Format**. The Format menu will appear.

2. Click on **Font**. The Font dialog box will open.

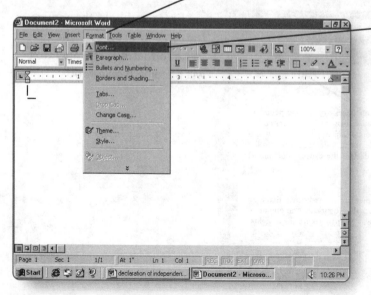

3. If necessary, **click** on the **Font tab**. The Font tab will come to the front.

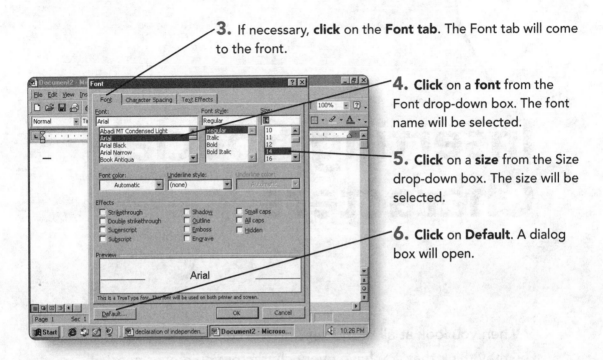

4. Click on a **font** from the Font drop-down box. The font name will be selected.

5. Click on a **size** from the Size drop-down box. The size will be selected.

6. Click on **Default**. A dialog box will open.

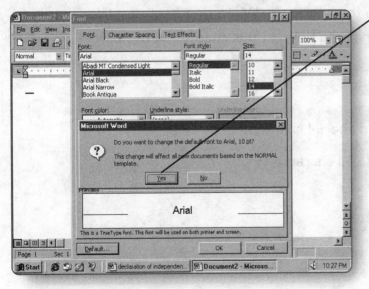

7. Click on **Yes**. The dialog box will close and the next time you create a new document, the font you selected will be the current font.

9

Inserting Special Characters

When you look at all of the keys on the computer keyboard, you may think that you have every character you'd ever need at your fingertips. Occasionally however, you'll need a special character that isn't on the keyboard. When that happens, Word has several features that can help. In this chapter, you'll learn how to:

- Use drop caps
- Insert symbols and special characters
- Insert frequently used characters

Using Drop Caps

If you're writing a newsletter, preparing a special report, or creating a letterhead, you may want to use a *drop cap*, an enlarged first letter.

Creating a Drop Cap

Only the first letter of a paragraph can be formatted as a drop cap.

1. Click in the **paragraph** where you want to have a drop cap. The blinking insertion point will appear in the paragraph.

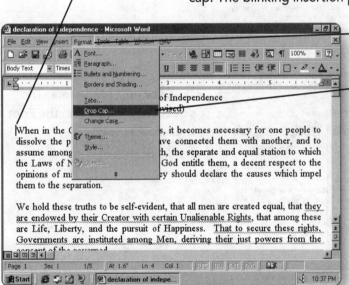

2. Click on **Format**. The Format menu will appear.

3. Click on **Drop Cap**. The Drop Cap dialog box will open.

> ### TIP
> If Drop Cap does not immediately appear on your Format menu, hold the mouse over the word Format for a couple of seconds. The menu will expand and the Drop Cap option will be displayed.

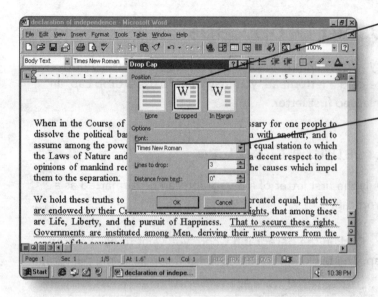

4. Click on a **position** for the Drop Cap character. The selected option will have a box around it.

5. Optionally, **click** on the **Font drop-down arrow**. A list of font choices will appear.

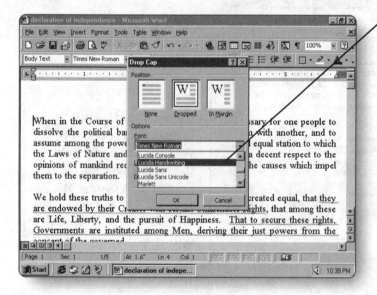

6. Click on a **font name**. The selection will appear in the Font drop-down list box.

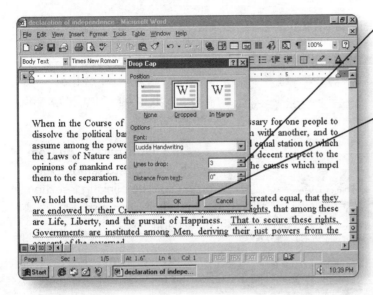

7. **Click** on the **up or down arrows** in the Lines to drop list box. The number specifies how large the drop cap should be.

8. **Click** on **OK**. The first character of the paragraph will be changed to a drop cap character.

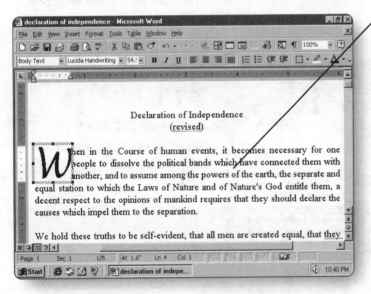

9. **Click** in the **body** of the paragraph. The box surrounding the drop cap will disappear.

Removing a Drop Cap

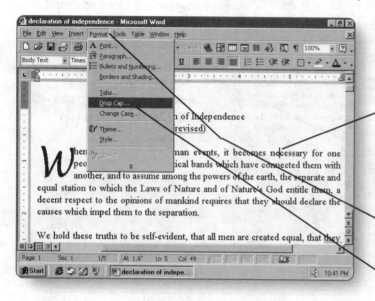

If you later decide you don't want the first letter of the paragraph to be a drop cap, you can remove it.

1. Click in the **paragraph** from which you want to remove the drop cap. The blinking insertion point will appear in the paragraph.

2. Click on **Format**. The Format menu will appear.

3. Click on **Drop Cap**. The Drop Cap dialog box will open.

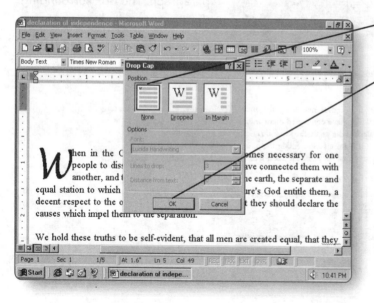

4. Click on **None**. The option will have a box around it.

5. Click on **OK**. The first character of the paragraph will return to normal.

Inserting Special Characters and Symbols

Word includes hundreds of special characters and symbols for you to include in your document. Symbols include things like copyright or trademark symbols, stars, checkmarks, or airplanes.

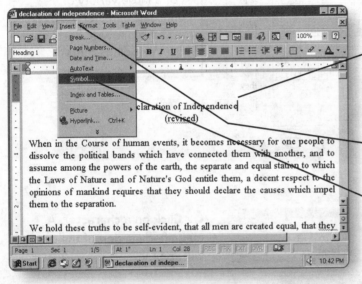

1. **Click** the **mouse** where you want the special character to appear. The blinking insertion point will appear.

2. **Click** on **Insert**. The Insert menu will appear.

3. **Click** on **Symbol**. The Symbol dialog box will open.

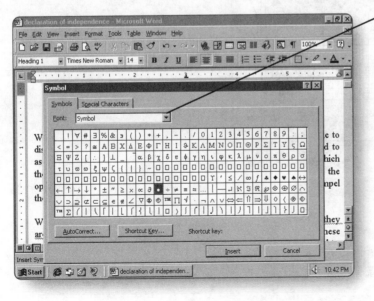

4. **Click** on the **Font drop-down arrow**. A list of fonts will appear.

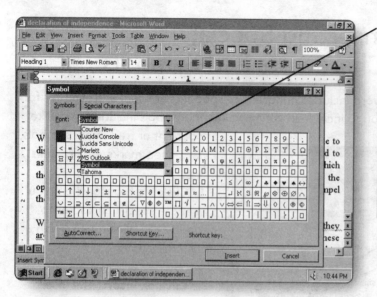

5. Click on a **font**. The symbols available for that font will display.

TIP

For a large variety of unusual characters, look at the Monotype Sorts or the Wingdings fonts.

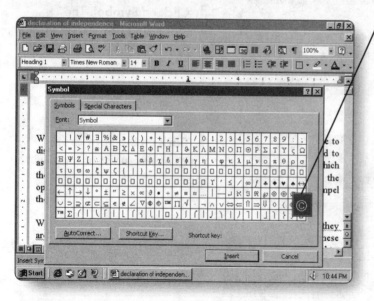

6. Click on a **character**. A magnified version of the symbol will appear.

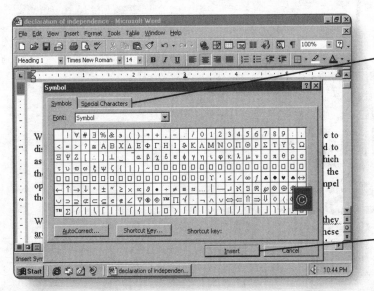

NOTE
Additional special characters are available under the Special Characters tab. To insert one of these special characters, click on the Special Characters tab and then choose the character you want.

7. Click on **Insert**. The symbol or character will be inserted into your document.

8. Click on **Close**. The symbol dialog box will close.

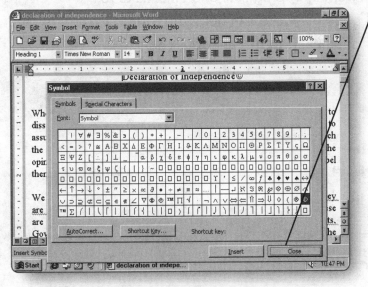

10

Working with Lists

Everyone uses lists—from shopping lists and checklists to meeting agendas and outlines. Word can help you format lists in your documents automatically. In this chapter, you'll learn how to:

- Use AutoFormat
- Create a bulleted or numbered list
- Modify the bullet style
- Add pictures to a list
- Create a multilevel numbered list
- Remove bullets or numbering

Using AutoFormat As You Type

Word 2000 includes a feature called AutoFormat As You Type, which guesses what you're trying to do from what you type. This can be a substantial time saver when you're creating lists.

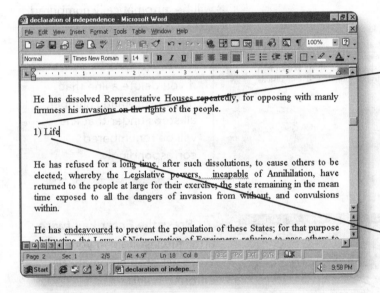

Using AutoFormat to Create a List

1. Type a **number**, then a **closing parenthesis**, a **period**, or a **hyphen**. The number will display in your document.

2. Press the **spacebar** or **Tab key**. The insertion point will move accordingly.

3. Type the **text** for the first item on your list. The text will display in the document.

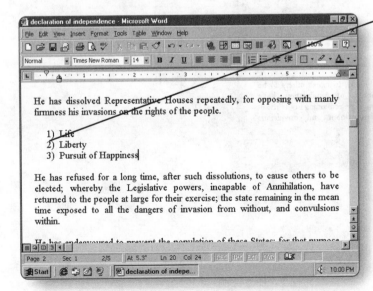

4. Press the **Enter key**. Word will assume you are trying to create a numbered list and will begin the next line with the next item number. Numbered items are also indented.

For example, if you typed a 1 in the first step, then the next line will be a 2; however if you typed a 6 in the first step, the next line will be a 7.

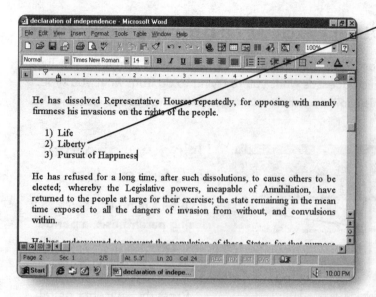

5. Type the **text** for the second item on your list. The text will display in the document.

6. **Repeat steps 4 and 5** for each item on your list. The items will be automatically numbered.

NOTE

If you delete a line that has an automatic number, all steps under that line will be renumbered correspondingly.

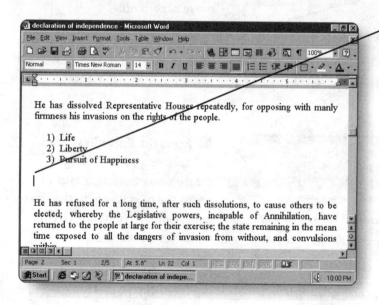

7. **Press** the **Enter key twice** after the last item in your list. Word will stop automatically entering numbers.

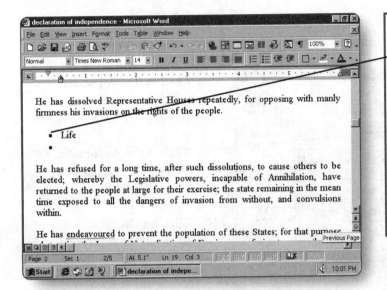

TIP

To begin a bulleted list, instead of typing a number at the first item, type an asterisk, hyphen or a dash. Word will continue the list with the same character. Note that when using the asterisk key, Word will convert that to a round filled-in bullet.

Turning Off AutoFormat

If the AutoFormat As You Type feature is adding numbers or bullets when you don't want numbers or bullets, you can easily turn off the feature.

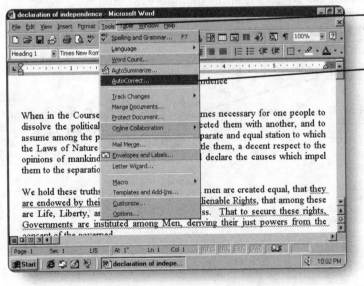

1. Click on **Tools**. The Tools menu will appear.

2. Click on **AutoCorrect**. The AutoCorrect dialog box will open.

3. Click on the **AutoFormat As You Type tab**. The AutoFormat As You Type tab will come to the front.

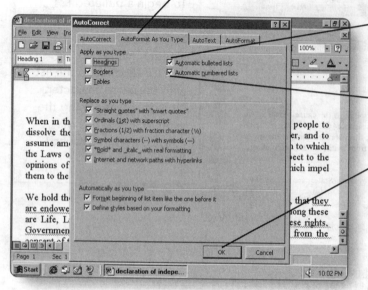

4. Click in the **Automatic bulleted lists check box**. The check mark will be removed.

5. Click in the **Automatic numbered lists check box**. The check mark will be removed.

6. Click on **OK**. The AutoFormat As You Type feature will be disabled.

Working with Bulleted or Numbered Lists

If you've typed text without bullets or numbering, you can use the toolbar to quickly apply them to your list.

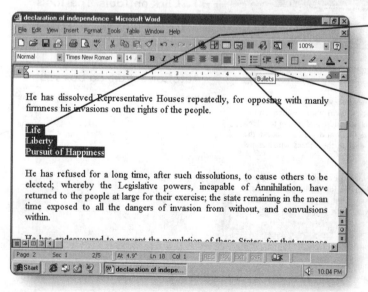

1. Select the **list** to be bulleted or numbered. The text will be highlighted.

2a. Click on the **Bullets button** on the toolbar. The list will have bullets applied to it.

OR

2b. Click on the **Numbering button** on the toolbar. The list will have numbers applied to it.

Switching between Bulleted and Numbered Lists

If you created a bulleted list and would prefer it to be numbered, it's easy to change it.

1. Select the **list** to be changed. The list will be highlighted.

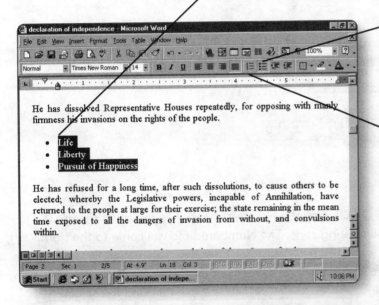

2a. Click on the **bullet button** if the list is currently numbered. The list will change to bulleted.

OR

2b. Click on the **numbering button** if the list is currently bulleted. The list will change to numbered.

Changing a List Style

By default, Word places a round bullet at the beginning of each item in a bulleted list and uses Arabic numbers for numbered lists. There are many other styles of bullets and numbers you can choose from.

1. Select the **list**. The list will be highlighted.

2. Click on **Format**. The Format menu will appear.

3. Click on **Bullets and Numbering**. The Bullets and Numbering dialog box will open.

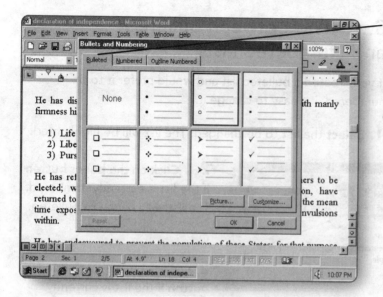

4a. **Click** on the **Bulleted tab** if you want to change the style of bullet. The Bulleted tab will come to the front.

OR

4b. **Click** on the **Numbered tab** if you want to change the numbering style. The Numbered tab will come to the front.

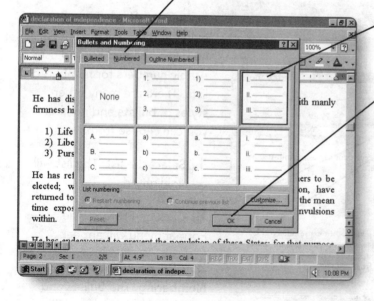

5. **Click** on a **style**. A frame will appear around the selected style.

6. **Click** on **OK**. The dialog box will close.

Word will apply the new style to the existing list and any new lists of that type will be formatted the same way.

Customizing a Bulleted Style

Didn't see a bullet style you liked? There's lots more to choose from!

1. Select the **list** to be modified. The list will be highlighted.

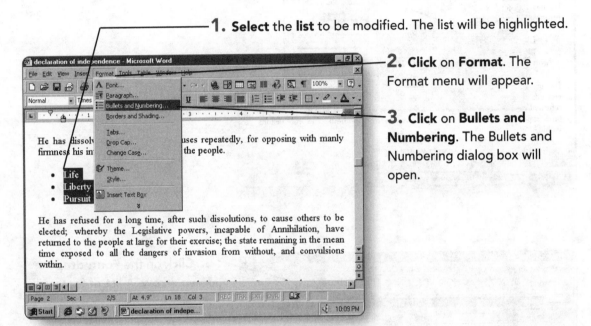

2. Click on **Format**. The Format menu will appear.

3. Click on **Bullets and Numbering**. The Bullets and Numbering dialog box will open.

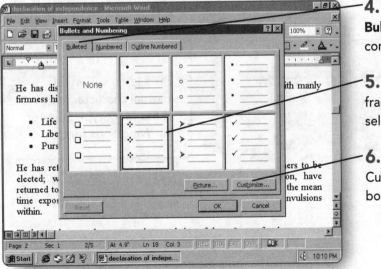

4. If necessary, **click** on the **Bullets tab**. The Bullets tab will come to the top.

5. Click on a **bullet style**. A frame will appear around the selected style.

6. Click on **Customize**. The Customize Bulleted List dialog box will open.

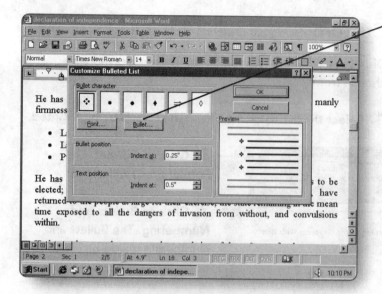

7. Click on **Bullet**. The Symbol dialog box will open.

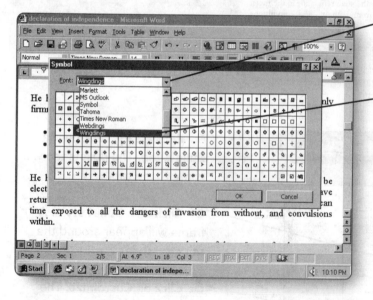

8. Click on the **Font: drop down arrow**. A list of fonts will appear.

9. Click on a **font**. The symbols available for that font will display.

TIP

For a large variety of unusual characters, look at the Monotype Sorts or the Wingdings fonts.

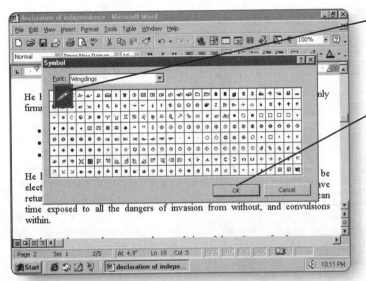

10. Click on a **character** to be used as a bullet. A magnified version of the symbol will appear.

11. Click on **OK**. The Symbol dialog box will close.

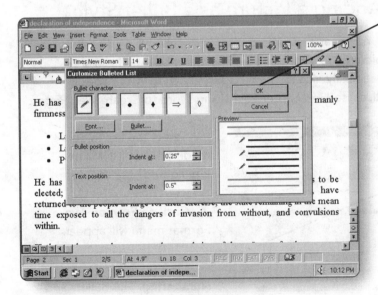

12. Click on **OK**. The Customize Bulleted List dialog box will close.

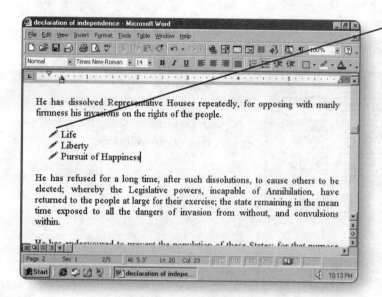

The new style will be applied to your list.

Adding a Picture as a Bullet Style

A new feature to Word 2000 is the ability to add small pictures to a list as a special type of bullet. These are especially nice for Web pages. Creating Web pages is discussed in Chapter 25, "Using Word to Create Web Pages."

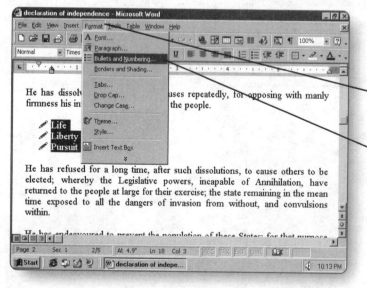

1. Select the **list** to be modified. The list will be highlighted.

2. Click on **Format**. The Format menu will appear.

3. Click on **Bullets and Numbering**. The Bullets and Numbering dialog box will open.

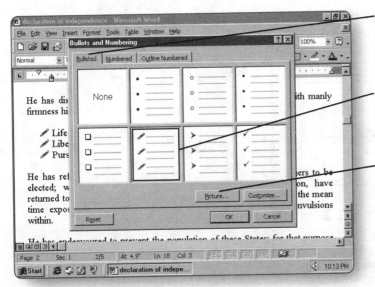

4. If necessary, **click** on the **Bulleted tab**. The Bulleted tab will come to the top.

5. Click on a **bullet style**. A frame will appear around the selected style.

6. Click on **Picture**. The Picture Bullet dialog box will open.

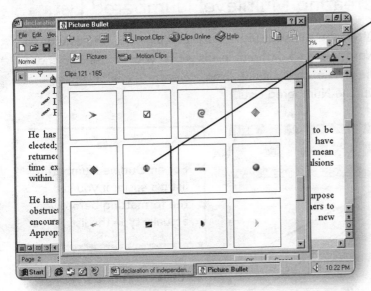

7. Click on a **Picture clip**. The picture will be highlighted and a small picture menu will appear.

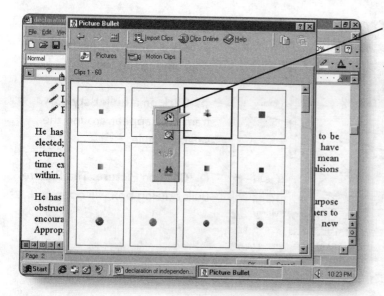

8. Click on **Insert Picture**. The picture style will be applied to the list.

Creating Multilevel Numbered Lists

Often you will want to have a list within a list. You can tell Word to create different levels within your lists and to choose the style of those levels. Word calls these multilevel lists Outline Numbered Lists.

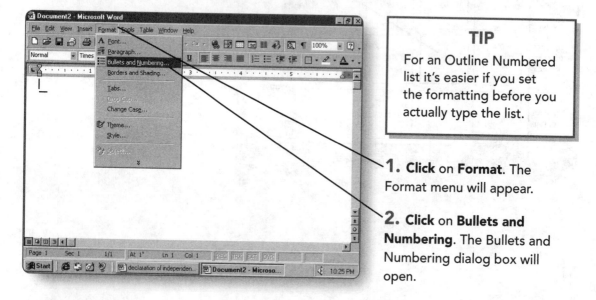

TIP

For an Outline Numbered list it's easier if you set the formatting before you actually type the list.

1. Click on **Format**. The Format menu will appear.

2. Click on **Bullets and Numbering**. The Bullets and Numbering dialog box will open.

3. **Click** on the **Outline Numbered tab**. The Outline Numbered tab will be on top.

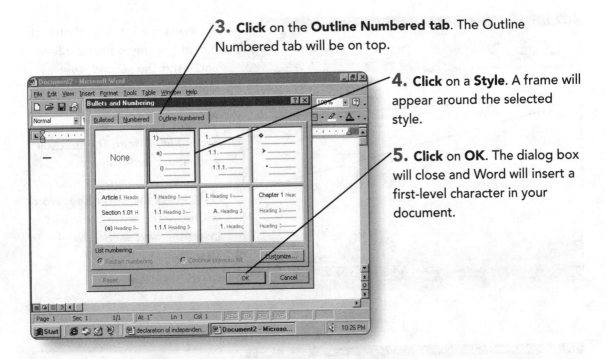

4. **Click** on a **Style**. A frame will appear around the selected style.

5. **Click** on **OK**. The dialog box will close and Word will insert a first-level character in your document.

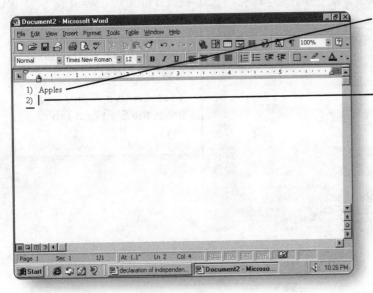

6. **Type** the **text** of the first-level item. The text will appear in the document.

7. **Press** the **Enter key**. Word will move to the next line and insert another first-level character.

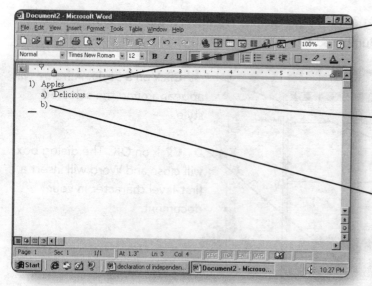

8. Press the **Tab key**. Word will indent the line to the next level and insert the second-level character.

9. Type the **text** for the second-level item. The text will appear in the document.

10. Press the **Enter key**. Word will move to the next line and insert the next second-level character.

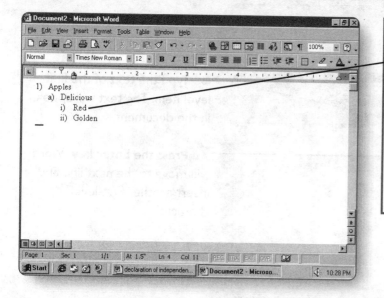

TIP

Each time you want to move another level inward, press the Tab key. Word will shift to the next level character.

To revert to a higher level, press the Shift and Tab keys.

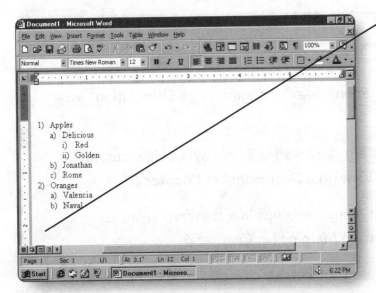

11. Press the **Enter key twice** after the last item in the list has been added. The Outline Numbered list will stop.

Removing Bullet or Number Formatting

If you no longer want the bullet or numbering style applied to your list, it only takes a click to remove it.

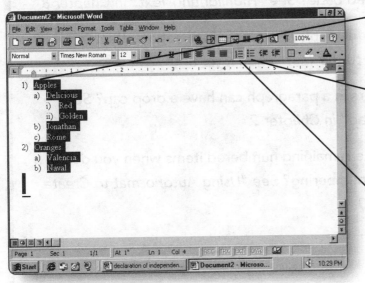

1. Select the **list** to be cleared of bullets or numbers. The text will be highlighted.

2a. Click on the **Bullets button** on the toolbar. The bullets will be removed.

OR

2b. Click on the **Numbering button** on the toolbar. The numbers will be removed.

Part II Review Questions

1. What is Page Orientation? *See "Changing Page Orientation" in Chapter 6*

2. What types of items are displayed in Print Layout view but not in Normal view? *See "Viewing a Document" in Chapter 6*

3. What are the default margin settings in a standard Word document? *See "Setting Margins" in Chapter 6*

4. What are the keyboard shortcuts to change line spacing? *See "Changing Line Spacing" in Chapter 7*

5. What happens to justified text? *See "Aligning Text" in Chapter 7*

6. How large is a font point? *See "Choosing a Font Size" in Chapter 8*

7. When printing to a black and white printer, how does highlighting appear on the printed page? *See "Highlighting Text" in Chapter 8*

8. How must a document display to see text animation effects? *See "Adding Animation to the Text" in Chapter 8*

9. How many characters in a paragraph can have a drop cap? *See "Creating a Drop Cap" in Chapter 9*

10. What happens to the remaining numbered items when you delete a line with automatic numbering? *See "Using AutoFormat to Create a List" in Chapter 10*

PART III

Adding Visual Interest

11

Communicating Your Ideas with Clip Art

In a world where everyone is frantically busy, you need to communicate your ideas quickly. Pictures help you do this. No time to draw? That's not a problem. Word 2000 comes with a wide variety of clip art. *Clip art* is simply a collection of computer pictures or graphics that are ready to use. You just select an appropriate picture and insert it in your document. In this chapter, you'll learn how to:

- Insert clip art
- Move and size the clip art object
- Adjust the contrast and brightness
- Add or remove a border
- Wrap text around the clip art
- Create a watermark

Inserting Clip Art

Clip art pictures can be inserted into a document in any view, although the best place to view visual elements is the Page Layout view. Often, Word will automatically switch you into this view so that you can see visual elements such as clip art.

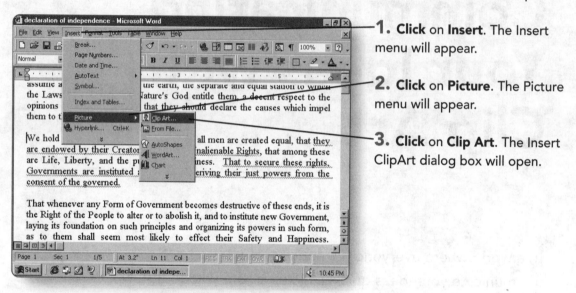

1. Click on **Insert**. The Insert menu will appear.

2. Click on **Picture**. The Picture menu will appear.

3. Click on **Clip Art**. The Insert ClipArt dialog box will open.

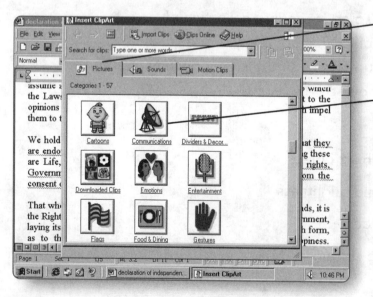

4. If necessary, **click** on the **Pictures tab**. The Pictures tab will come to the front.

5. Click on a **category** in the pictures box. An assortment of pictures will appear in the central viewing area.

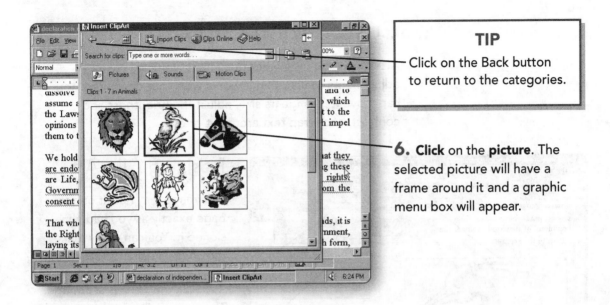

TIP

Click on the Back button to return to the categories.

6. **Click** on the **picture**. The selected picture will have a frame around it and a graphic menu box will appear.

7. **Click** on **Insert Clip**. The clip will be inserted into your document.

8. **Click** on the **Close button**. The Insert ClipArt dialog box will close.

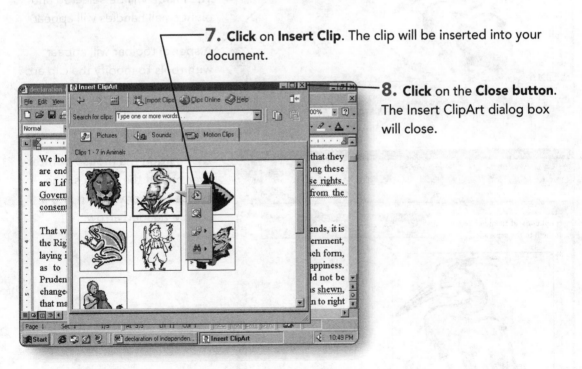

Customizing Clip Art

After the image is in your document, you can make adjustments to it so that it works with your document. You can move it, change its size, adjust the brightness and contrast, and wrap text around it or over it.

Resizing Clip Art

The image may not fit on the page exactly as you had envisioned it. You can easily make the image smaller or larger.

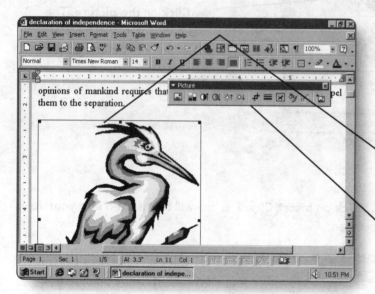

1. Click on the **clip art image**. The image will be selected and eight small handles will appear.

A special toolbar will appear with tools to modify the clip art.

2. Position the **mouse pointer** over one of the handles. The mouse pointer will turn into a double-headed arrow.

3. Press and **hold** your **mouse button** down on one of the selection handles. The pointer will turn into a plus sign.

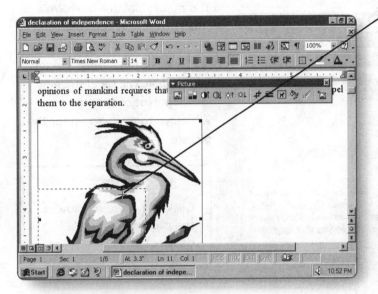

4. Drag the **selection handle** out to make the picture larger, or inward to make it smaller. A dotted box will indicate the new size.

> ### NOTE
>
> Dragging on any corner handle will resize the height and width of the object at the same time; dragging on any side handle will resize the clip art in a single direction.

Moving Clip Art

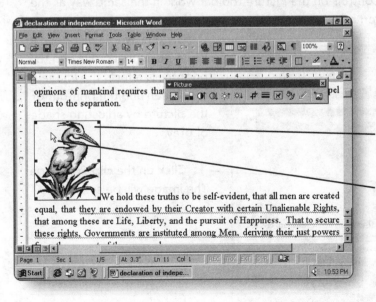

The picture you choose may need to be moved. As the clip art is inserted into the document, surrounding text adjusts to make room for it.

1. Click on the **clip art image**. The image will be selected.

2. Position the **mouse pointer** anywhere inside the frame of the graphic. Do not position it over one of the selection handles.

3. **Press** and **hold** the **mouse button** and **drag** the insertion point (in the form of a gray dotted line) to the new location. The mouse pointer will have a small box at the end of it.

4. **Release** the **mouse button**. The graphic will be in the new location. Notice that the text will move to make room for the picture.

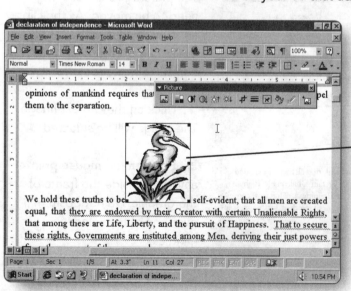

TIP
Click anywhere outside of the clip art image to deselect it.

Adjusting the Brightness or Contrast

Controls on the Picture toolbar work in the same way as the controls on your TV that adjust the brightness and contrast of the picture. With a picture in a Word document, adjusting this brightness affects the image on the screen and the printout of the picture by adjusting shades of gray.

1. **Click** on the **clip art image**. The image will be selected.

2a. Click on the **More Contrast button**. The contrast will brighten.

OR

2b. Click on the **Less Contrast button**. The contrast will lighten.

3a. Click on the **Less Brightness button**. The brightness will decrease.

OR

3b. Click on the **More Brightness button**. The brightness will increase.

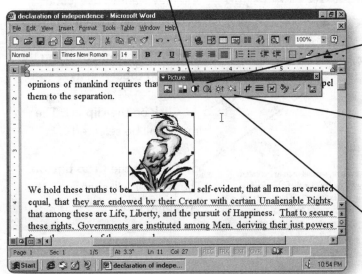

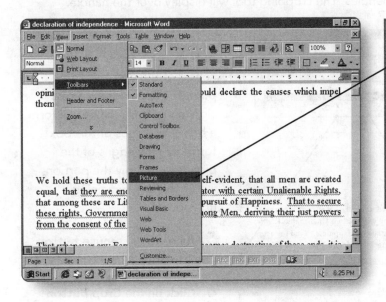

TIP

If the Picture toolbar does not appear when you click on the picture object, click on View, and then click on Toolbars. Click on Picture to return the Picture toolbar to the screen.

Cropping the Picture

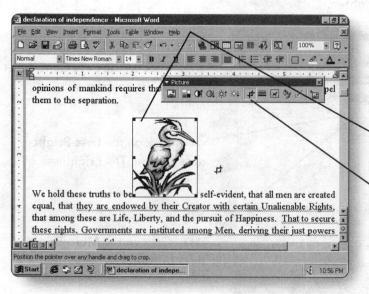

You may want to use just a portion of the entire picture you've selected. You can easily modify the picture by using the Cropping tool.

1. Click on the **clip art**. The image will be selected.

2. Click on the **Crop button**. The pointer will change to the Cropping tool.

3. Position the **mouse pointer** over one of the selection handles. The cropping tool will display over the handle.

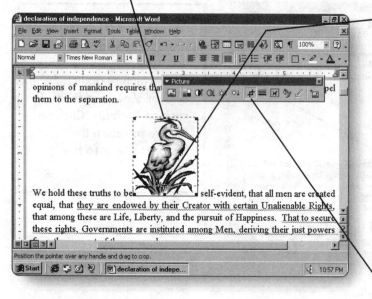

4. Press and **hold** the **mouse button** and **drag toward** the center of the graphic. The pointer will change to a plus sign, and a dashed line will form a box. The edges of this box form the new edges of the picture, with only the portion inside the box remaining uncropped.

5. Release the **mouse button**. The clip art will be cropped.

6. Click on the **Crop button** again. The Cropping tool will be turned off.

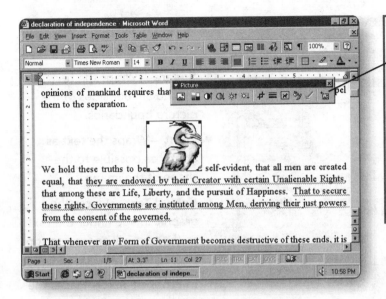

TIP
Click on the Reset Picture button on the Picture toolbar if you don't like any of the adjustments that you've made to your clip art and would like to start again. The clip art will go back to the way it was originally inserted.

Wrapping Text Around Clip Art

When you insert clip art into a document, lines of text move up or down to accommodate the clip art. Depending on the size of the clip art and the length of the lines of text, this effect may not be quite what you want. You might prefer to have the clip art sit within the lines of text, with the text stopping before the picture and starting again on the other side. This is called text-wrapping.

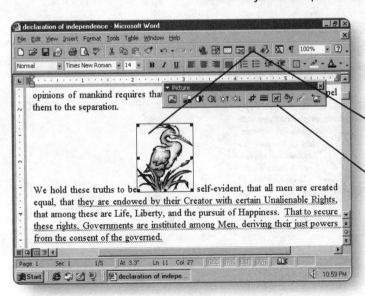

1. Click on the **clip art**. The image will be selected.

2. Click on the **Text Wrapping button**. A list of text wrapping selections will appear.

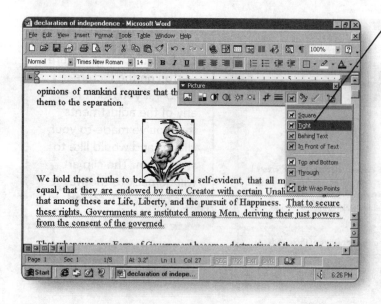

3. Click on **one** of the following options:

- **Square**—Wraps the text around all four sides of the picture boundaries.

- **Tight**—Wraps the text as tightly as possible to the shape of the image.

- **Behind Text**—Places the graphic image under the text so the text will appear on top of the image.

- **In Front of Text**—Places the graphic image on top of the text so the text will appear under the image.

- **Top and Bottom**—Places the text above and below the graphic object but not on either side.

- **Through**—Places text around the perimeter of the graphic object and through any open areas of the object.

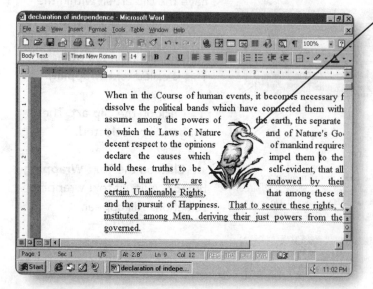

The image here has the text wrapped "tight" around the graphic.

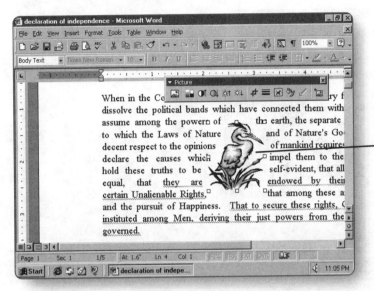

Deleting Clip Art

It's easy to delete any unwanted clip art from your document.

1. Click on the **clip art**. The image will be selected.

2. Press the **Delete key**. The image will be deleted.

Creating a Watermark

Sometimes rather than wrapping text around a picture, you might prefer to have the picture appear more in the background of the text, like images you sometimes see on fine stationery when you hold the stationery up to the light.

Another option, which can look very professional and eliminate the need for wrapping, is the watermark.

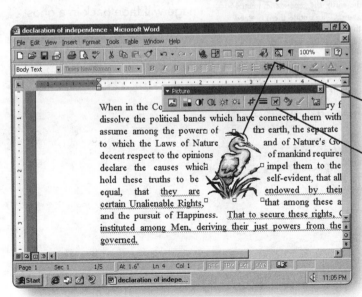

1. Click on the **clip art**. The image will be selected.

2. Click on the **Text Wrapping button**. A list of text wrapping selections will appear.

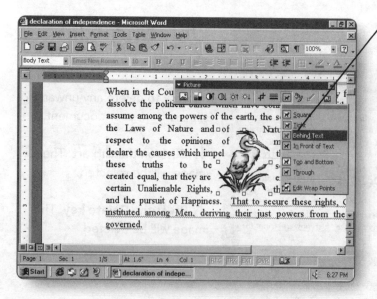

3. Click on **Behind Text.** The text will flow over the picture.

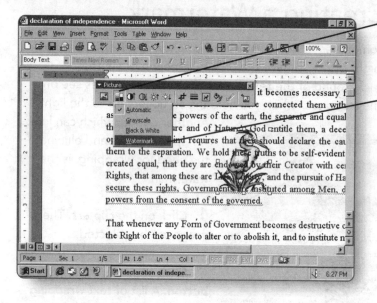

4. Click on the **Image Control button.** A list of Image Control options will appear.

5. Click on **Watermark.** The image will fade back in a ghost-like effect.

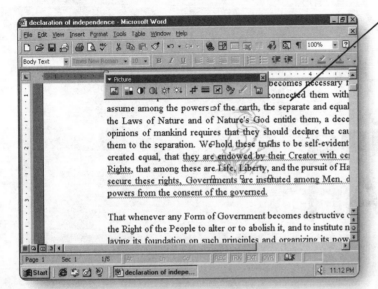

6. Click anywhere outside the picture to deselect the image. The Picture toolbar will close.

12

Creating WordArt

Adding clip art to a document is one way to add visual excitement, but if you're the creative type, you might want to draw your own pictures using Word's drawing tools. If you want your text to have more impact, WordArt may be your solution. With WordArt, you can take headings or key words and add wonderful color schemes, shapes, and special effects. In this chapter, you'll learn how to:

- Create a WordArt object
- Change the object's size and shape
- Rotate and change the direction of a WordArt object

Adding WordArt

Adding WordArt to your document is simply a matter of selecting a predefined style and typing your text.

1. Click on **Insert**. The Insert menu will appear.

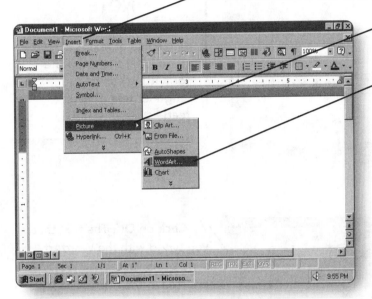

2. Click on **Picture**. The Picture submenu will appear.

3. Click on **WordArt**. The WordArt Gallery dialog box will open, containing predefined styles in which formats such as shape, color, or shadows are used to enhance text.

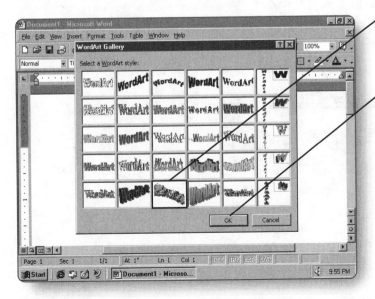

4. Click on a **WordArt style**. The selection will have a box around it.

5. Click on **OK**. The Edit WordArt Text dialog box will open. A placeholder in the Text box will say, "Your Text Here."

6. Click in the **Text box** and **type** in the **text** that you want to appear as WordArt. The text will appear.

> **NOTE**
>
> Limiting WordArt to a single line of text is a good idea; the elaborate formatting can make lengthier text difficult to read.

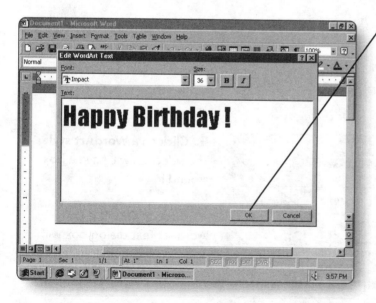

7. Click on **OK**. The text that you typed with the WordArt style you selected will be inserted in the document.

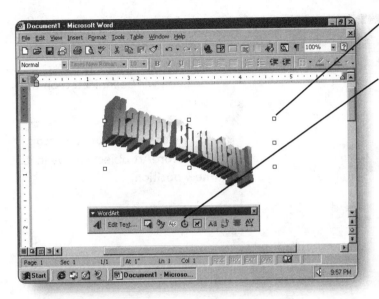

The WordArt object will have selection handles around it.

The WordArt toolbar will appear.

Making Adjustments to the WordArt

Even though it looks as though you've made a very specific design selection in the WordArt dialog box, you can actually make lots of adjustments to your selection.

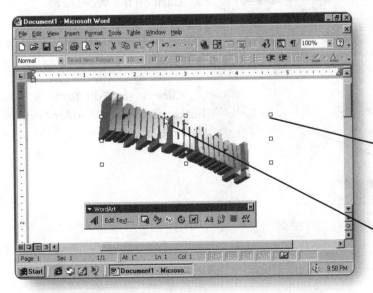

Moving Objects on a Page

You can easily move any object, including a WordArt object, around your document.

1. Click on the **WordArt object**. The object will be highlighted with selection handles.

2. Position the **mouse pointer** over the middle of the WordArt object. The mouse pointer will turn into a four-headed arrow.

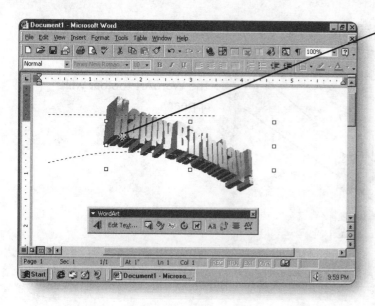

3. Press and **hold** the **mouse button** and **drag** the object to another position. The new position will be indicated on the screen.

4. Release the **mouse button**. The WordArt object will be in its new position.

Editing WordArt

If you made a typing error or you want to adjust the size or font of the text, you can easily open the WordArt feature again.

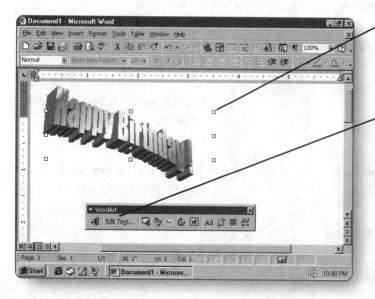

1. Click on the **WordArt object**. The object will be highlighted with selection handles.

2. Click on the **Edit Text button**. The Edit WordArt Text dialog box will open.

3. **Click** on the **down arrow** to the right of the Size drop-down box. A list of font sizes will appear.

4. **Click** on a **font size**. The font size will change.

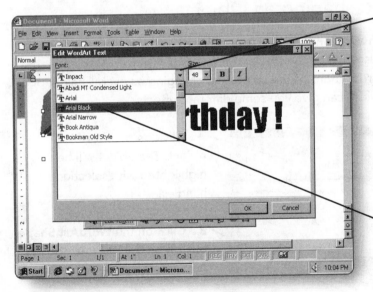

5. **Click** on the **down arrow** to the right of the Font drop-down box. A list of fonts will appear.

NOTE
Your selection of fonts may vary from the ones shown.

6. **Click** on a **font**. The font will change.

7. Make any **changes** to your text in the Text box. The text box will reflect the changes.

8. Click on **OK**. The object will be modified.

Reshaping an Object

In addition to changing the size of the WordArt text, you can also change the shape of the WordArt object. Modifying the proportions of the object and changing its overall height or width can give you some different effects.

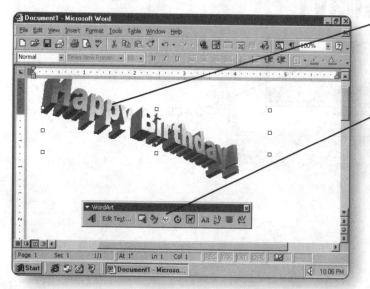

1. Click on the **WordArt object**. The object will be highlighted with selection handles.

2. Click on the **WordArt Shape button** on the WordArt toolbar. A palette of shapes will appear.

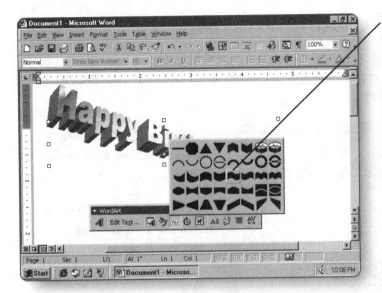

3. Click on a **shape**. Your WordArt will change to the shape you selected.

NOTE

Some shapes will make your text hard to read, whereas others will add an exciting or fun tone to your words.

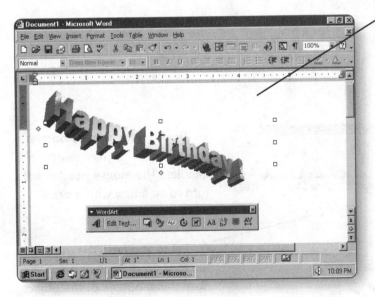

4. Click anywhere on the document outside of the WordArt object. The object will be deselected.

Rotating WordArt

Because WordArt is an object, it can be rotated to give you greater flexibility in designing the layout of your document page.

1. **Click** on the **WordArt object**. The object will be selected.

2. **Click** on the **Free Rotate button**. The square selection handles will become rounded.

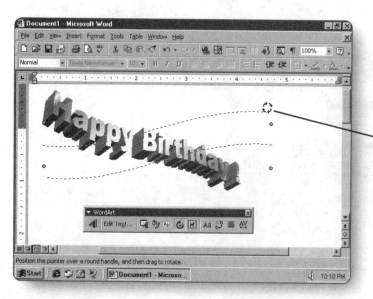

3. **Position** the **mouse button** on one of the circular selection handles. The mouse pointer will turn to an arrow with a circle around it.

4. **Press** and **hold** the **mouse button** and **drag** the object. A dotted-line outline of the object in its new position will appear.

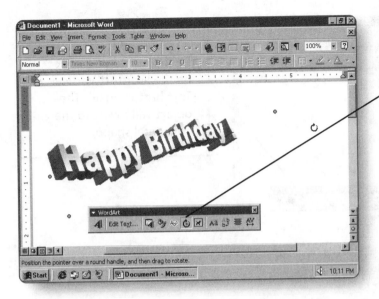

5. Release the **mouse button**. The object will display in its new position.

6. Click on the **Free Rotate button**. The rotate feature will be turned off.

Changing the Direction of WordArt Text

If you want your text to run up and down instead of left to right, you can easily change the text's direction.

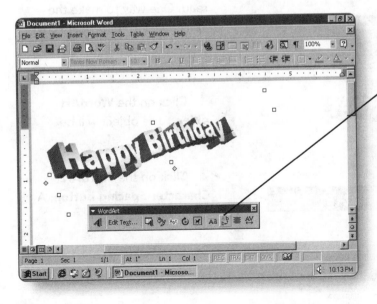

1. Click on the **WordArt object**. The object will be selected.

2. Click on the **WordArt Vertical Text button**. The text will now run from top to bottom.

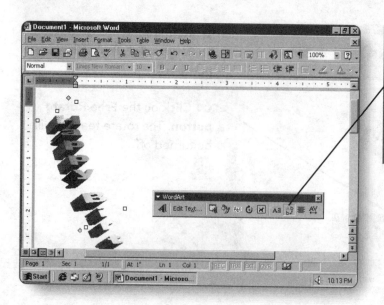

Changing WordArt Character Spacing

In some cases, depending on your text and the WordArt style you've selected, the WordArt text might be a little difficult to read. One way to make the individual letters clearer is by adjusting the spaces between the letters.

1. Click on the **WordArt object**. The object will be selected.

2. Click on the **WordArt Character Spacing button**. A menu will appear.

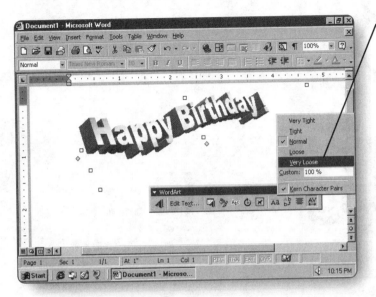

3. Click on a **spacing setting**. The menu will close.

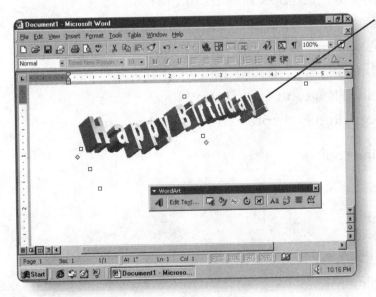

The text will appear with more space between letters if you choose a loose spacing or less space if you choose a tighter spacing.

13

Using the Drawing Toolbar

WordArt is a nice shortcut to applying sets of predefined text effects. Many of those same effects, such as shadows, can be added to objects that you create in your Word document using the toolbar. This toolbar offers predefined drawing shapes, called AutoShapes, as well as tools to draw and format lines, boxes, circles, and more. In this chapter, you'll learn how to:

- Display the drawing toolbar
- Draw Autoshapes
- Add to a drawing
- Give shapes a shadow effect
- Make a shape 3-dimensional

Displaying the Drawing Toolbar

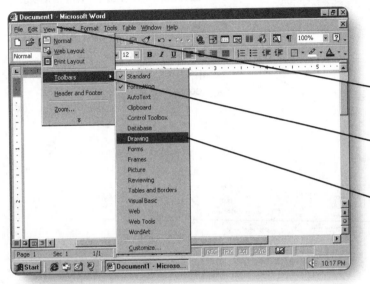

The easiest way to work with drawn objects is to use the toolbar.

1. **Click** on **View**. The View menu will appear.

2. **Click** on **Toolbars**. A list of available toolbars will display.

3. **Click** on **Drawing**. The toolbar will display at the bottom of your screen.

Working with Autoshapes

Word has built-in sets of drawing shapes that make it easy to click and drag to draw anything from a fancy banner to a pyramid on your document page.

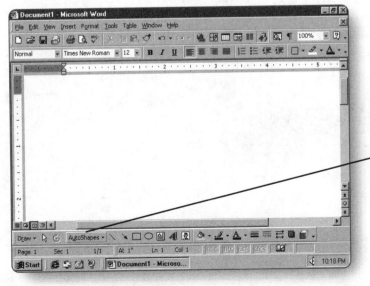

Drawing Autoshapes

Autoshapes can help you create flow charts or text callout buttons.

1. **Click** on **AutoShapes**. A list of AutoShapes categories will appear.

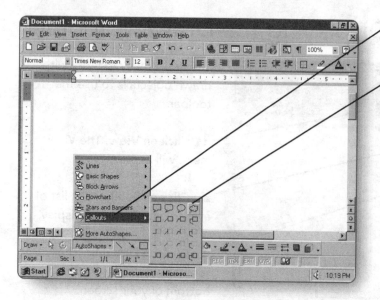

2. Click on a **Category**. A selection of shapes will appear.

3. Click on a **shape**. The palette will close, and the pointer will change to a large crosshair.

4. Click and **drag** the **mouse**. A shaped object will appear.

5. Release the **mouse button**. The new drawing shape will display.

Adding Text to Objects

In addition to drawing shapes, the toolbar contains a tool that enables you to draw boxes in which you can enter text. Because these text boxes are objects and not regular text, you can use drawing features such as rotating and layering with them to create interesting effects. You can even add text inside an AutoShape.

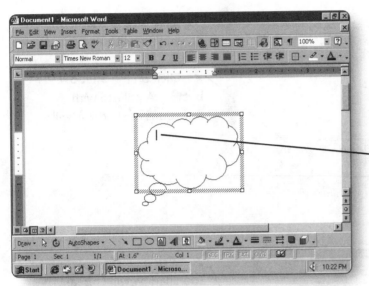

1. Click in the **drawn shape**. A framed box outside the AutoShape and a blinking pointer will appear.

2. Type some **text**. The text will appear in the object.

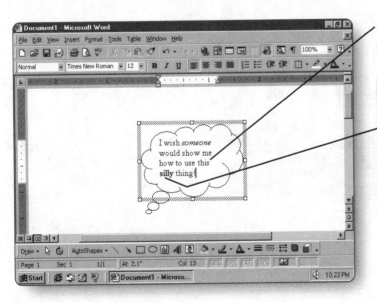

TIP

You can format the text font, size, color, or alignment in the same manner as any other document text.

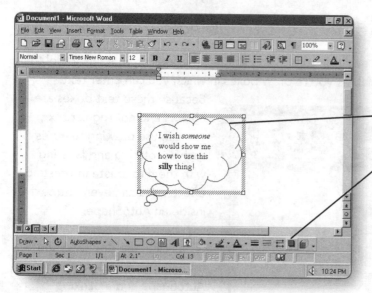

Creating Shadows

Shadows can add depth and visual interest to objects.

1. Click on the **shape object**. The object will be selected.

2. Click on the **Shadow button**. A palette with selections of shadows will appear.

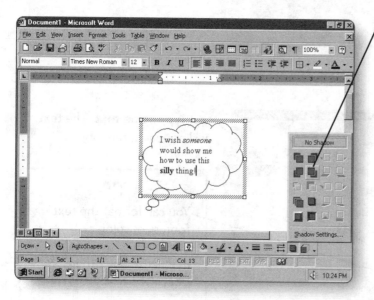

3. Click on a **shadow option**. The Shadow will appear.

Making Shapes 3-Dimensional

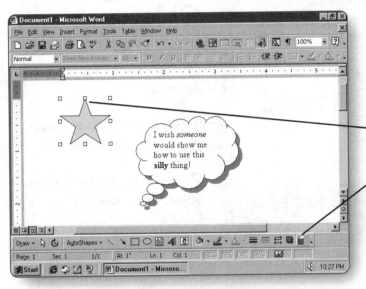

Make objects come alive by adding 3-dimensional effects! Some objects won't work with 3-dimensional shapes, so the feature will not be available.

1. **Click** on the **shape object**. The object will be selected.

2. **Click** on the **3-D button**. A palette with selections of 3-D settings will appear.

3. **Click** on a **3-D option**. The object will take on the added dimension.

TIP

Remove 3-D settings by choosing No 3-D from the 3-D pallet.

Deleting an Object

Don't want the drawn object in your document? You can easily delete it.

1. Click on the **shape object**. The object will be selected.

2. Press the **Delete key**. The object will be deleted.

Part III Review Questions

1. Where do you place your mouse pointer when you want to resize clip art? *See "Resizing Clip Art" in Chapter 11*

2. What happens to surrounding text when you move a clip art object? *See "Moving Clip Art" in Chapter 11*

3. What does "cropping" a picture do? *See "Cropping the Picture" in Chapter 11*

4. Where does text appear when you elect to wrap text tight around a picture. *See "Wrapping Text Around Clip Art" in Chapter 11*

5. Why should text be kept short in a Word Art object? *See "Adding Word Art" in Chapter 12*

6. What can you do to Word Art to make the text vertical? *See "Changing the Direction of Word Art Text" in Chapter 12*

7. When choosing character spacing for Word Art, are letters closer together or farther apart if you choose "loose spacing?" *See "Changing Word Art Character Spacing in Chapter 12*

8. How can you display the Drawing toolbar? *See "Displaying the Drawing Toolbar" in Chapter 13*

9. What are AutoShapes? *See "Working with AutoShapes" in Chapter 13*

10. How do you format text in a text box? *See "Adding Text to Objects" in Chapter 13*

Using Tables, Charts, and Columns

14

Working with Tables

Tables are great for organizing information. When you need to compare data or follow information across several columns, it's easier if the information is displayed in a table. Tables can be used to place information side by side in a document, for example, in creating the various sections of an invoice or address list. In this chapter, you'll learn how to:

- Create a simple table
- Use the AutoSum feature
- Format a table
- Add and delete rows and columns
- Add borders and shading

Creating a Simple Table

You can insert a table in any of three different ways. You can insert it from a menu selection, create it from the toolbar, or draw it manually.

Inserting a Table Using the Menu

To create a simple table, all you need to do is estimate the number of rows and columns that you want to start working with, and you're ready to go. You don't even need to be accurate; you can add or delete columns and rows as you work.

1. Click on **Table**. The Table menu will appear.

2. Click on **Insert**. The Insert submenu will appear.

3. Click on **Table**. The Insert Table dialog box will open.

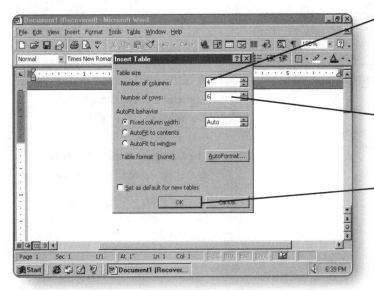

4. Enter the **number of columns** in the Number of columns text box. The number will be displayed.

5. Enter the **number of rows** in the Number of rows text box. The number will be displayed.

6. Click on **OK**. The table will be created.

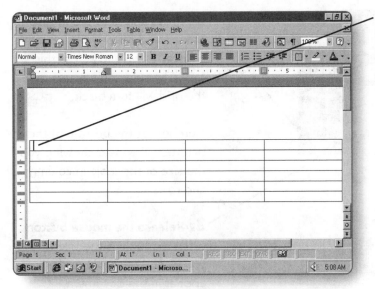

The table will appear in the Word document with the blinking insertion point ready to enter table information.

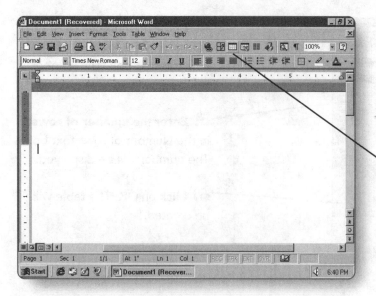

Creating a Table Using the Toolbar

A button is located on the Word standard toolbar to help you quickly create a table.

1. Click on the **Insert Table button**. A small grid will appear.

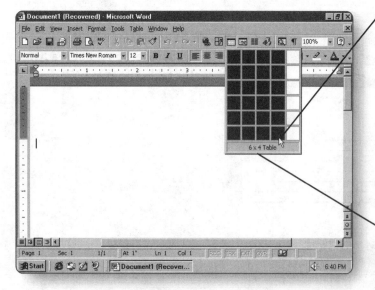

2. Press and **hold** the **mouse button** and **move** your **mouse pointer** down and across this grid. The selected squares of the grid will turn black.

Numbers at the bottom of the palette will appear showing you the size of the table in columns and rows.

3. Release the **mouse button** when the table is the size that you want. Your table grid will appear in the document.

Using the Draw Table Feature

The Draw Table feature enables you to just draw the grid you need on the screen by hand. This is particularly useful if you don't want all the lines inside the grid. With the Draw Table feature, not only are you able to quickly draw lines, but you can also quickly erase any parts of those lines that you don't need.

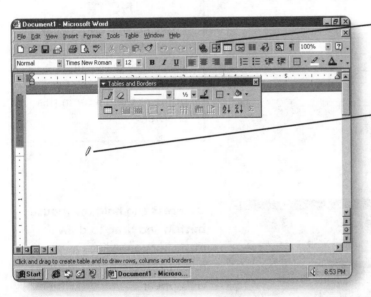

1. Click on the **Tables and Borders button**. The Tables and Borders toolbar will be displayed.

The pointer will immediately change to a pen.

> ### NOTE
> If you're not already in it, the view will automatically change to Print Layout view. Views were discussed in Chapter 6, "Working with Pages."

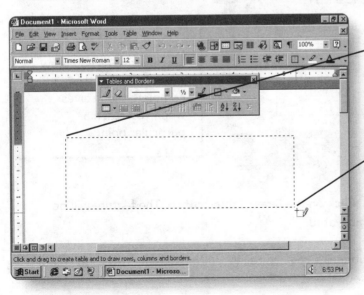

2. Press and **hold** the **mouse button** to anchor the top left corner of the table. The mouse pointer will turn into an arrow with a small box at the tip of it.

3. Press the **mouse button** and **drag** to draw a box that is the approximate size you need for your table. A dotted box will represent the table size.

4. Release the **mouse button**. The table border will appear.

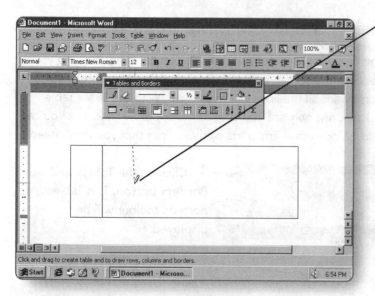

5. Press and **hold** the **mouse button** and **drag** to draw as many vertical lines as you need to create columns. The lines will appear as you draw them.

NOTE

Don't be concerned over exact placement and spacing of drawn lines. You'll learn how to space or move them later in this chapter.

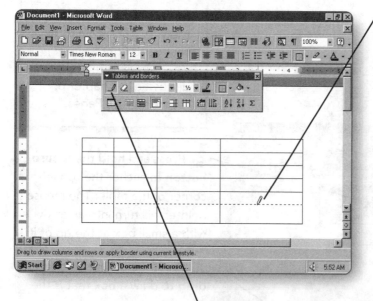

6. Press and **hold** the **mouse button** and **drag** to draw as many horizontal lines as you need to create rows. The lines will appear as you draw them.

NOTE

You'll notice as you draw these lines that they complete themselves when you reach a particular point.

7. **Click** on the **Draw Table button**. The feature will be deactivated.

Optionally, you can tell Word to make the rows and columns an equal size.

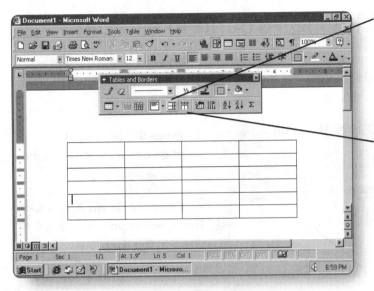

8a. **Click** on the **Distribute Rows Evenly button**. All of the rows you've created will be of equal size.

AND/OR

8b. **Click** on the **Distribute Columns Evenly button**. The table columns will be of equal size.

Entering Text

Each intersection of a column and row is called a cell. Text is typed into the individual cells. As you enter text in the cells, if you have more characters than will fit horizontally, the text automatically wraps to the next line, and the cell and the row it lies in expand vertically to hold the text.

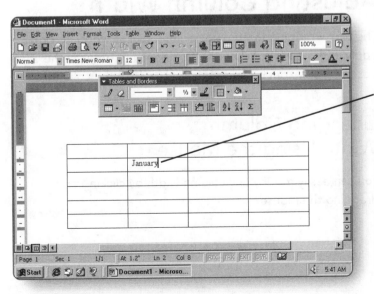

1. **Click** the **mouse pointer** in a cell. The blinking insertion point will appear.

2. **Type** some **text**. The text will display in a single cell.

NOTE

You edit text in cells in the same manner that you edit text in a regular document.

Moving Around in a Table

You can use your keyboard or mouse to move around in a table. To use the mouse, simply click in the cell you want to work with.

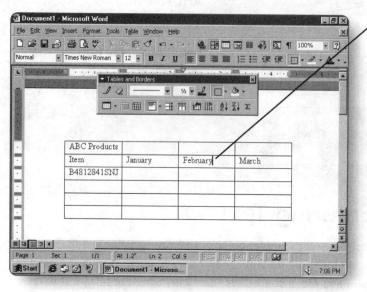

1. **Press** the **Tab key**. The insertion point will move to the cell to the right.

2. **Press** the **Down Arrow key**. The insertion point will move down to the next row.

3. **Press** the **Shift + Tab key**. The insertion point will move to the cell to the left.

4. **Press** the **Up Arrow key**. The insertion point will move up a row.

Adjusting Column Width

The text-wrapping feature sometimes causes words to break oddly in the middle. When the text does not break in the position you expect, you may need to widen the column.

Changing Column Width Using the Mouse

You can easily modify any column width by clicking and dragging the mouse.

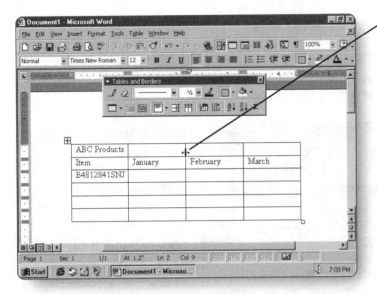

1. Place the **insertion point** over the border line of the column. The mouse pointer will change to a double-headed arrow.

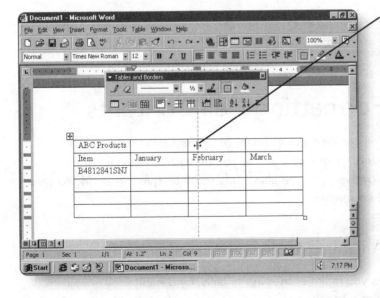

2. Press and hold the **mouse button** and **drag** to the right to increase the column width or to the left to decrease the column width. A dotted line will indicate the new position.

3. Release the **mouse button** when the column is at the width you want. The column width will change.

NOTE

Widening one column may make an adjacent column shrink so the table fits the document width.

Using AutoFit

A new feature to Word 2000 is the Table AutoFit feature. AutoFit will automatically adjust all columns to fit your text or the width of the document.

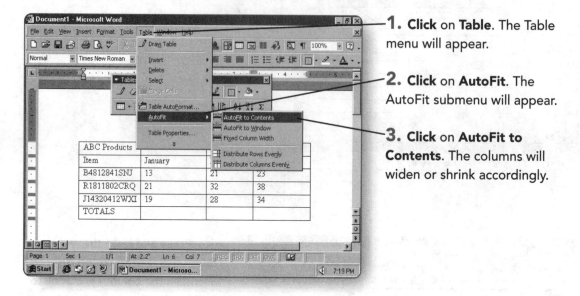

1. **Click** on **Table**. The Table menu will appear.

2. **Click** on **AutoFit**. The AutoFit submenu will appear.

3. **Click** on **AutoFit to Contents**. The columns will widen or shrink accordingly.

Formatting Cell Contents

You can perform a variety of formatting effects on the contents of a cell, just as you do with any text in Word. However, you can also apply some unique formatting to cells themselves.

Aligning Cell Contents

As you make entries in the cells, by default they are all aligned at the top of the cell, along the left side. If you're using numbers in your table, you may want to make them right-align, or maybe you would like to center-align column headings. You'll align your text both horizontally and vertically in each cell. You can align the contents of each cell separately.

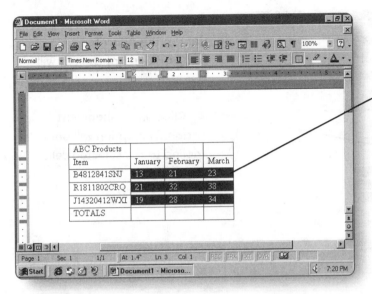

1. Click in the **first cell** you want to format. The blinking insertion point will appear.

2. Press and hold your **mouse button** and **drag** across any other cells that you want to format. The selected cells will be highlighted.

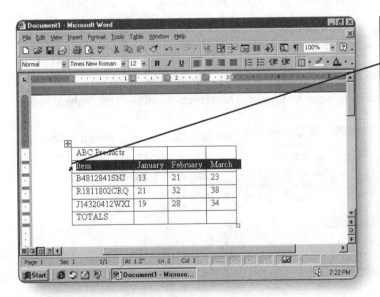

TIP

You can also select a whole row at a time by moving your insertion point to the left of the row until it becomes a white arrow and then clicking. This works the same for selecting a column by moving the insertion point to the top of the column until you see the same arrow.

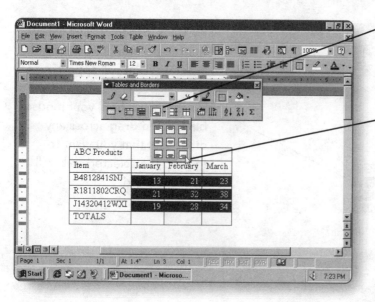

3. Click on the **arrow** to the right of the **Align Top Left button**. A grid of choices will appear.

4. Click on an **alignment option**. The option will be applied to the selected cells.

Formatting Text in Cells

Text inside tables is formatted exactly the same way any other text in the document is formatted.

1. Press and **hold** the **mouse button** and **drag** across any cells that you want to format. The selected cells will be highlighted.

2. Click on the **down arrow** to the right of the Font or Font size text box. A list of choices will appear.

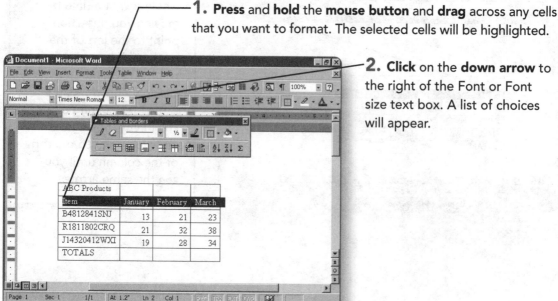

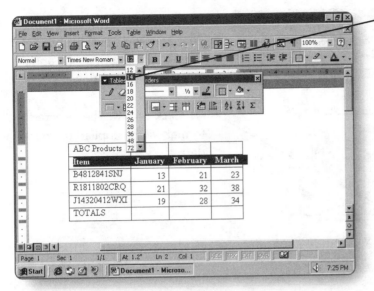

3. Click on the desired **choice**. The option will be applied to the selected cells.

Using AutoFormat

You can add formatting to the lines that divide your rows and columns, and even add color or patterns to the interior of the cells. Of course, you don't want to spend hours trying different line sizes, colors, and patterns. Instead, you can use AutoFormat.

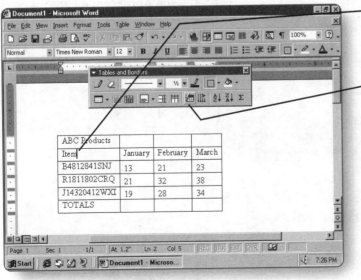

1. Click in any **table cell**. The blinking insertion point will appear.

2. Click on the **Table AutoFormat button**. The Table AutoFormat dialog box will open.

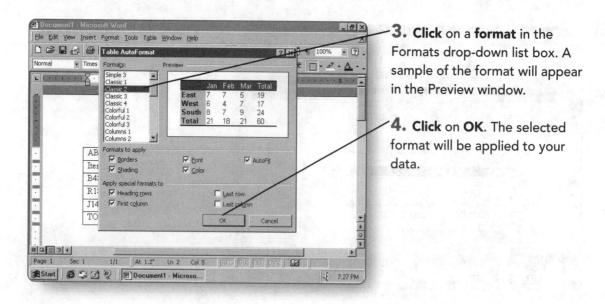

3. Click on a **format** in the Formats drop-down list box. A sample of the format will appear in the Preview window.

4. Click on **OK**. The selected format will be applied to your data.

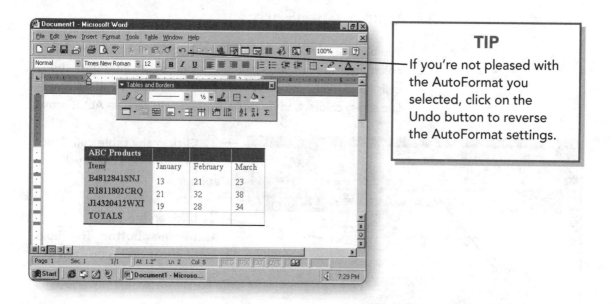

TIP

If you're not pleased with the AutoFormat you selected, click on the Undo button to reverse the AutoFormat settings.

Using AutoSum

Frequently, tables contain numbers that need to be added.
For this reason, Word includes an AutoSum button on the
Tables and Borders toolbar.

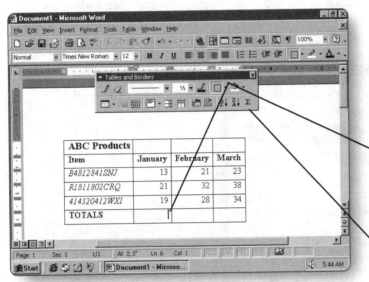

Totaling Cells with AutoSum

The AutoSum feature will add
the cells directly above it or to
the right of it.

1. Click in the **cell** where you
want the total to appear. The
blinking insertion point will
appear.

2. Click on **AutoSum**. The total
will be calculated.

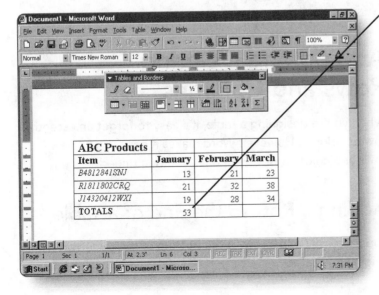

The answer will be displayed in
the selected cell.

Updating AutoSum Totals

If you change any of the values in the cells that are totaled, the cell that has the total does not automatically update. You must update it manually.

1. **Click** in the **cell** with the current total. Depending on exactly where you click in the cell, either a blinking insertion point will appear or a gray highlight will surround the total.

2. **Click** on **AutoSum**. The new total will be displayed.

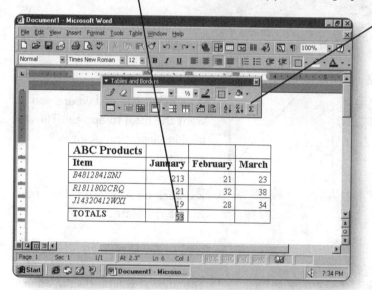

Adding and Deleting Rows and Columns

When you're designing a table, it's easy to forget an essential row or column. However, Word makes it easy to add new rows and columns or delete ones you don't need.

Adding a Row to the End of a Table

You can easily add a row to the bottom of the table you originally created.

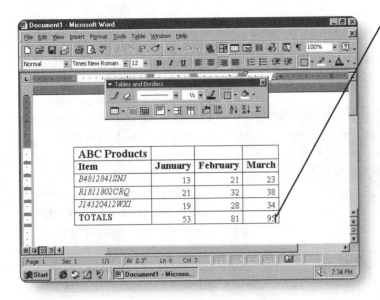

1. Click in the **last cell** of the last row. The blinking insertion point will appear.

2. Press the **Tab key**. A new row will automatically appear.

Inserting a Row Between Existing Rows

You may want to add a row at the beginning or in the middle of a table.

1. Click in the **row** below where you want to insert a new row. The blinking insertion point will appear.

2. Click on **Table**. The Table menu will appear.

3. Click on **Insert**. The Insert submenu will appear.

4. Click on **Rows Above**. The new row is inserted above the row where your insertion point rested.

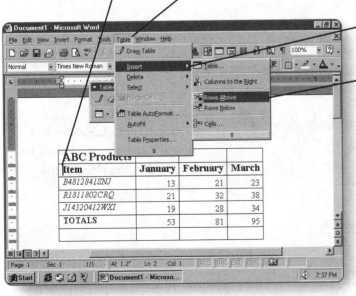

Inserting a Column

What if you decide you need another category of information in your table? That calls for a new column. Again, you can easily add a column between two existing columns or add one on to the end of a set of existing columns.

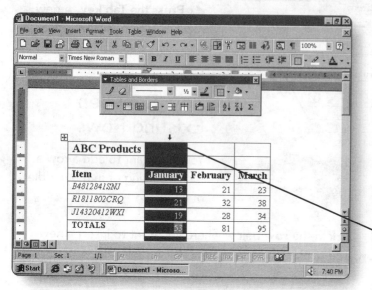

1. Move the **mouse pointer** above the column before where you want to insert a new column. The pointer will change to a black, downward-pointing arrow.

2. Click the **mouse pointer**. The column will be selected.

3. Click on **Table**. The Table menu will appear.

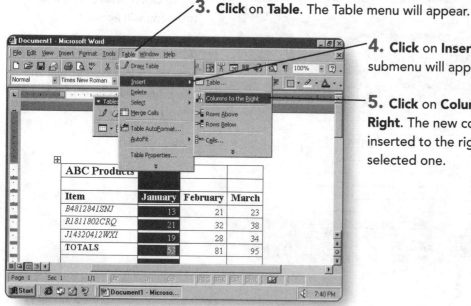

4. Click on **Insert**. The Insert submenu will appear.

5. Click on **Columns to the Right**. The new column will be inserted to the right of the selected one.

Deleting a Row

Deleting a row will delete an entire row across a table.

1. **Click** the **mouse pointer** in the row that you want to delete. The blinking insertion point will appear.

> ### TIP
> Optionally, select multiple rows to delete them at the same time.

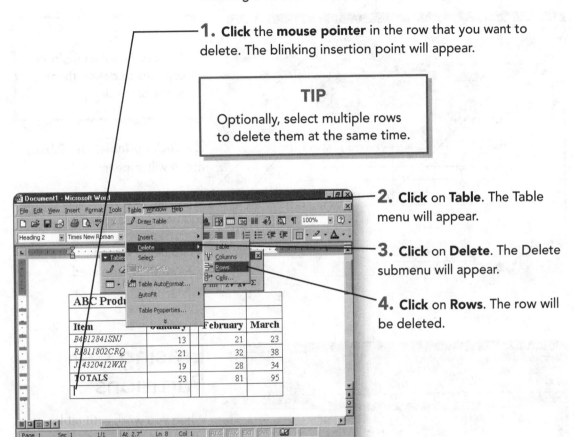

2. **Click** on **Table**. The Table menu will appear.

3. **Click** on **Delete**. The Delete submenu will appear.

4. **Click** on **Rows**. The row will be deleted.

Deleting a Column

You may decide, for example, that you only need six months of columns, not 12. In that case, you can also easily delete columns.

1. Click the **mouse pointer** in the column that you want to delete. The blinking insertion point will appear.

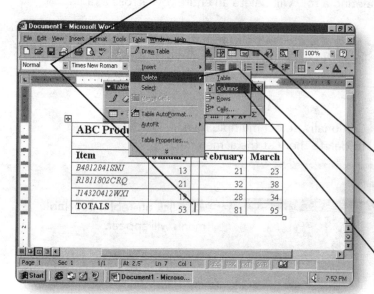

2. Click on **Table**. The Table menu will appear.

3. Click on **Delete**. The Delete submenu will appear.

4. Click on **Columns**. The column will be deleted.

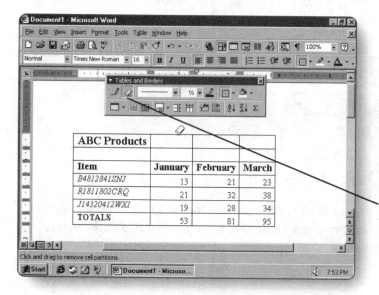

Erasing Cell Partitions

When you work with tables, you often find that you don't want all of the lines that divide cells. Erasing lines will combine connecting cells.

1. Click on the **Eraser button**. The pointer will change shape to look like an eraser.

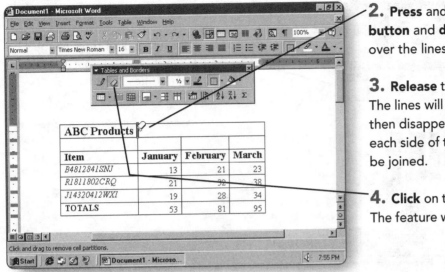

2. Press and **hold** the **mouse button** and **drag** the eraser over the lines you don't need.

3. Release the **mouse button**. The lines will change color and then disappear. The cells on each side of the erased line will be joined.

4. Click on the **Erase button**. The feature will be deactivated.

Changing the Direction of Your Text

It may be more effective to have the text in some cells run vertically rather than horizontally.

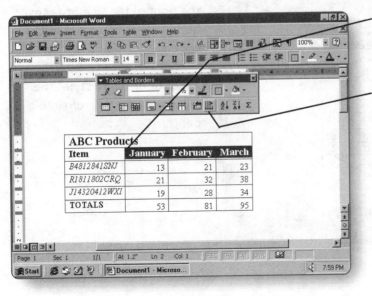

1. Select the **text** to be modified. The text will be highlighted.

2. Click on the **Change Text Direction button**. The text will display vertically.

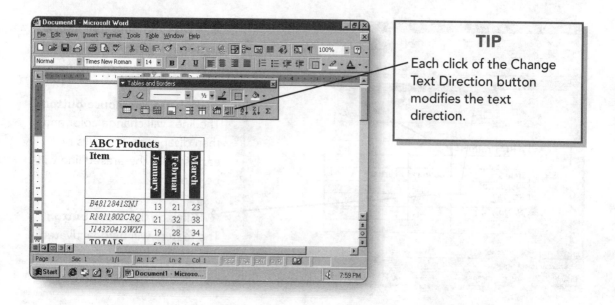

TIP

Each click of the Change Text Direction button modifies the text direction.

Modifying Table Cell Borders

You can modify the styles of the lines that surround your table cells.

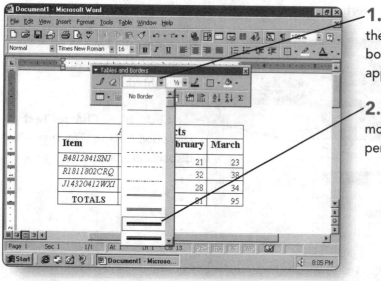

1. Click on the **down arrow** to the right of the Line Style text box. A list of line styles will appear.

2. Click on a **line style**. The mouse pointer will turn into a pencil.

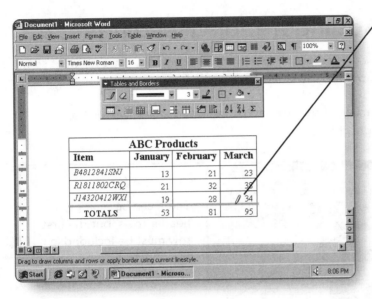

3. Press and **drag** the **mouse** across the lines to have the new border line style. A gray line will appear.

4. Release the **mouse button**. The style will be applied to the selected cells.

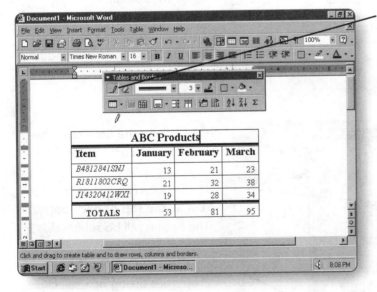

5. Click on the **Draw button**. The feature will be deactivated.

Adding a Table Heading Row

If a table extends to more than one page, you may want some of the top rows to repeat on each page.

1. Select the **rows** to be repeated. The rows will be highlighted.

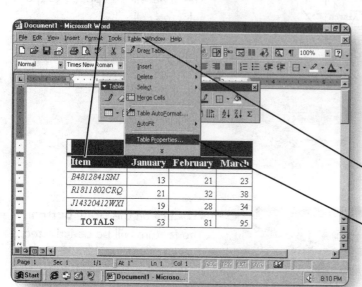

2. Click on **Table**. The Table menu will appear.

3. Click on **Table Properties**. The Table Properties dialog box will open.

NOTE

There can be multiple header rows, but the first row must be included in the selection.

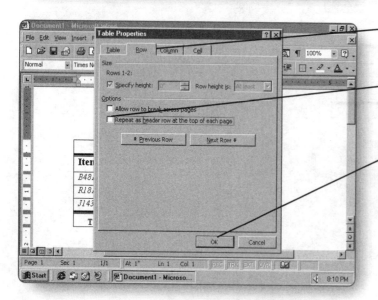

4. Click on the **Row tab**. The Row tab will come to the front.

5. Click on **Repeat as header row at the top of each page**. The option will be selected.

6. Click on **OK**. The Table Properties dialog box will close.

15

Creating Charts

Charts summarize data and make it easy for the reader to compare results. They also add color and interest to what otherwise may be a dull document. In this chapter, you'll learn to:

- Create a column chart from the data in a table
- Add a chart title
- Adjust the size of your chart and format elements
- Create a chart without creating a table first

Creating a Chart from a Table

You can make a column chart from a table you've already created. Column charts are easy for readers to understand and are often used for comparing data from one year to another, one quarter to another, or estimated budget data against actual data.

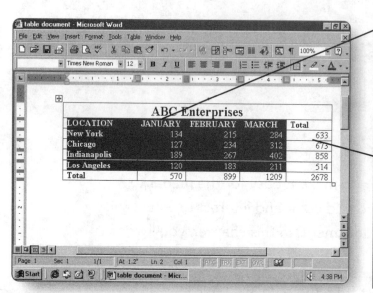

1. Select the **data, column heads**, and **row labels** of your table. The data will be highlighted.

> **TIP**
>
> When selecting data for your chart, be careful not to include data that you don't want to chart. For example, including totals can distort the overall chart picture.

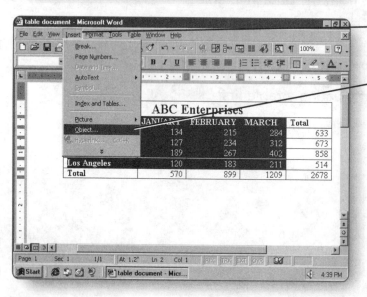

2. Click on **Insert**. The Insert menu will appear.

3. Click on **Object**. The Object dialog box will open.

4. If necessary, **click** on the **Create New tab**. The Create New tab will come to the front.

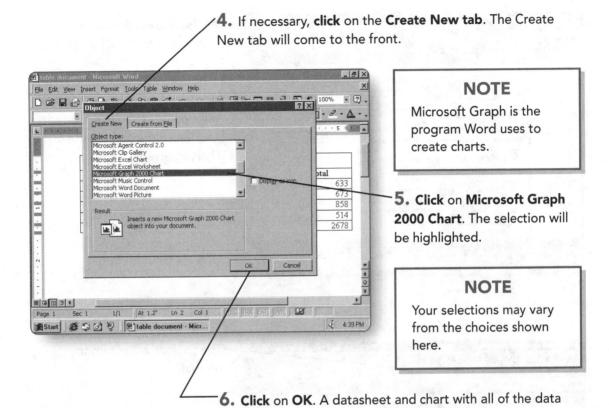

NOTE

Microsoft Graph is the program Word uses to create charts.

5. **Click** on **Microsoft Graph 2000 Chart**. The selection will be highlighted.

NOTE

Your selections may vary from the choices shown here.

6. **Click** on **OK**. A datasheet and chart with all of the data that you selected in the table will appear.

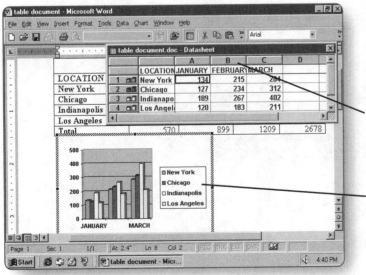

If you work with spreadsheet software such as Excel, the datasheet will look familiar. Notice the differences in the window now:

- The datasheet is set up with letters labeling the columns and numbers labeling the rows.

- The chart is complete with legend and category labels.

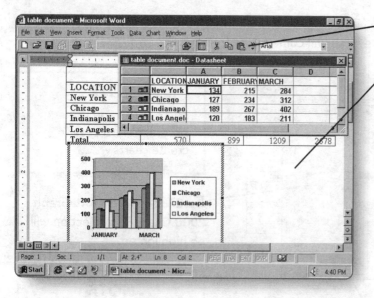

• The Standard toolbar changes to the Chart toolbar.

7. **Click** anywhere in the **document body**. The datasheet will close and you will return to your Word document with a chart inserted.

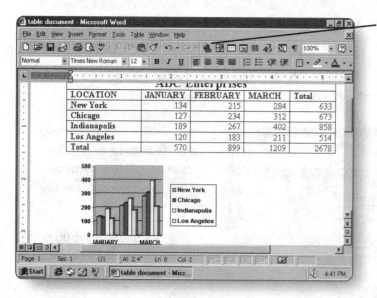

The toolbar will return to normal.

Resizing a Chart

The chart is created automatically and won't always be the exact size you need in your document. Not only is it sometimes the wrong size, but you may need to adjust the width so that all the category labels are visible. In the example shown here, the word "February" is not displayed due to size constraints.

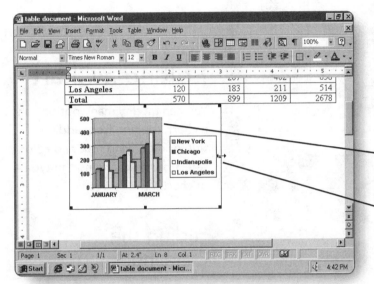

1. **Click** on the **chart**. Eight small handles will appear.

2. **Position** the **mouse pointer** over any of the handles. The mouse pointer will turn into a black double-headed arrow.

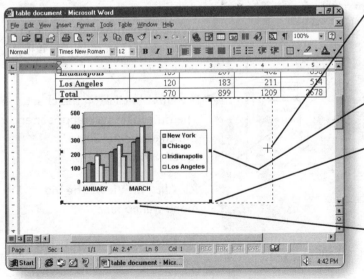

3. **Press** and **hold** the **mouse button** and **drag** the **handle**. A dotted line will indicate the new chart size.

• Dragging a side handle will modify the width only.

• Dragging corner handles will enlarge or shrink the window in both height and width in proportion to its original size.

• Dragging a top or bottom handle will modify the height only.

4. **Release** the **mouse button**. The chart will be resized.

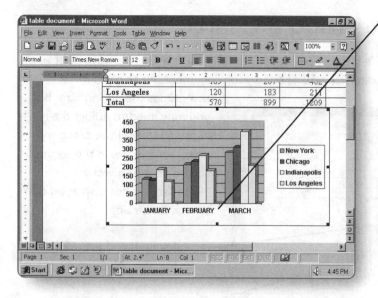

The category label "February" is now displayed.

Editing a Chart

You can modify many options on a chart, ranging from adding a title or modifying font and color selections to changing the type of chart.

Hiding the Datasheet

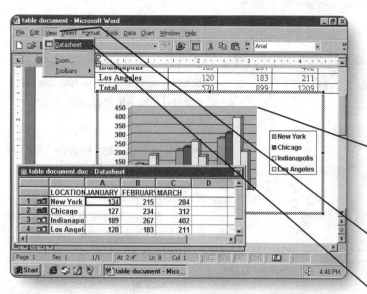

Frequently the datasheet is lying on top of the chart, making it difficult to work with the elements of the chart. You can hide it and then redisplay it if necessary.

1. Double-click on the **chart**. The datasheet will reappear and the chart menu will be reactivated.

2. Click on **View**. The View menu will appear.

3. Click on **Datasheet**. The Datasheet will close.

Repeat the previous steps to redisplay the Datasheet.

Adding a Chart Title

A chart title helps your reader quickly interpret the information displayed in the chart.

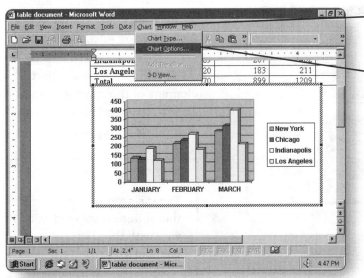

1. Click on **Chart**. The Chart menu will appear.

2. Click on **Chart Options**. The Chart Options dialog box will open.

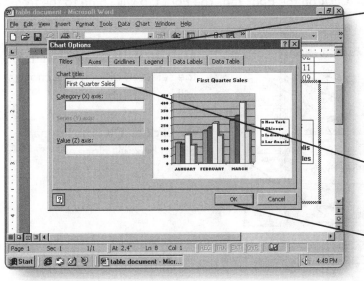

3. If necessary, **click** on the **Titles tab**. The Titles tab will come to the front.

4. Click in the **Chart title text box**. A blinking insertion point will appear.

5. Type a **title** for your chart. The title will display in the chart preview box.

6. Click on **OK**. The new title will be added to your chart.

Formatting Chart Text

Similar to standard Word documents, you can change the font, size, style, color, and other attributes for text on a chart. You can change the formatting of the Title, Legends, Category Axis, or Value Axis.

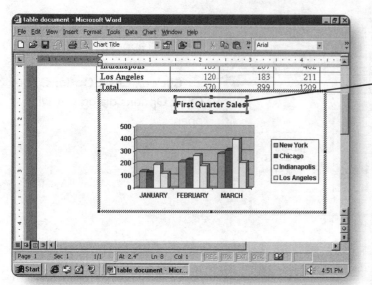

1. Double-click on the **text element** of the chart that you want to format. The Format dialog box will open.

> **NOTE**
>
> The dialog box name and the options displayed will vary with the chart element you selected.

2. Click on the **Font tab**. The Font tab will come to the front.

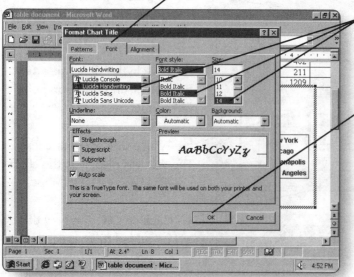

3. Click on the **Font, Font Style, or Font Size** you want for the selected object. The choices will be highlighted.

4. Click on **OK**. The Format dialog box will close.

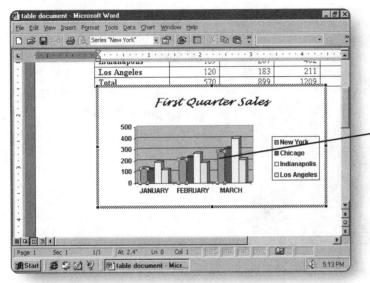

Modifying Chart Colors

The series in the chart can be of any color you specify.

1. Double-click on the **first bar** of any series in the chart. The Format Data Series dialog box will open.

2. If necessary, **click** on the **Patterns tab**. The Patterns tab will come to the front.

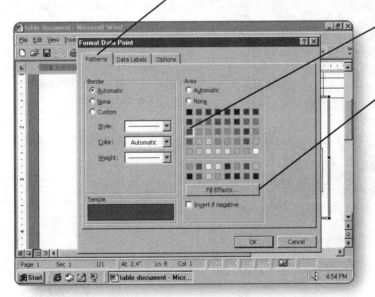

3. Click on a **color** for the selected series. A preview will display in the Sample box.

4. Click on the **Fill Effects button**. The Fill Effects dialog box will open.

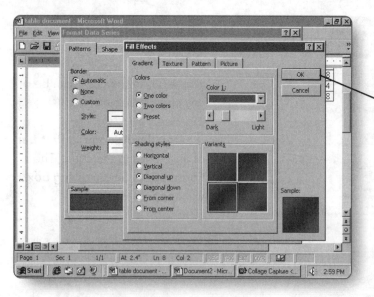

5. Click on a **fill choice** for the selected bar series. A sample will be displayed.

6. Click on **OK**. The Fill Effects dialog box will close.

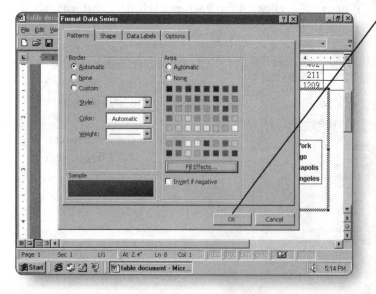

7. Click on **OK**. The Format dialog box will close and the series, including the legend, will change to the new color.

8. Repeat steps 1–7 for each series to be modified.

Selecting Bar Shapes

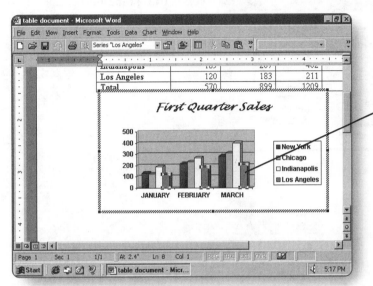

Word 2000 includes several fun shapes you can use for column charts instead of the default rectangular bars.

1. Double-click on the **first bar** of any series in the chart. The Format Data Series dialog box will open.

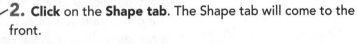

2. Click on the **Shape tab**. The Shape tab will come to the front.

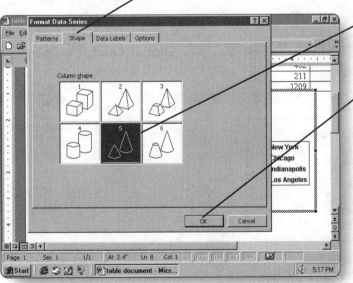

3. Click on a **shape** for the selected series. The option will be selected.

4. Click on **OK**. The selected series on the chart will change to the new shape.

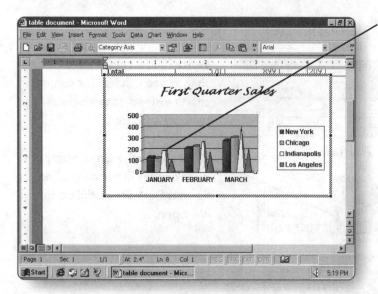

5. Repeat steps 1–4 for each series to be modified.

Changing the Chart Type

Several types of charts are available to you. Column charts are fine for comparing sets of data, and line charts are useful to show trends, such as population growth. Pie charts, on the other hand, show percentages that make up a whole.

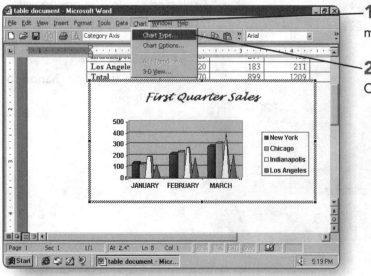

1. Click on **Chart**. The Chart menu will appear.

2. Click on **Chart Type**. The Chart Type dialog box will open.

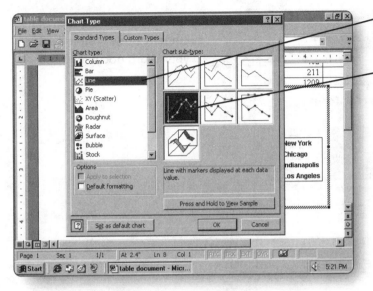

3. **Click** on a **Chart Type**. A selection of options will appear.

4. **Click** on a **style** for your chart. The option will be selected.

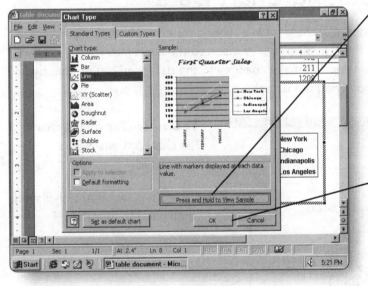

5. **Press** and **hold** the **mouse button** on **Press and Hold to View Sample**. A representative chart with your "live" data will display.

6. **Release** the **mouse button**. The options will reappear.

7. **Click** on **OK**. Your chart type will change.

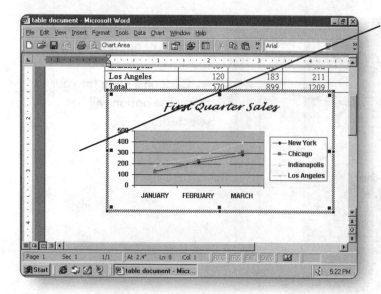

8. Click anywhere in the **document body**. You will return to your Word document.

Editing Chart Data

Changing the data in a table does not automatically reflect in a chart. If, after you've inserted the chart into your document, you need to make changes to the data, you can do that by modifying the datasheet.

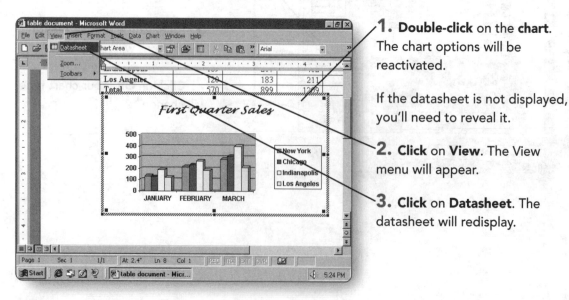

1. Double-click on the **chart**. The chart options will be reactivated.

If the datasheet is not displayed, you'll need to reveal it.

2. Click on **View**. The View menu will appear.

3. Click on **Datasheet**. The datasheet will redisplay.

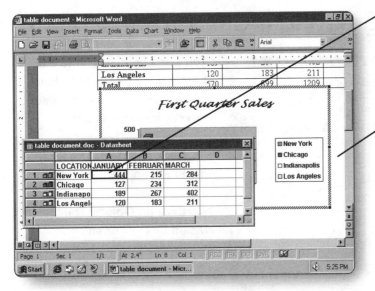

4. Click in any **cell** of the datasheet and **type** any **desired changes**. The chart will automatically update to reflect the changes.

5. Click anywhere in the **document body**. You will return to your Word document.

Deleting a Chart

If at any time a chart is no longer necessary, you can easily delete it.

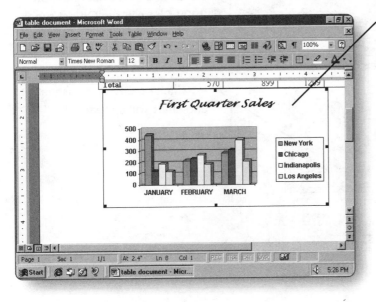

1. Click on the **chart**. The chart will be selected with eight black handles.

2. Press the **Delete key**. The chart will be deleted from the Word document.

Creating a Chart from Scratch

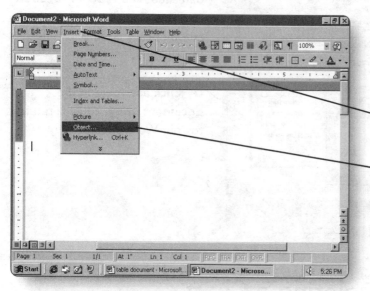

You don't need to create a table before you can create a chart. You can simply type your data directly into the datasheet.

1. Click on **Insert**. The Insert menu will appear.

2. Click on **Object**. The Object dialog box will open.

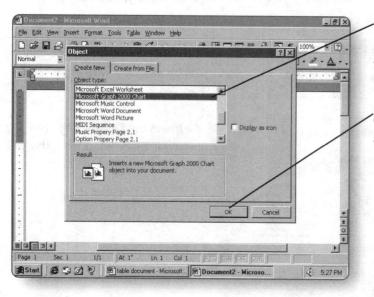

3. Click on **Microsoft Graph 2000 Chart** in the Object type: text box. The selection will be highlighted.

4. Click on **OK**. A datasheet and chart will appear.

The datasheet will contain data, but not your data. This is sample data to help you figure out where to enter your data to create the chart. Notice the following:

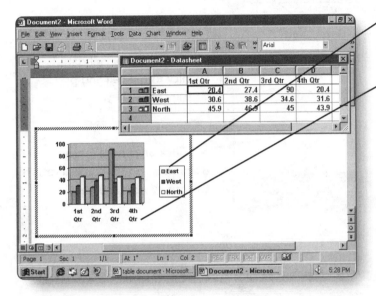

- The East, West, and North row labels appear as the legend.

- The column labels appear as category labels at the bottom of the chart.

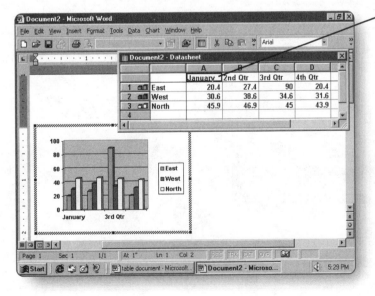

6. Click in a **cell** in the datasheet. A black border will appear around the selected cell.

7. Replace the **sample data** with your data. You will immediately see the changes applied in the chart.

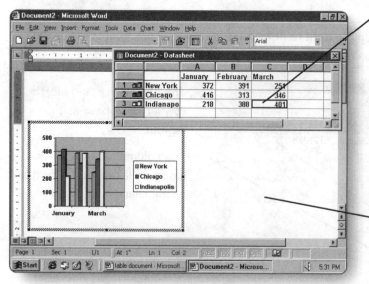

8. Continue clicking in cells and **replacing** data. The chart will be updated.

TIP

To delete any cell data, click in the cell and press the Delete key.

9. Click anywhere in the **document body**. You will return to your Word document.

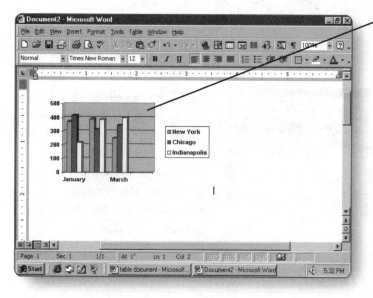

You can now edit the chart size, data, or formatting as you learned earlier in this chapter.

16

Using Newspaper Columns

When you think of columns you probably think of newspapers or newsletters, the kind that arrive through the mail from hospitals, schools, insurance companies, and other local businesses. These documents use columns to break up stories, with the text flowing from the bottom of one column to the top of the next. Of course, columns can be used for many other things, such as creating attractive forms or marketing materials. In this chapter, you'll learn how to:

- Create newspaper columns
- Change the number and width of columns
- Add headings that span more than one column
- Add vertical lines between columns
- Remove newspaper columns

Creating Newspaper Columns

Newspaper columns will apply to the entire document unless you select a portion before creating the columns.

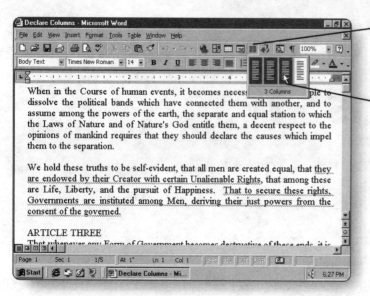

1. Click on the **Columns button.** A palette of column choices will appear.

2. Press and **hold** the **mouse button** and **drag across the palette** to select the number of columns. The number at the bottom of the palette will change as you drag over the selections.

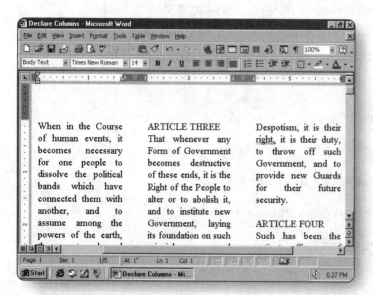

3. Release the **mouse button** on the number of columns that you want to use. The columns palette will close.

The selected text will flow into the number of columns that you chose, from the top to the bottom of the left-most column, and then up to the top of the column to its right, and so on.

Changing the Number of Columns

Perhaps you decide after formatting text in columns that you want one more column or one less column. Word enables you to change the number of columns easily.

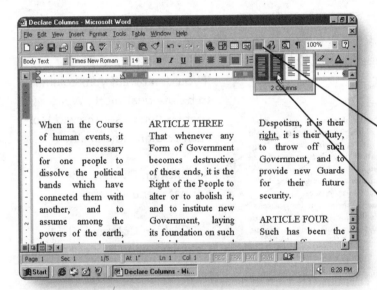

Again, if you want to make this change to only a portion of the document, you must select that portion before continuing with these steps.

1. Click on the **Columns button.** The palette of column choices will appear.

2. Press and **hold** the **mouse button** and **drag across the palette** to make your new selection. The number at the bottom of the palette will change as you drag over the selections.

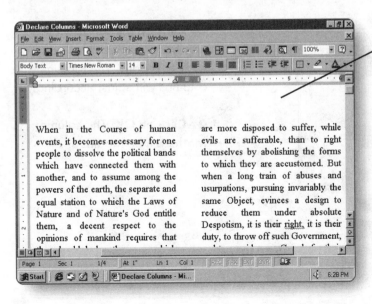

3. Release the **mouse button** on your new column choice. The selected text will flow into the new number of columns that you chose.

Changing Column Width

When you select the number of columns to be created, Word divides the text into columns of equal width. However, you can modify column width, and you can adjust the space between columns, called the *gutter*.

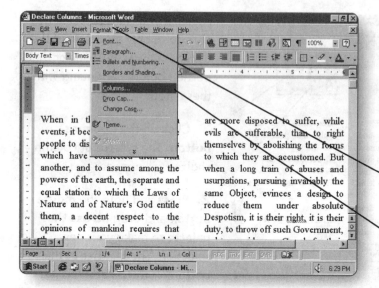

Changing the Width of Columns

If you don't want your columns to be of equal width, Word enables you to set the width of each column individually.

1. Click on **Format**. The Format menu will appear.

2. Click on **Columns**. The Columns dialog box will open.

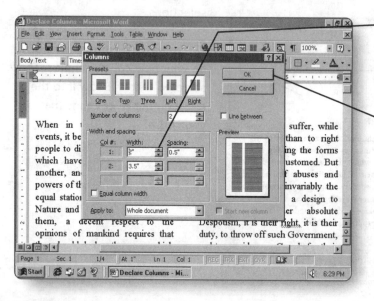

3. Click on the **up/down arrows** for each column you want to modify. The remaining columns will adjust accordingly.

4. Click on **OK**. The column widths will be modified.

Changing the Width of Space Between Columns

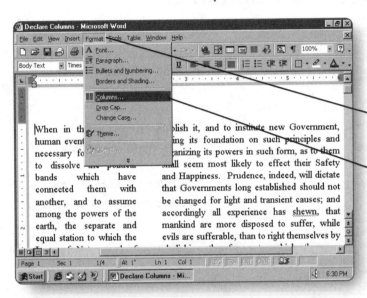

The space between each column is called the gutter. You can individually adjust the gutter between any two columns.

1. Click on **Format**. The Format menu will appear.

2. Click on **Columns**. The Columns dialog box will open.

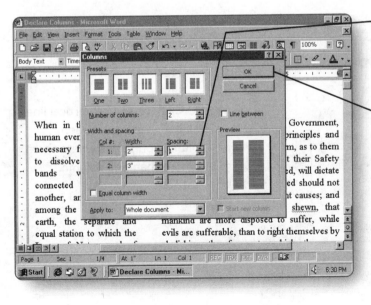

3. Click on the **up/down arrows** for each gutter spacing you want to modify. The width of the gutter will be displayed.

4. Click on **OK**. The gutter widths will be modified.

Creating Vertical Lines Between Columns

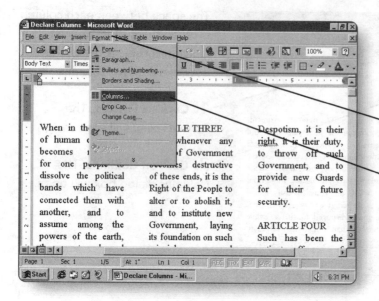

Newspapers and magazines often add vertical lines between columns to make it easier to read the text.

1. Click on **Format**. The Format menu will appear.

2. Click on **Columns**. The Columns dialog box will open.

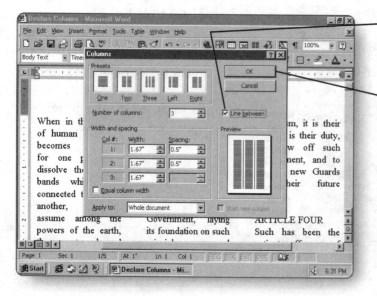

3. Click in the **Line between check box**. The option will be selected.

4. Click on **OK**. A vertical line will be inserted between columns on pages where there is more than one column.

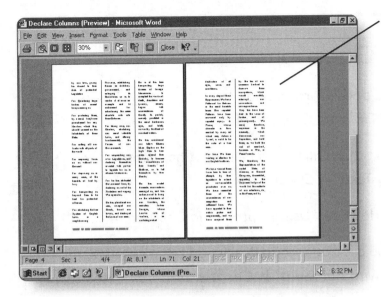

On the final page, if all columns are not used, the vertical line will not appear in front of the last column.

Removing Newspaper Columns

If you prefer your text without multiple columns, the columns and vertical lines can be easily removed. This is really just a matter of returning the text to a one-column format.

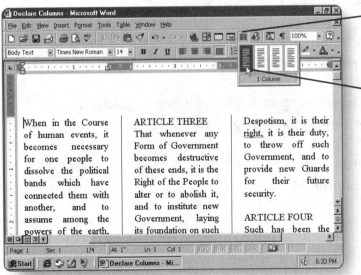

1. Click on the **Columns button**. The Columns palette will appear.

2. Click on **One Column**. The vertical line(s) will disappear and the text will expand across the entire page.

Part IV Review Questions

1. How many methods does Word provide to create a table? *See "Creating a Simple Table" in Chapter 14*

2. If you type more text than will fit in a cell, what happens to the text? *See "Entering Text" in Chapter 14*

3. What does AutoFit do? *See "Using AutoFit" in Chapter 14*

4. What button can you click to automatically add table cell values? *See "Totaling Cells with AutoSum" in Chapter 14*

5. When might you use a table heading row? *See "Adding a Table Heading Row" in Chapter 14*

6. What is the default style of chart? *See "Creating a Chart From a Table" in Chapter 15*

7. What happens to the standard toolbar when you create a chart? *See "Creating a Chart From a Table" in Chapter 15*

8. What type of data is traditionally represented in a pie chart? *See "Changing the Chart Type" in Chapter 15*

9. How does text flow when using multiple newspaper columns? *See "Using Newspaper Columns" in Chapter 16*

10. What is the blank space in between columns called? *See "Changing Column Width" in Chapter 16*

PART V

Using the Word Tools

17

Discovering Tools for Speed

Word 2000 includes tools that help speed up the process of creating and editing documents. In this chapter, you'll learn how to:

- Work with AutoCorrect
- Use AutoText
- Create executive summaries using AutoSummarize
- Make corrections quickly with Find and Replace
- View document statistics

Working with AutoCorrect

AutoCorrect is a great feature. You type something wrong, and Word automatically corrects it. Or, you type something like (c), and Word understands that what you really want is a symbol for copyright, and it inserts ©.

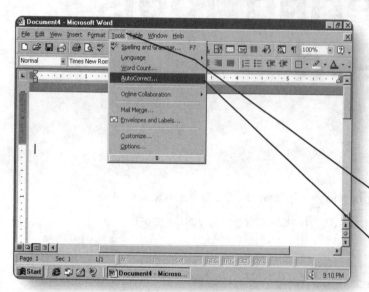

Turning AutoCorrect Features On and Off

To take full advantage of this wonderful automatic correction feature, you have to understand how it works and how to customize it.

1. Click on **Tools**. The Tools menu will appear.

2. Click on **AutoCorrect**. The AutoCorrect dialog box will open with the AutoCorrect tab in front.

A check mark will appear next to the features that are activated.

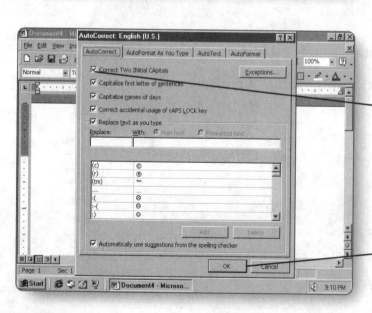

4. Click on an **option** to remove the check mark. The option will be turned off. If an option doesn't have a check mark next to it, **click** on the **option** to add a check mark. The option will be turned on.

5. Click on **OK**. The AutoCorrect dialog box will close.

Adding AutoCorrect Entries

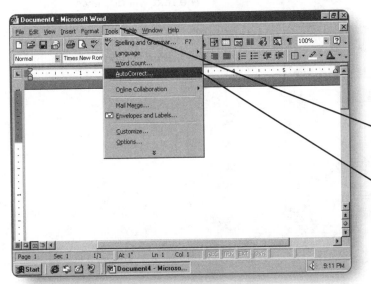

If you know that you commonly make the same typing mistake, such as "clcik" when it should be "click," you can tell Word to fix it for you.

1. Click on **Tools**. The Tools menu will appear.

2. Click on **AutoCorrect**. The AutoCorrect dialog box will open with the AutoCorrect tab in front.

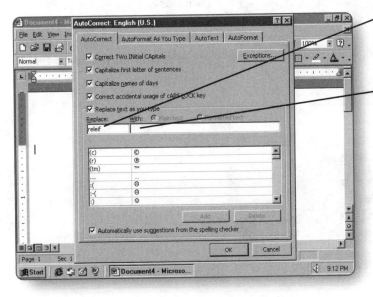

3. Type your **common mistake** in the Replace: text box. The text will display.

4. Click in the **With: text box**. A blinking insertion point will display.

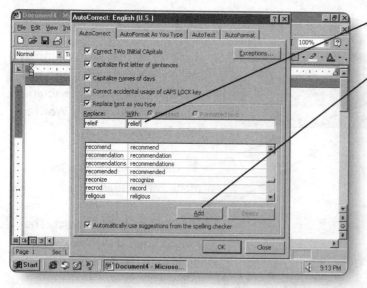

5. Type the **correct version.** The text will display.

6. Click on **Add.** The word will be added to your permanent AutoCorrect list.

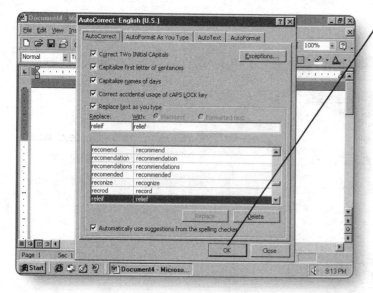

7. Click on **OK**. The dialog box will close.

Now, Word will automatically correct your mistake each time you type it.

Deleting AutoCorrect Entries

What if you're typing an article on common misspellings and you *want* to type the word "the" spelled "teh?" Or, you use "(c)" to indicate headings in a report, and Word keeps changing this to the copyright symbol?

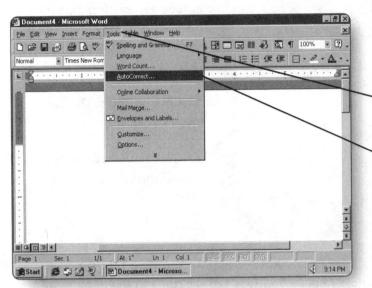

1. Click on **Tools**. The Tools menu will appear.

2. Click on **AutoCorrect**. The AutoCorrect dialog box will open with the AutoCorrect tab in front.

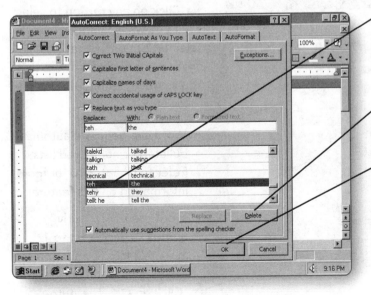

3. Click on an **entry** from the AutoCorrect list. The entry will appear in the Replace: and With: text boxes.

4. Click on **Delete**. The entry will be deleted.

5. Click on **OK**. The AutoCorrect dialog box will close.

Exploring AutoFormat as You Type

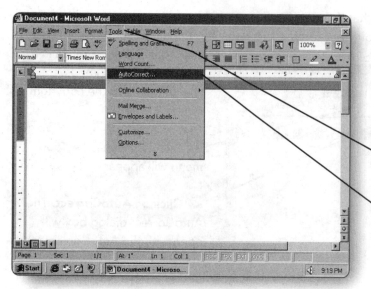

Word can also format text as you are typing it. This can include automatically creating bulleted and numbered lists or replacing fractions with fraction characters.

1. Click on **Tools**. The Tools menu will appear.

2. Click on **AutoCorrect**. The AutoCorrect dialog box will open.

3. Click on the **AutoFormat As You Type tab.** The AutoFormat As You Type tab will come to the front. More automatic features will be available from this tab.

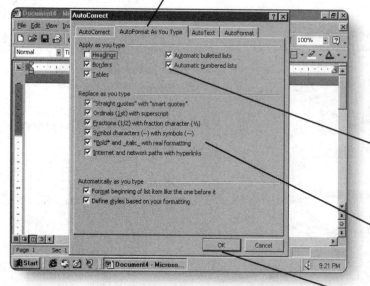

4. Click on any **option** to select what you want to apply. A selected option will have a check mark in the box next to it. You'll notice options such as the following:

- Word can generate automatic bulleted or numbered lists (refer to Chapter 10 for more information on this feature).

- Word can apply "curly quotes," change 1st to 1st, make 1/2 into ½, and more!

5. Click on **OK.** The Auto-Correct dialog box will close.

Using AutoText

Word 2000 is not only able to fix mistakes, it can also type commonly used text for you.

Creating Your Own AutoText Entry

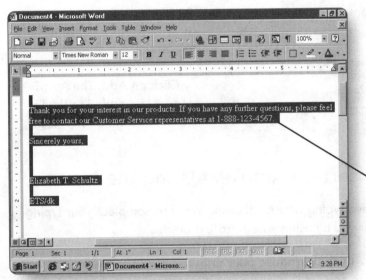

You can also add your own AutoText entries, for example, the address of a business you write to often or a paragraph you use every week in your weekly report. A standard letter closing is also a perfect entry for AutoText.

1. Type and **select** the **text** to be included as an AutoText entry. The text will be highlighted.

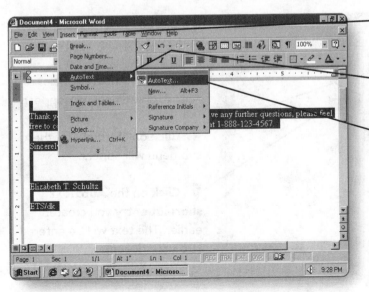

2. Click on **Insert**. The Insert menu will appear.

3. Click on **AutoText**. A submenu will appear.

4. Click on **AutoText.** The AutoCorrect dialog box will open.

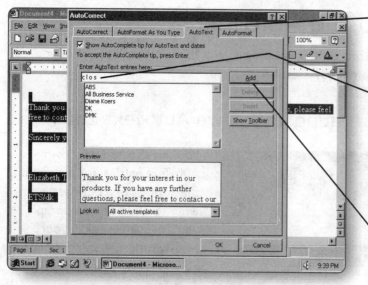

5. If necessary, **click** on the **AutoText tab**. The AutoText tab will come to the front.

6. Type an **abbreviation** you would like to use that represents the highlighted text. The abbreviation will appear in the Enter AutoText entries here: text box.

7. Click on **Add**. The AutoText entry will be added to the list and the dialog box will close.

Inserting AutoText Using the Menu

Save typing time by allowing Word to complete your typing for you by using your AutoText entries.

1. Click the **mouse pointer** in the document where the text is to appear. A blinking insertion point will appear.

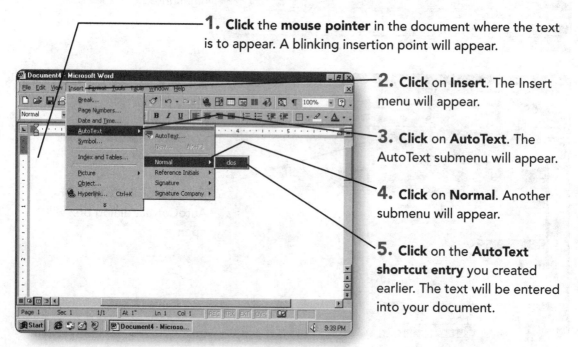

2. Click on **Insert**. The Insert menu will appear.

3. Click on **AutoText**. The AutoText submenu will appear.

4. Click on **Normal**. Another submenu will appear.

5. Click on the **AutoText shortcut entry** you created earlier. The text will be entered into your document.

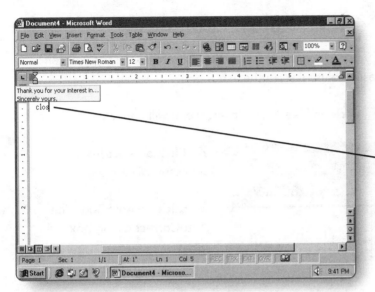

Inserting AutoText Using the Keyboard

Word tries to anticipate your needs when it comes to inserting AutoText.

1. Type the **AutoText shortcut entry** you created earlier. A ToolTip will appear displaying the AutoText entry.

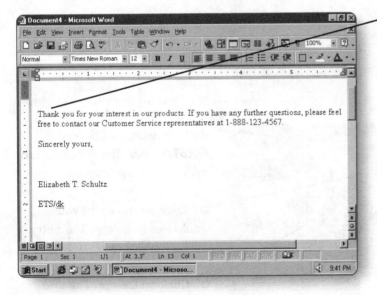

2. Press the **Enter key**. The AutoText entry will be completed.

Deleting AutoText Entries

If you no longer want a particular AutoText entry, you can easily delete it from the list.

1. Click on **Insert**. The Insert menu will appear.

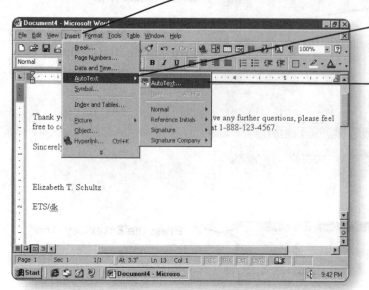

2. Click on **AutoText**. A submenu will appear.

3. Click on **AutoText**. The AutoCorrect dialog box will open.

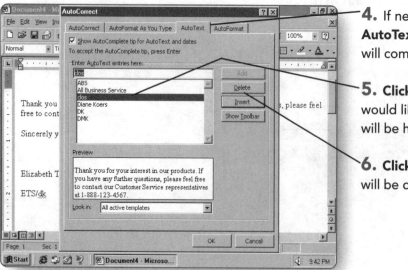

4. If necessary, **click** on the **AutoText tab**. The AutoText tab will come to the front.

5. Click on the **entry** you would like to delete. The entry will be highlighted.

6. Click on **Delete**. The entry will be deleted.

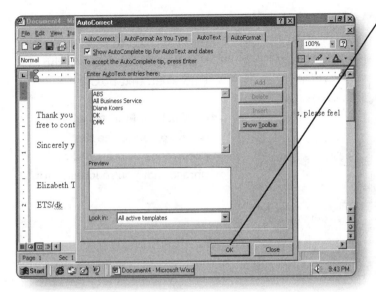

7. Click on **OK**. The dialog box will close.

Using Find and Replace

Find and Replace is a real time saver. You can quickly find out if you covered a topic in a lengthy report, and you can change names, dates, and prices throughout documents with just a few keystrokes.

Using Find

The Word Find command is useful to seek out text in a document you may have trouble visually locating. The Find command does not change any text; it simply locates and highlights it for you.

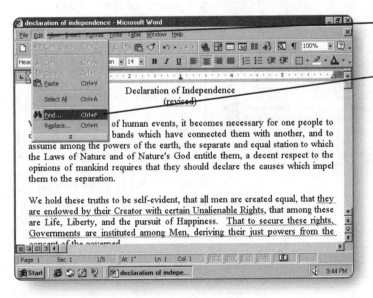

1. Click on **Edit**. The Edit menu will appear.

2. Click on **Find**. The Find and Replace dialog box will open.

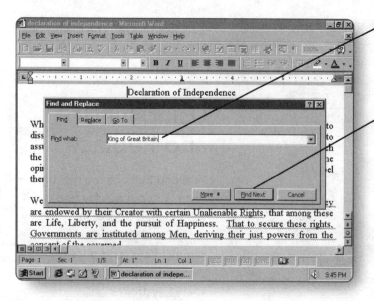

3. Type the **word** or **phrase** that you want to search for. The typed text will appear in the Find what: text box.

4. Click on **Find Next.** Word will take you to the first occurrence of the word or phrase that you're looking for.

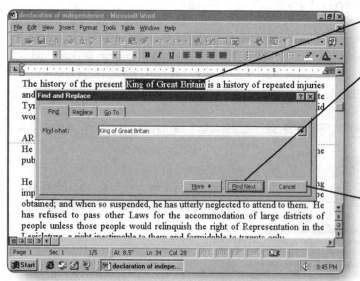

The first occurrence of the word or phrase is highlighted.

5. Click on **Find Next** again. Word will take you to the next occurrence of the word or phrase that you're looking for.

TIP

Click on Cancel if you want to discontinue the search.

Word will notify you when no more occurrences of the search text occur.

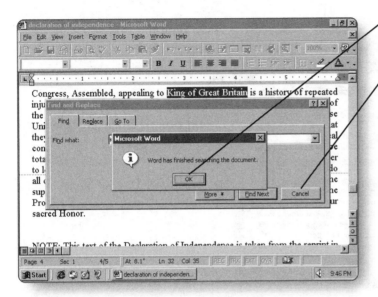

6. Click on **OK**. The message box will close.

7. Click on **Cancel**. The Find and Replace dialog box will close.

Using Replace

If you want to locate text and change it to something else, let Word do it for you with the Replace feature.

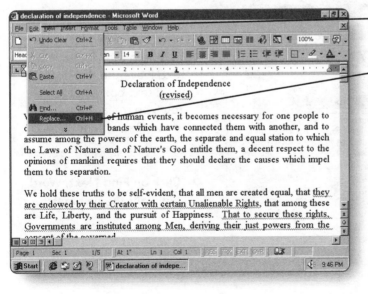

1. Click on **Edit**. The Edit menu will appear.

2. Click on **Replace**. The Find and Replace dialog box will open.

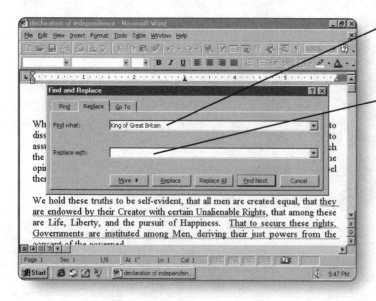

3. **Type** the **text** you want to search for. The text will appear in the Find what: text box.

4. **Click** in the **Replace with: text box**. The blinking insertion point will appear.

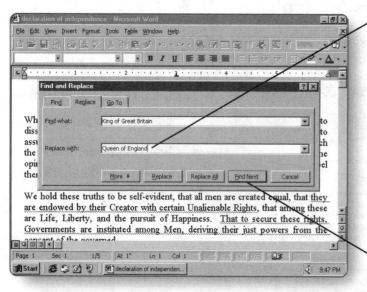

5. **Type** a **replacement word** or **phrase**. The text will appear in the Replace with: text box.

TIP

To delete the "found" text, leave the Replace with: text box empty. You'll be replacing the found text with nothing.

6. **Click** on **Find Next**. Word will highlight the first match.

7. Choose one of the following:

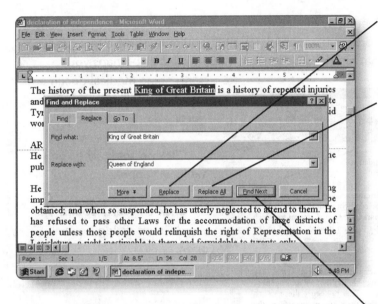

- **Click** on **Replace** if this is text you want to change. The text will be replaced and Word will highlight the next text match.

- **Click** on **Replace All**. Word will replace all occurrences of the found text with the "replace text" and notify you of the total number of replacements. Use this feature cautiously. Remember that Word will take you very literally. Make sure the find and replace options are exactly as you want them.

- **Click** on **Find Next**. Word will not make any changes and will locate the next occurrence of the text.

Word will notify you when no more occurrences of the search text occur.

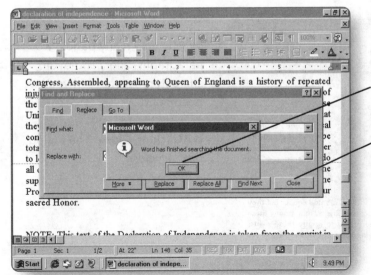

8. Click on **OK**. The message box will close.

9. Click on **Close**. The Find and Replace dialog box will close.

Finding Document Statistics

There may be occasions when you need to know how many words you've typed. Possibly, you're finishing a term paper that needs to be at least 1,000 words, or perhaps you're transcribing medical documents for which you'll be paid by the word.

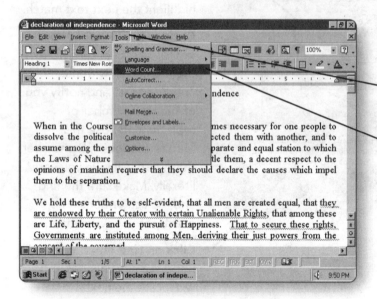

1. **Click** on **Tools**. The Tools menu will appear.

2. **Click** on **Word Count**. The Word Count dialog box will open.

The dialog box will tell you exactly how many pages, words, paragraphs, lines, and even characters you have in your document.

3. **Click** on **Close**. The dialog box will close.

18

Discovering Tools for Quality

Whether you're writing the great American novel, a standard business letter, or a resume, spelling or grammatical errors can ruin the impression that you're trying to create. Not only does Word have spelling and grammar checkers to correct these errors, but it also has an online Thesaurus so that you can find just the right word to convey your ideas. In this chapter, you'll learn how to:

- Find and correct spelling mistakes
- Identify and correct grammatical errors
- Use the Thesaurus

Correcting Spelling and Grammatical Errors

Word has built-in dictionaries and grammatical-rule sets that it uses to check your document. Word can identify possible problems as you type, and it also can run a special spelling and grammar check, which provides you with more information about the problems and tools for fixing them. These features aren't infallible; if you type air instead of err, Word probably won't be able to tell you that you're wrong. However, combined with a good proofreading, these tools can be very helpful.

Checking Spelling as You Go

By default, Word identifies problems right in your document as you type. Spelling errors have a red wavy line underneath them.

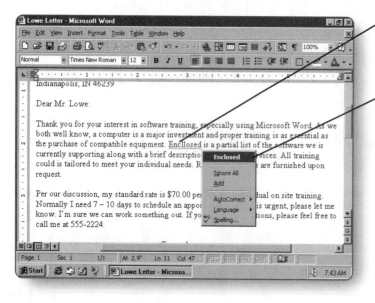

1. **Right-click** on the **word.** The shortcut menu will appear with suggested corrections.

2. **Click** on the **correct spelling** or **grammatical suggestion.** The erroneous word will be replaced with your selection.

Checking Grammar as You Go

Similar to spelling errors, Word identifies some grammatical errors with a green wavy line underneath them.

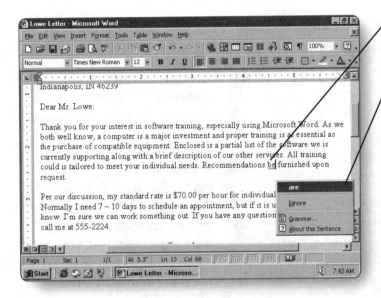

1. Right-click on the **word** or **phrase.** The shortcut menu will appear.

2. Click on the **grammatical suggestion.** The incorrect word or phrase will be replaced with your selection.

NOTE

Sometimes, Word cannot give a grammatical suggestion. In those cases, you'll need to correct the error yourself.

TIP

Do *not,* repeat do *NOT,* rely on the Spell Check and grammar features to catch all of your errors. They are far from perfect and can miss many items. They can also flag errors when your text is really OK and can suggest wrong things to do to fix both real problems and false error reports. You alone know what you want your document to say. Proofread it yourself!

Running a Spelling and Grammar Check

Word is set up to run both a spelling and grammar check at the same time.

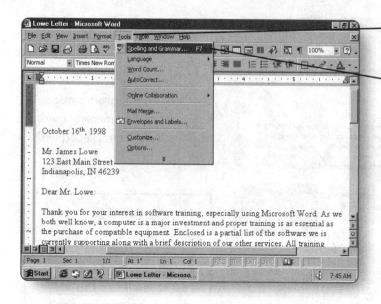

1. Click on **Tools**. The Tools menu will appear.

2. Click on **Spelling and Grammar**. The Spelling and Grammar dialog box will open.

The first error encountered, whether spelling or grammar, will be displayed. If the error is in spelling, it is identified in the Not in Dictionary: text box. In the Suggestions: text box, there are possible correct spellings for the word. In this case, the correct spelling is already highlighted.

3. Click on **one** of the following options:

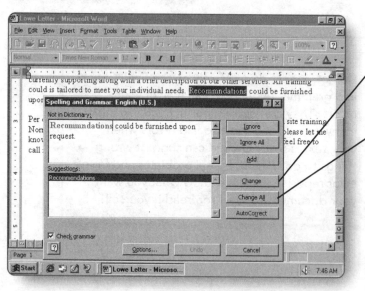

- **Click** on **Change** to change just this incident of the spelling mistake.

- **Click** on **Change All** if you think you could have made the mistake more than once.

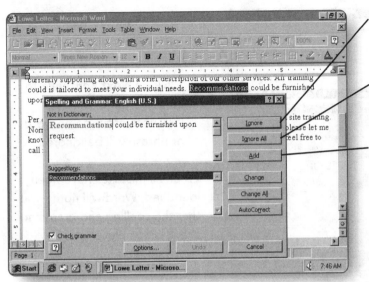

- **Click** on **Ignore** if you don't want to correct this instance of the spelling.

- **Click** on **Ignore All** if you don't want to correct any instances of the spelling.

- **Click** on **Add** to add a word, such as a proper name or legal term, to Word's built-in dictionary so that it won't be flagged as an error in the future.

After you choose one of these actions, the check will proceed to the next possible error.

If Word finds a grammatical error, it will display it in the top text box, with a suggested revision or explanation of the error in the Suggestions: text box.

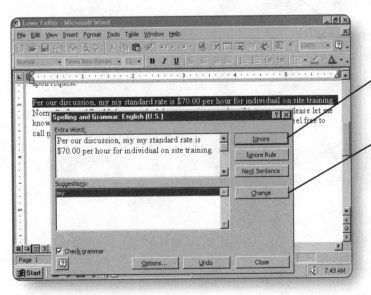

4. Click on **one** of the following:

- **Click** on **Ignore** if you don't want to change this instance of the grammatical problem.

- **Click** on **Change** to make the suggested change.

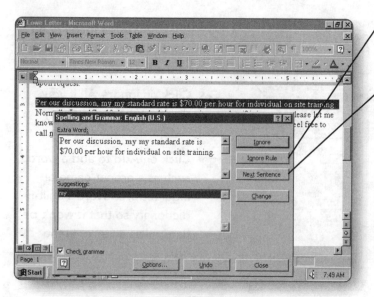

- **Click** on **Ignore Rule** to ignore all instances of the grammatical problem.

- **Click** on **Next Sentence** to continue the check. All instances of the same word or phrase will be ignored.

When all mistakes have been identified, Word will notify you that the spelling and grammar check is complete.

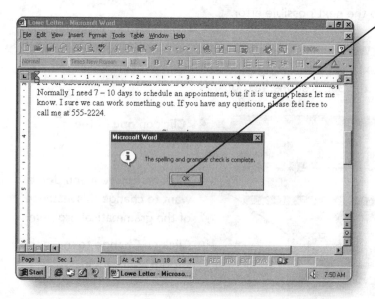

5. Click on **OK**. The message box will close.

Disabling Grammar Check

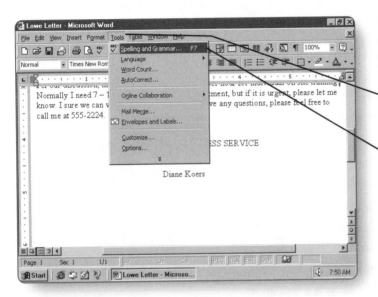

If you want to have a spelling check but not grammar check, you can disable it.

1. Click on **Tools**. The Tools menu will appear.

2. Click on **Spelling and Grammar**. The Spelling and Grammar dialog box will open.

3. Click in the check box next to **Check grammar**. The check mark will be removed and the spell check will begin.

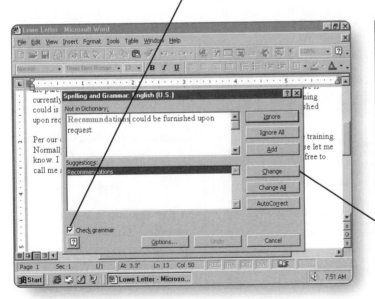

NOTE

In some instances, a message box may appear. Click on Yes. The grammar check will be disabled, and Word will look only for misspelled words.

4. Continue with the **spell check** as covered in the previous section. A message box will display.

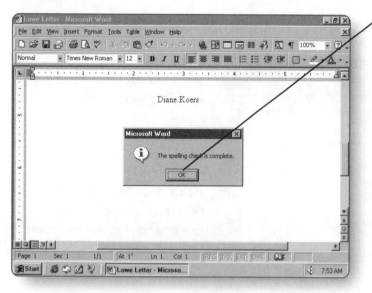

5. Click on **OK**. The spell check will be complete.

Finding that Elusive Word with the Thesaurus

When you just can't remember the word you need, the Thesaurus is invaluable.

1. Select the **word** that you want to replace with a better word. The word will be highlighted.

2. Click on **Tools**. The Tools menu will appear.

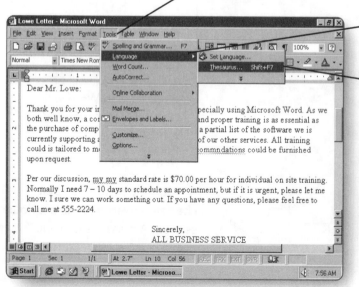

3. Click on **Language**. A submenu will appear.

4. Click on **Thesaurus**. The Thesaurus dialog box will open.

TIP

If the Thesaurus is not installed, you'll be prompted to install it. You'll need your Word CD to install the feature.

Many words have multiple meanings. Word frequently lists many of the possible meanings of your word.

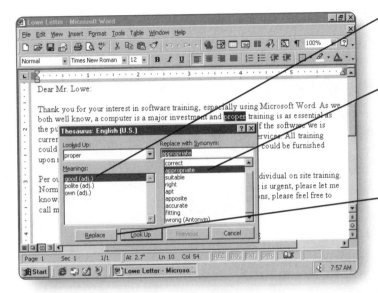

5. **Click** on a **meaning**. A selection of synonyms will appear on the right.

6. **Click** on a **word** in the Replace with Synonym: text box that fits your document better than the original. The word will be highlighted.

7. **Click** on **Replace**. The word will be replaced with the suggestion.

19

Using Mail Merge to Create Form Letters

You know the letter you get from the famous celebrity telling you that you have won TEN MILLION DOLLARS! (OK, in teeny tiny print it says you "may" have won ten million dollars.) It has your name printed in big letters right there on the certificate!

You need two things to create a personalized mailing with a mail merge: a letter, which is called the *main document* and contains the information that doesn't change, and codes, called *merge fields*, that act as placeholders for the variable information. This variable information is usually a list of names and addresses, called the *data source*, and contains the information that does change for each letter. When you merge the two, the result is the individualized form letters, called the *merge document*. In this chapter, you'll learn how to:

- Create a main document
- Create a data source
- Insert merge fields
- Merge the data with the document to create a form letter

Creating the Main Document

You can use a letter that you've previously created as the main document, or you can create a letter from scratch. Type your letter without filling in any return address or name in the salutation. If you want to add variables in the body of the letter, such as the addressee's first name, you can do this too. You just need to remember to leave a space for a field.

1. Type or **open** the **letter** to be used as the main document. The document will appear on the screen.

2. Click on **Tools.** The Tools menu will appear.

3. Click on **Mail Merge.** The Mail Merge Helper dialog box will open.

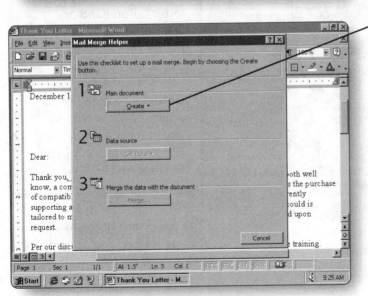

4. Click on **Create.** A drop-down list of selections will appear.

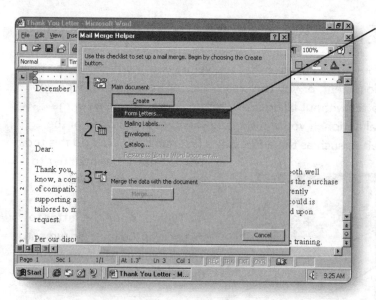

5. **Click** on **Form Letters**. A dialog box will open telling you that you can use the active document window or a new document window.

6. **Click** on **Active Window**. The letter you created will be the main document for your mail merge.

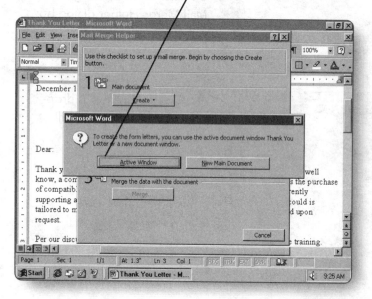

NOTE

If you hadn't created a letter beforehand or wanted to start a mail merge with a brand-new document, you could select New Main Document instead of Active Window. Word would supply a new document, ready for you to enter text.

You will return to the Mail Merge Helper. You're ready for the next step.

Specifying Data for Your Mail Merge

The next stage of the mail-merge process is to create the data source and then enter the names and addresses that will be merged into your letter.

Creating the Data Source

Fields and records are two of the common terms used with merge data files. A *field* is an individual piece of information about someone or something, such as zip code or first name. A *record* is the complete picture of information about someone with all the fields put together.

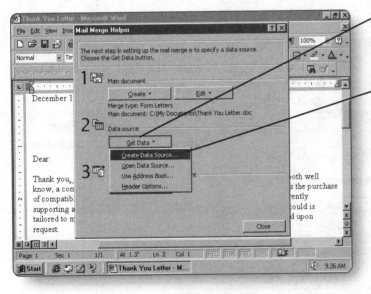

1. Click on **Get Data**. A drop-down list of selections will appear.

2. Click on **Create Data Source**. The Create Data Source dialog box will open.

Word has tried to anticipate your needs by providing the most commonly used fields.

You will need to customize the data source by removing fields that you don't need and adding fields that aren't included.

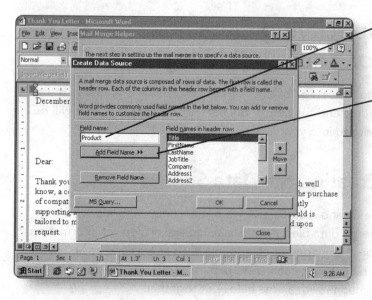

3. Type a **field name** to be added. The text will appear in the Field name text box.

4. Click on **Add Field Name**. The field will be added to the list.

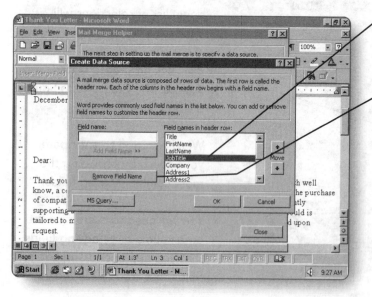

5. Click on a **field** you don't want. The field name will be highlighted.

6. Click on **Remove Field Name**. The field will be deleted.

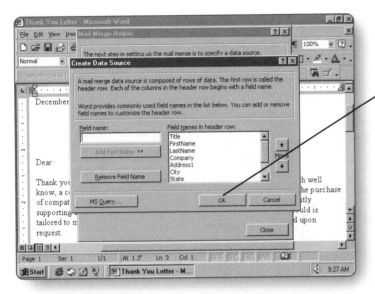

7. Repeat steps 3 through 6 for any fields to be added or deleted.

8. Click on **OK**. The Save As dialog box will open.

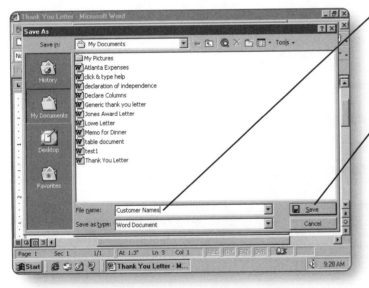

9. Type a **name** for the Word file that contains the data source that you're creating. The file name will appear in the File name text box.

10. Click on **Save**. A Microsoft Word dialog box will open.

The data source file has been designed, but no records have been entered. You'll need to do this next.

Entering Data

After you've determined the fields in the data source, you can enter individual data records in a form that Word has designed for you.

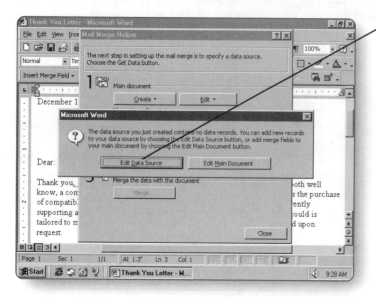

1. **Click** on **Edit Data Source** to add your data. The Data Form dialog box will open.

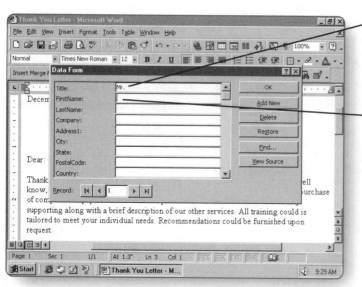

2. **Enter** the first **field information** for your first recipient. The text will appear in the first text box.

3. **Press** the **Enter or Tab key**. The insertion point will move to the next field.

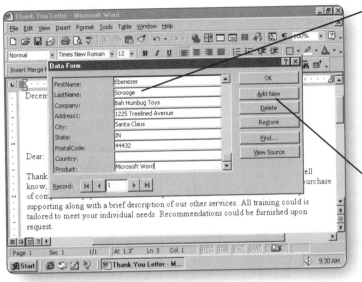

4. Enter the next **field information**. The text will appear in the first text box.

5. Continue entering data until the first record is complete. Data does not need to be entered in every field.

6. Click on **Add New**. A new, blank record will appear.

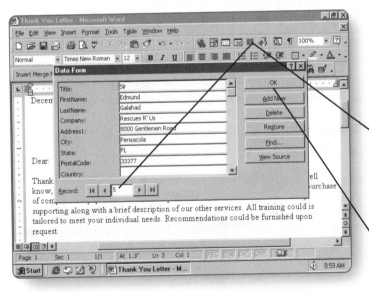

7. Repeat steps 2 through 5 until you've entered all the data records that you want to use for your mail merge.

TIP

An indicator at the bottom displays the current record number.

8. Click on **OK**. The dialog box will close.

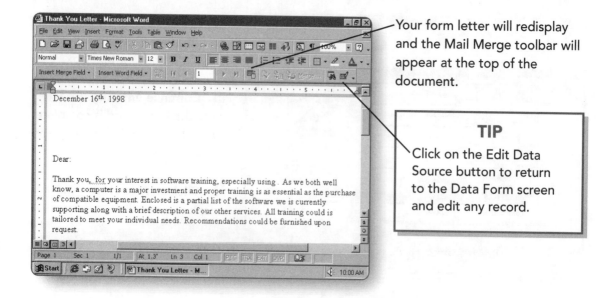

Your form letter will redisplay and the Mail Merge toolbar will appear at the top of the document.

TIP

Click on the Edit Data Source button to return to the Data Form screen and edit any record.

Merging the Letter with the Data Source

You've now created a main document (a letter) and a data source. The next step is to enter the codes (merge fields) into your form letter for the data source fields.

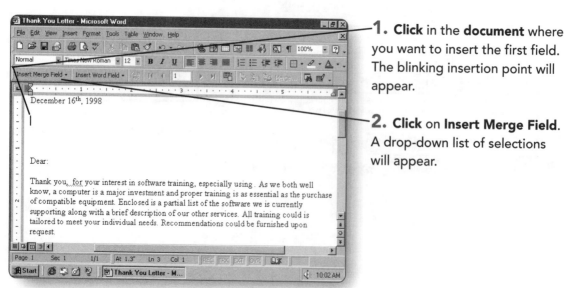

1. Click in the **document** where you want to insert the first field. The blinking insertion point will appear.

2. Click on **Insert Merge Field**. A drop-down list of selections will appear.

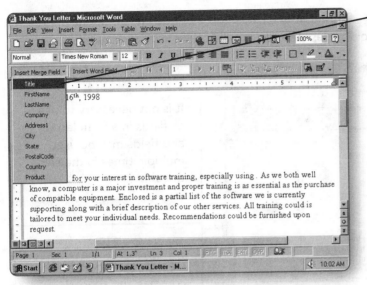

3. **Click** on the first **field** that you want. The field name will be inserted in the document.

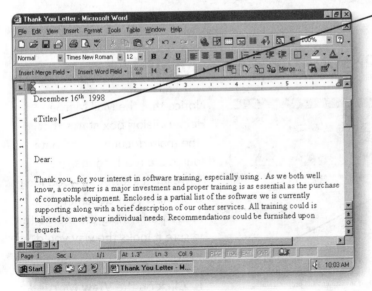

4. **Insert** appropriate **spaces and punctuation** between fields. This is important so the final documents read correctly.

5. Repeat steps 1 through 4 to add any additional merge field codes. The codes will appear in your document.

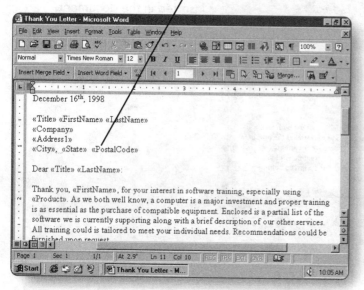

NOTE

It is not necessary to use all fields in a form letter, and fields may be used multiple times in the same document.

TIP

Don't forget to add commas and spaces!

Previewing the Mail Merge

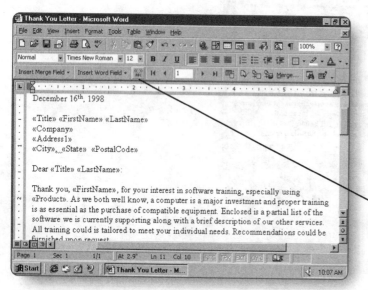

Notice that the Mail Merge Helper dialog box states that "the main document and data source are ready to merge." However, it's always a good idea to preview your document before performing the merge to be sure it looks the way you'd like it to.

1. Click on the **View Merged Data button**. You're first record will be merged with the main document and appear on the screen.

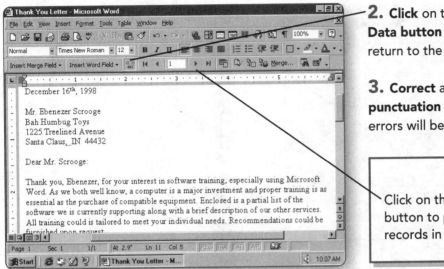

2. Click on the **View Merged Data button** again. You will return to the main document.

3. Correct any **spacing** or **punctuation problems**. The errors will be corrected.

> **TIP**
> Click on the Next Record button to preview other records in the data source.

Performing the Merge

Now that you've created the documents and previewed them for errors, it's time to actually merge them together.

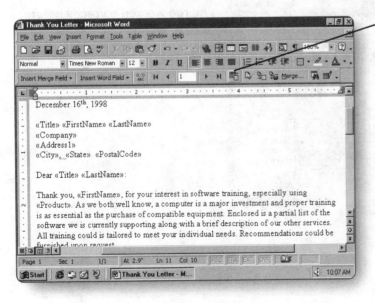

1. Click on the **Mail Merge Helper button.** The Mail Merge Helper dialog box will open.

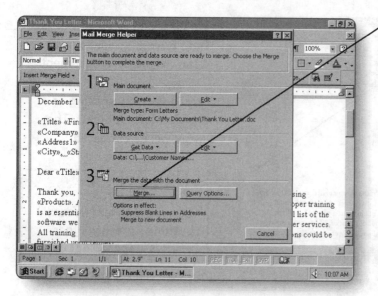

2. Click on **Merge**. The Merge dialog box will open.

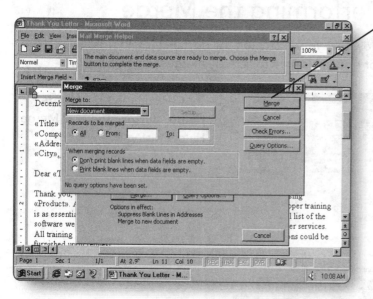

3. Click on **Merge**. The merge letters will appear on your screen so that you can see if the merge worked correctly before you print.

4. Click on the **Print button.** Your letters will be sent to the printer.

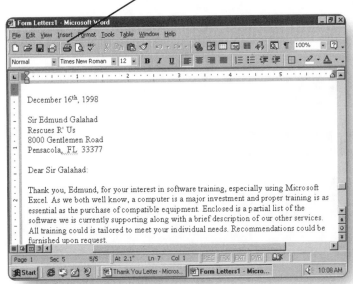

20

Merging Envelopes and Labels

Now that you have created your form letters, you'll need envelopes in which to mail them. Or maybe you'd prefer to use mailing labels. Either way, Word makes it easy to create them using the mail merge feature. In this chapter, you'll learn how to:

- Open an existing data source file
- Create and print envelopes for your merged letters
- Merge labels from a data source file

Creating Envelopes

You can use the mail-merge process to go back and create an envelope main document using the same data source.

1. Click on **New Document**. A new blank document will appear.

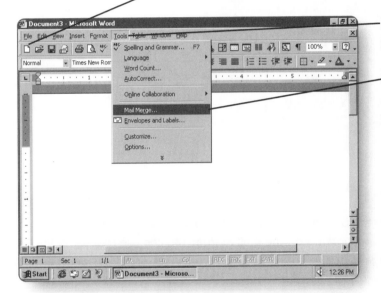

2. Click on **Tools**. The Tools menu will appear.

3. Click on **Mail Merge**. The Mail Merge Helper dialog box will open.

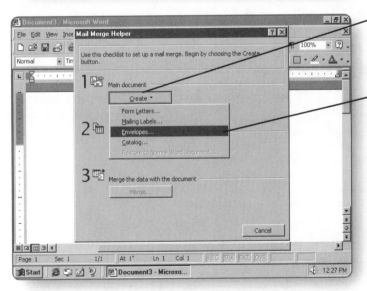

4. Click on **Create**. A drop-down list of selections will appear.

5. Click on **Envelopes**. A dialog box will open telling you that you can use the active document window or a new document window.

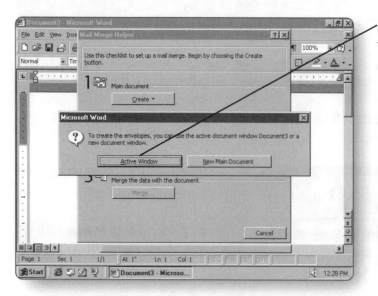

6. Click on **Active Window**. The Mail Merge Helper will return.

Opening a Data File

In the previous chapter, you created a data source file as you were working on the mail merge. You can use that same file again, or even open an Excel worksheet or Access database to use as your data source.

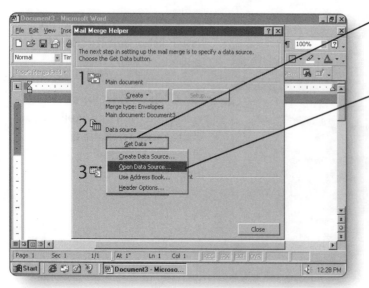

1. Click on **Get Data**. A drop-down list of selections will appear.

2. Click on **Open Data Source**. The Open Data Source dialog box will open.

3. Locate and **click** on the **file name** to be used for your data source. The file name will be highlighted.

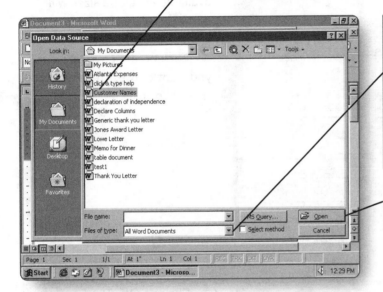

TIP

If you're going to use an Excel or Access file for the data source, change the Files of type to MS Excel Worksheets or MS Access Databases.

4. Click on **Open**. A message box will appear.

Setting Up the Envelope

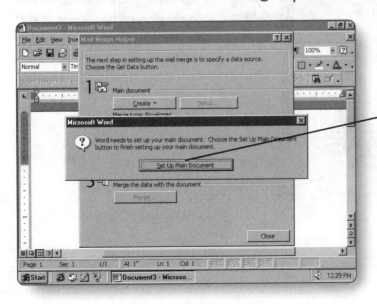

Next you'll need to tell Word what size envelope you'll be using and how you want it addressed.

1. Click on **Set Up Main Document**. The Envelope Options dialog box will open.

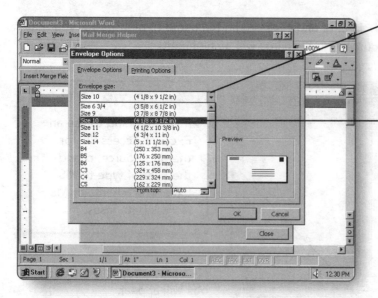

2. Click on the **Envelope size drop-down list arrow**. A list of available envelope sizes will display.

3. Click on the Envelope **size** you want to use. The envelope size will display.

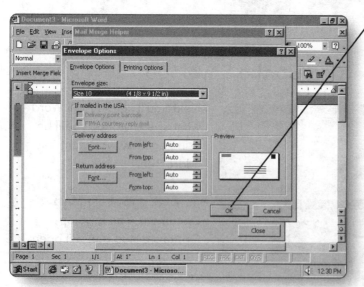

4. Click on **OK**. The Envelope address dialog box will open.

From here, you'll need to lay out the envelope address just like you did in the letter.

Inserting Merge Fields

In Chapter 19, "Using Mail Merge to Create Form Letters," you learned how to insert the fields from the data source. You'll need to repeat that process when creating an envelope.

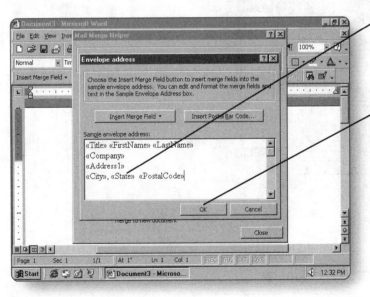

1. Click on **Insert Merge Field**. A list of field names will display.

2. Click on the first **field name** to be used when addressing the envelope. The merge code will appear in the Sample envelope address box.

3. Continue entering the **address** information including spaces and punctuation as needed.

4. Click on **OK**. The Envelope address dialog box will close.

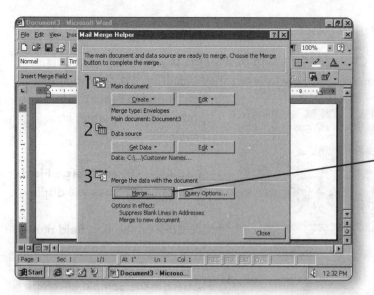

Merging the Envelopes

The final step is to merge the envelope layout and the data source file together.

1. **Click** on **Merge**. The Merge dialog box will open.

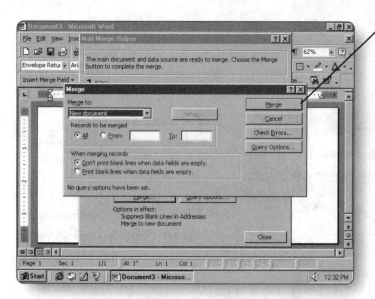

2. **Click** on **Merge**. An envelope will be created for each name in your data source file.

3. **Click** on the **Print button**. The envelopes will print.

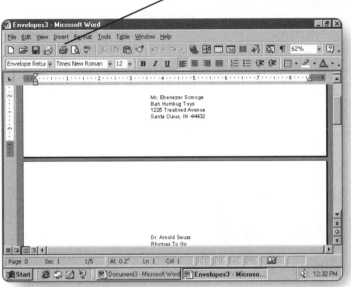

Creating Merged Mailing Labels

Now that you can buy sheets of labels that feed easily into both inkjet and laser printers, mailing labels and envelopes are equally easy to produce using Word's Mail Merge feature. Labels can be especially useful if you have large quantities of letters to mail.

1. **Click** on the **New Document button**. A new blank document will appear.

2. **Click** on **Tools.** The Tools menu will appear.

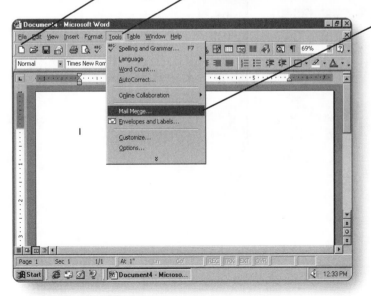

3. **Click** on **Mail Merge.** The Mail Merge Helper dialog box will open.

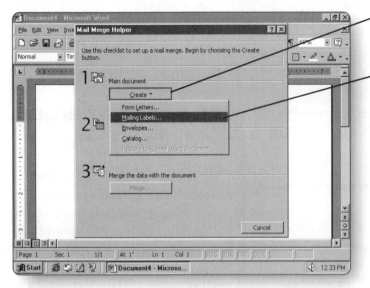

4. Click on **Create**. A list of selections will appear.

5. Click on **Mailing Labels**. A dialog box will open telling you that you can use the active document window or a new document window.

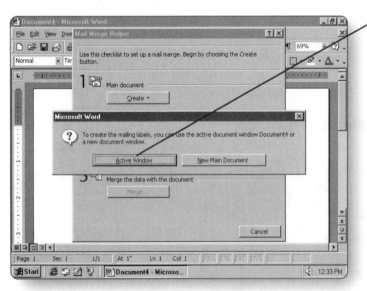

6. Click on **Active Window**. Your document will be the mailing label main document.

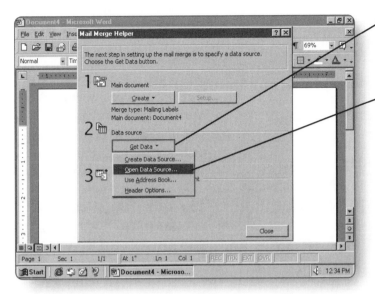

7. **Click** on **Get Data**. A drop-down list of selections will appear.

8. **Click** on **Open Data Source**. The Open Data Source dialog box will open.

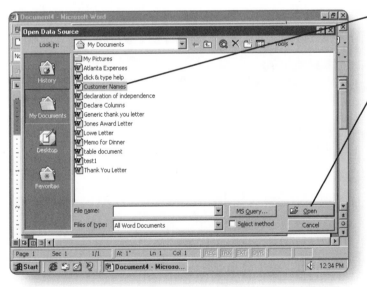

9. **Click** on the **document** that contains the data. The file name will be highlighted.

10. **Click** on **Open**. A Microsoft Word dialog box will open.

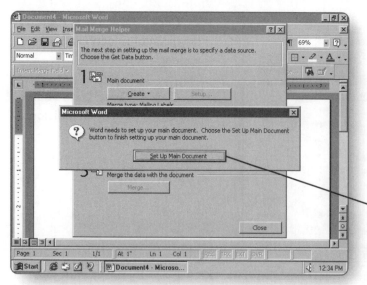

Setting Up the Label

Before you can print the mailing labels, you need to specify the type of labels you will be using because Word automatically sets up the main document in a table according to the size and number of labels on each sheet.

1. **Click** on **Set Up Main Document**. The Label Options dialog box will open.

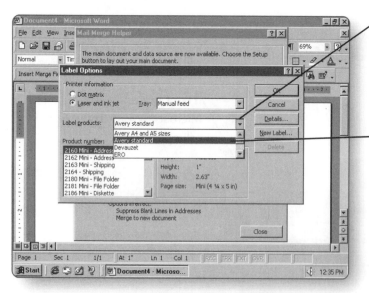

2. **Click** on **the drop-down list arrow** to the right of the Label products: text box. A list of label product brands will appear.

3. **Click** on a **label product**. The selection will be highlighted.

4. Click on a **selection** in the Product number: text box. This is the label product number you will be using.

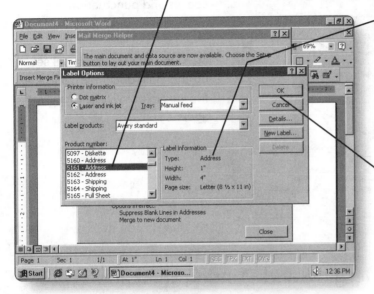

More information, such as the size of the label and the size of the sheet, is in the Label information box if you know only the dimensions of the labels and not the manufacturer's product number.

5. Click on **OK**. The Create Labels dialog box will open.

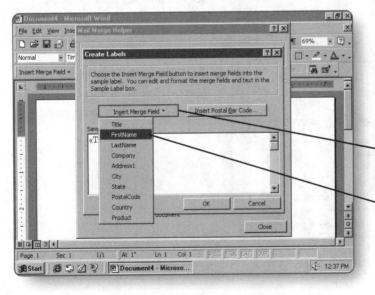

You now need to identify what information in the data source you want to use and exactly where you want to place it in the document by inserting merge fields.

6. Click on **Insert Merge Field**. A list of field names will display.

7. Click on the first **field name** of the address. The merge code will appear in the Sample label box.

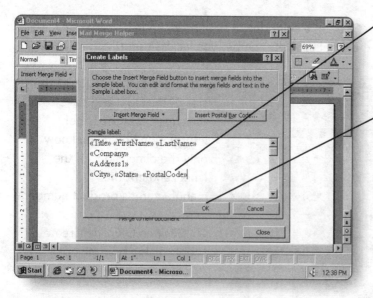

8. Continue entering the **address** information including spaces and punctuation as needed. The fields will display.

9. Click on **OK**. Word will set up the main document, and Mail Merge Helper will be displayed again.

Merging and Printing the Labels

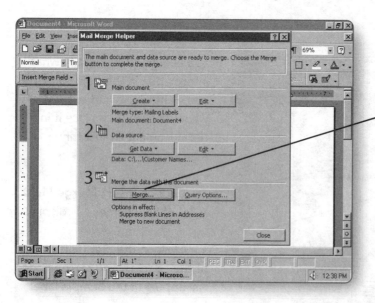

After you've opened the data source and set up the labels, you're ready to merge the two documents.

1. Click on **Merge** in the Mail Merge Helper dialog box. The Merge dialog box will open.

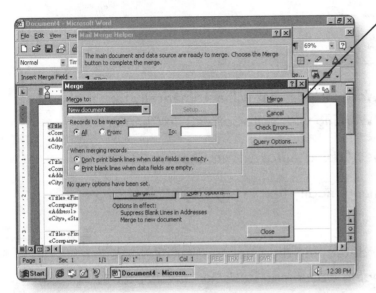

2. Click on **Merge** to accept the default setting to merge to a new document. You will see the merge document displayed. You can edit and format this document.

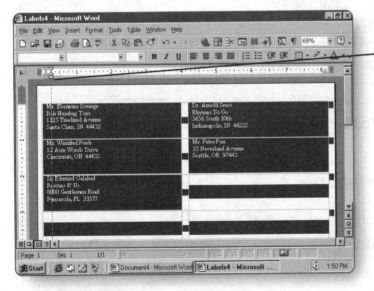

TIP

These labels have a tendency to print too close to the left edge of the label. Press Ctrl + A (to select all the labels) and drag the left indent mark a little to the right.

3. Click on the **Print button** after making sure that you have your label paper loaded in your printer. The labels will print.

Part V Review Questions

1. What feature does Word include that will automatically fix common typing errors? *See "Working with AutoCorrect" in Chapter 17*

2. What is AutoText? *See "Using AutoText" in Chapter 17*

3. Does the Find command modify text in any way? *See "Using Find" in Chapter 17*

4. How can you quickly determine the total number of words in a document? *See "Finding Document Statistics" in Chapter 17*

5. How does Word indicate potential spelling errors? *See "Checking Spelling As You Go" in Chapter 18*

6. What Word feature can locate a synonym? *See "Finding That Elusive Word with the Thesaurus" in Chapter 18*

7. What are the two documents needed to create a mail merge? *See "Using Mail Merge to Create Form Letters" in Chapter 19*

8. In a mail merge, what is the difference between a field and a record? *See "Creating the Data Source" in Chapter 19*

9. Besides a Word document, what other types of data source documents can Word use in a mail merge? *See "Opening a Data File" in Chapter 20*

10. Why might you want to indent mailing labels to the right? *See "Merging and Printing the Labels" in Chapter 20*

PART VI

Working with Long Documents

21

Working with Paragraph Styles

Whether you're creating a letter or a memo, a report or an invitation, each paragraph within that document has a *paragraph style*: a style can include its font, font size, any special effects, alignment, and spacing—any characteristics in the Font or Paragraph dialog box accessed through the Format menu. When you work with short documents, you probably need only one paragraph style. However, when you use Word to tackle longer documents, such as reports, you will find that paragraph styles can make formatting your document a breeze. In this chapter, you'll learn how to:

- Display the style area
- Apply a Word style
- Modify a style
- Use an example to create a new style
- Use the New Style dialog box to create a new style

Displaying the Style Area

The first text box on the Formatting toolbar shows only the style of the paragraph where the insertion point is. To see all the styles used in your document, you need to display the style area.

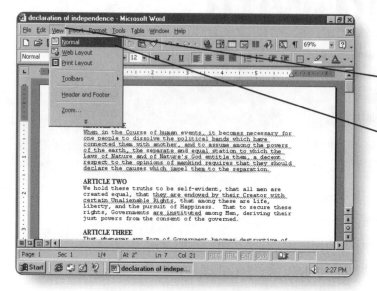

To view the style area, you'll need to be in Normal view.

1. Click on **View**. The View menu will appear.

2. Click on **Normal**. The onscreen document will be displayed in Normal view.

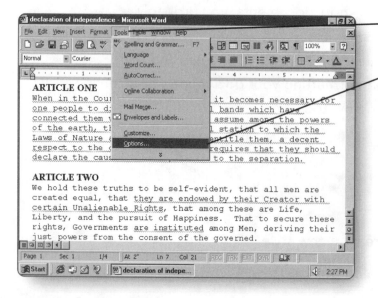

3. Click on **Tools**. The Tools menu will appear.

4. Click on **Options**. The Options dialog box will open.

5. **Click** on the **View tab**. The View tab will come to the front.

6. **Click** on the **up arrow** in the Style Area width text box until .4" appears in the text box.

7. **Click** on **OK**. The Options dialog box will close.

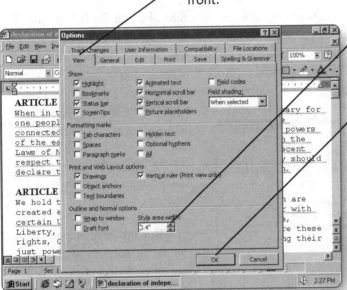

The style area will appear in every document until you change the Style Area width.

In this example you can see some of the text is set in the style called "Normal" while other text is set as "Heading 1".

Working with Word Styles

Word comes with a wide selection of styles for formatting titles, section heads, and so on. Remember that Word's definition of a paragraph isn't the one taught in grammar classes, where two or more sentences are set apart. To Word, a paragraph is any body of text ended by a pressing of the Enter key. Even one word can be a paragraph to Word.

The default style applied to all newly typed text is called "Normal."

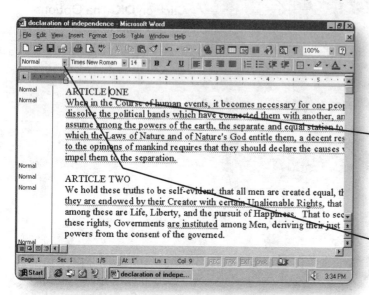

1. Click the **mouse pointer** in the paragraph that you want to format with one of the Word styles. The blinking insertion point will appear.

2. Click on the **drop-down list arrow** to the right of the Style text box. A list of styles will appear.

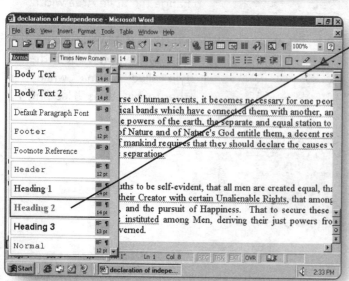

3. Click on the **style** you want. Word will apply the style to the paragraph.

4. Repeat steps 1 through 3 for any paragraphs to which you want new styles applied. Those selections will have the new styles applied.

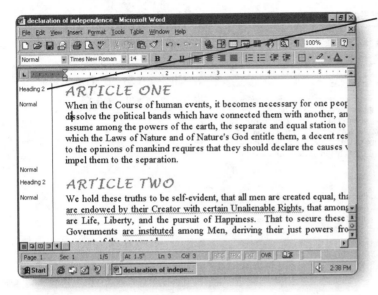

In this example, the Heading 2 style, changed the font name, size, and color attributes.

Creating New Styles

Sometimes you may find that the style Word offers doesn't exactly meet your needs. Word can create a new style by using an example, or it can create a new style from scratch.

Using an Example to Create a New Style

You can create new styles in several ways. One way is to format a paragraph with the attributes you need, then tell Word to look at that paragraph and create a new style from it.

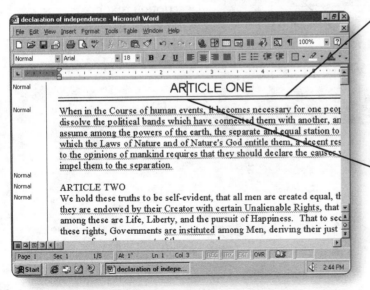

1. **Format** a **paragraph**. Formatting attributes will be applied to the text. In this example, the font is changed to 18 point Arial, a border is applied, and the paragraph spacing is centered.

2. **Click** the **mouse pointer** in the formatted paragraph. The blinking insertion point will appear.

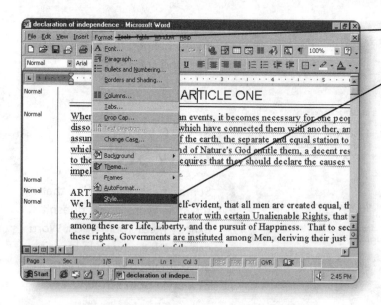

3. Click on **Format**. The Format menu will appear.

4. Click on **Style**. The Style dialog box will open.

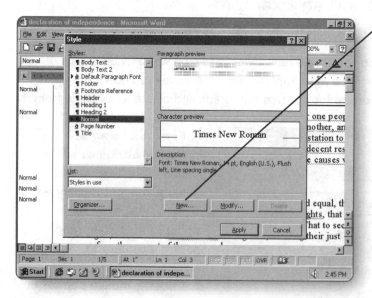

5. Click on **New**. The New Style dialog box will open with the formatting of the selected paragraph shown in the Preview areas and listed in the Description text box.

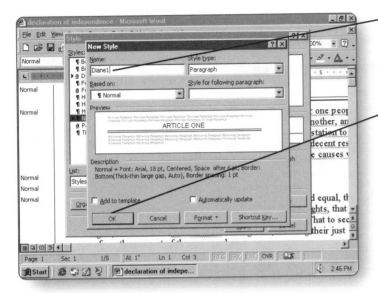

6. Type a **name** for the style in the Name text box. The new name will appear in the Name: text box.

7. Click on **OK**. The new style name will appear in the Styles: text box in the Style dialog box.

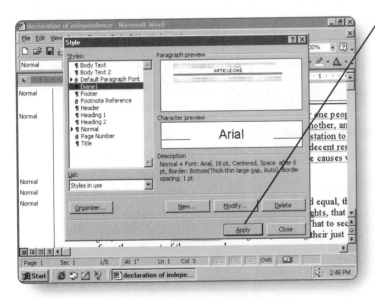

8. Click on **Apply**. The Style dialog box will close.

The new style will appear in the Style drop-down list in the Formatting toolbar. You can now apply this style to any other paragraphs using the techniques you learned in the previous section.

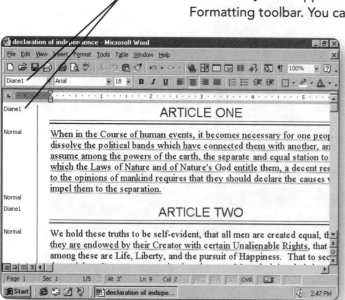

Creating a New Style from Scratch

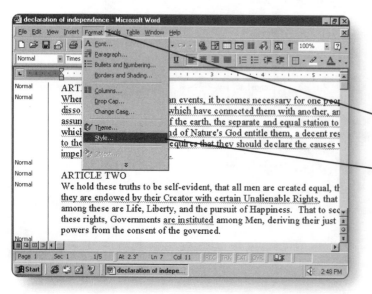

Another way to create a style is to simply create a style name and tell Word exactly what formatting you want applied.

1. Click on **Format**. The Format menu will appear.

2. Click on **Style**. The Style dialog box will open.

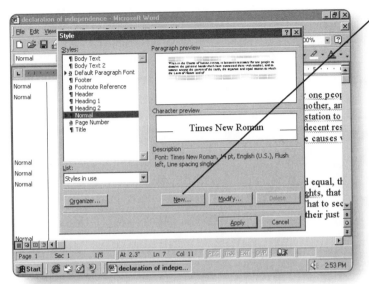

3. **Click** on **New**. The New Style dialog box will open with the formatting of the selected paragraph shown in the Preview area and listed in the Description text box.

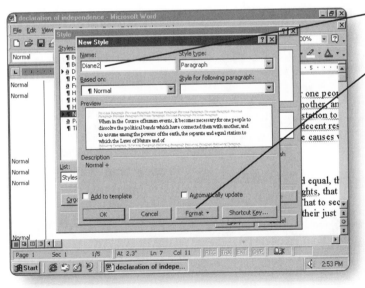

4. **Type** a **name** for the new style in the Name text box.

5. **Click** on the **Format button**. A list of Formatting Options will appear.

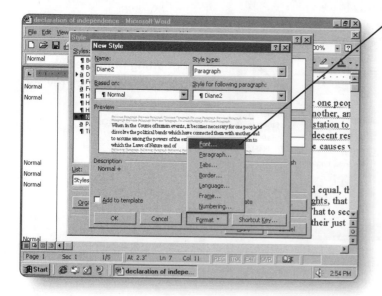

6. Click on **Font**. The Font dialog box will open.

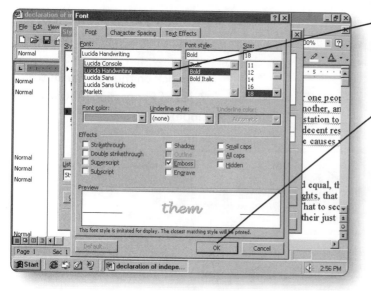

7. Select the **font characteristics** for the new style. A sample of the text will display in the Preview box.

8. Click on **OK**. The New Style dialog box will open with the selected font settings shown in the Preview area and listed in the Description text box.

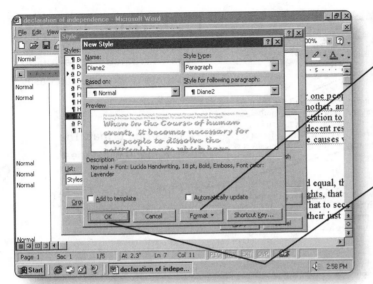

TIP

TIP
Additionally, you can click on Format and choose Paragraph or Border to choose any paragraph or border attributes.

9. Click on **OK**. The new style will appear in the Styles: text box in the Style dialog box.

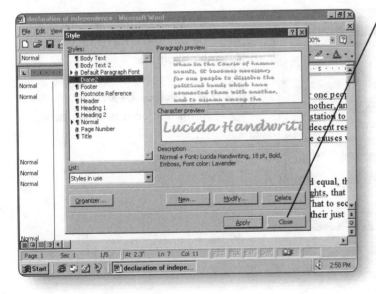

10. Click on **Close**. The Style dialog box will close, and the new style will appear in the Style drop-down list in the Formatting toolbar.

You can now apply the new style to any text in the document.

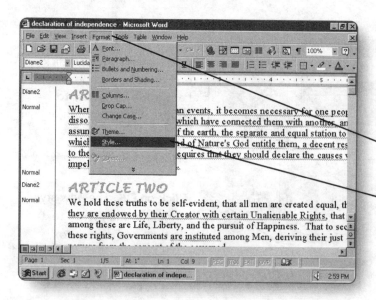

Deleting a Style

If you've created a style you no longer are using, you can easily delete it.

1. Click on **Format**. The Format menu will appear.

2. Click on **Style**. The Style dialog box will open.

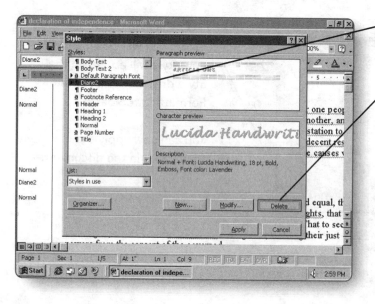

3. Click on the **style name** to be deleted. The name will be highlighted.

4. Click on **Delete**. A confirmation box will appear.

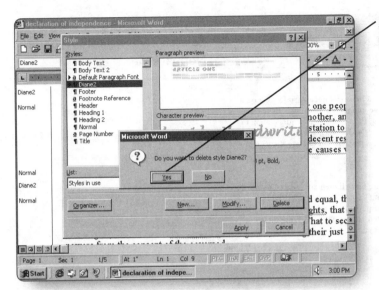

5. Click on **Yes**. The style will be deleted.

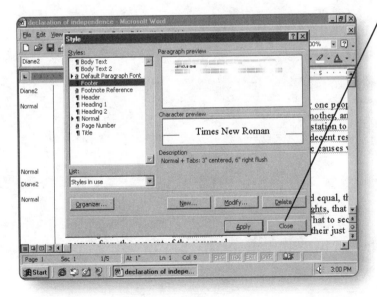

6. Click on **Close**. The Style dialog box will close.

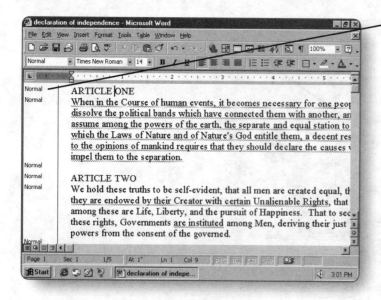

Any paragraphs that had the deleted style will return to the Normal style.

22

Discovering Templates

Every Microsoft Word document is based on a template. A *template* determines the basic structure for a document and contains settings such as styles, AutoText, fonts, macros, menus, page layout, and special formatting. Word provides a variety of document templates, and you can create your own document templates. In this chapter, you'll learn how to:

- Save a file as a template
- Use and apply a template
- Edit a template

Saving a File as a Template

When you save a template, Word will switch to the User templates location as specified in the Options menu (Tools menu, Options command, File Locations tab), which by default is the Templates folder. If you save a template in a different location, the template will not appear in the New dialog box.

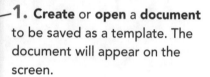

1. Create or **open** a **document** to be saved as a template. The document will appear on the screen.

2. Make any **changes** to the text, page setup, formatting or styles you want to be applicable to all new documents of this type. The new settings will be available in the current document.

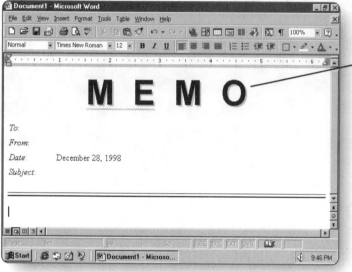

3. Click on **File**. The File menu will appear.

4. Click on **Save As**. The Save As dialog box will open.

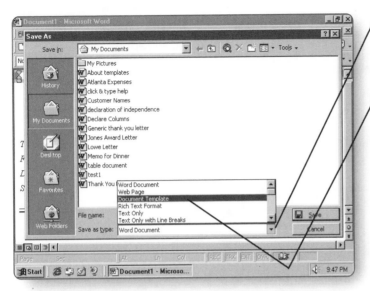

5. Click on the **Save as Type: arrow**. A list of choices will display.

6. Click on **Document Template**. The option will appear in the Save as Type: list box.

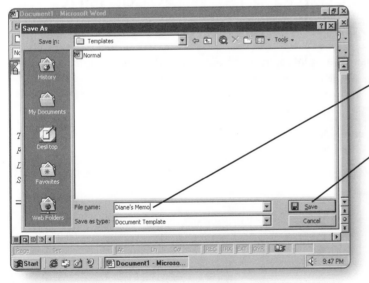

7. Click in the **File name: text box**. The blinking insertion point will appear.

8. Type a **name** for the new template. The name will appear in the File name: text box.

9. Click on **Save**. The document will be saved as a template.

Word will automatically add a file name extension of .dot to the end of any template.

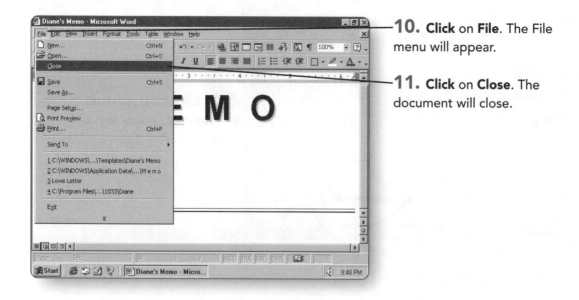

10. Click on **File**. The File menu will appear.

11. Click on **Close**. The document will close.

Creating a New Document Based on a Template

Using templates, you can automatically create memos, faxes, or other documents with the formatting already applied.

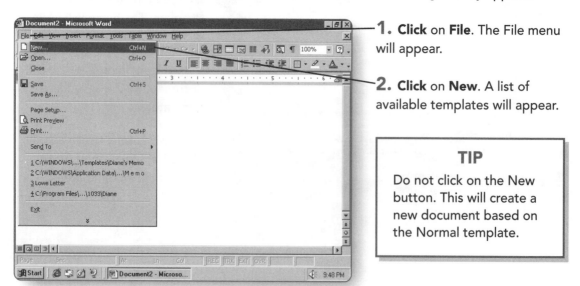

1. Click on **File**. The File menu will appear.

2. Click on **New**. A list of available templates will appear.

TIP

Do not click on the New button. This will create a new document based on the Normal template.

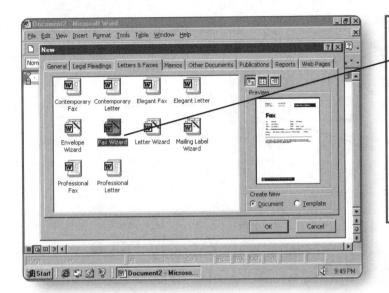

NOTE

Several categories of predefined templates are available for your use. Some templates are marked Wizards. You'll learn how to use a wizard in Chapter 25, "Using Word to Create Web Pages."

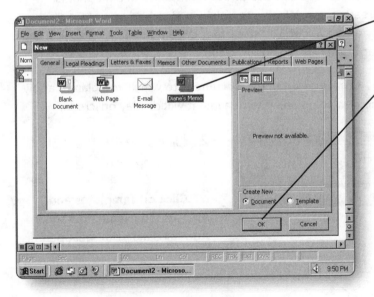

3. Click on the **template name** you want to use. The template name will be highlighted.

4. Click on **OK**. An untitled document will appear with the text, graphics, formatting, and other attributes applicable to that template.

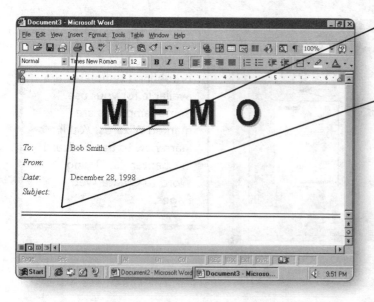

5. Add additional **text** or **edit** the **document** using methods you've already learned.

6. Click on the **Print button**. The document will print.

Applying a Template

As you've seen, you can open a document based on a template. You can also attach a template to a file that is already open. When a template is attached to a file, only the styles are added to the current document. Text, graphics, and page settings are not included.

1. Create or **open** the **document** to which you plan to apply the new template. The document will display onscreen.

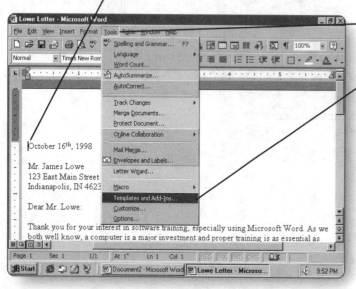

2. Click on **Tools**. The Tools menu will appear.

3. Click on **Templates and Add-ins**. The Templates and Add-ins dialog box will open.

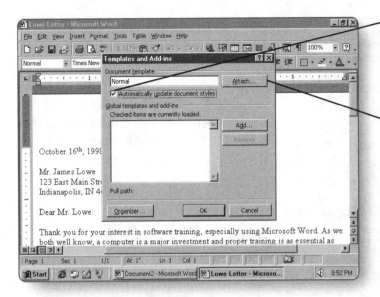

4. If not already checked, **click on Automatically update document styles**. The option will display a check mark.

5. **Click** on **Attach**. The Attach Template dialog box will open.

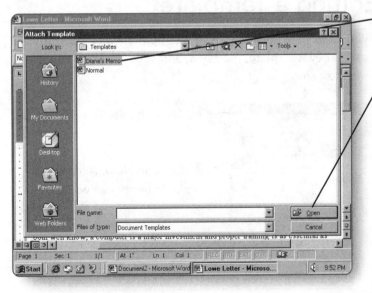

6. **Click** on the **template name** that you plan to attach to the document.

7. **Click** on **Open**. The selected template will appear in the Templates and Add-ins dialog box.

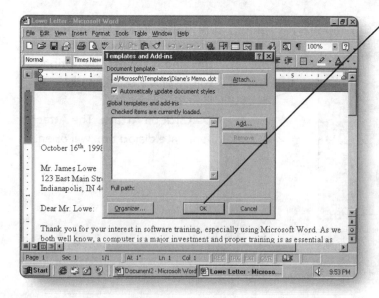

8. Click on **OK**. Word will attach the template to the open document.

Any styles from the attached template will now be available in the current document.

Editing a Template

If you need to make changes to a template, you'll need to create a new template, modify it, and save it with the old template name.

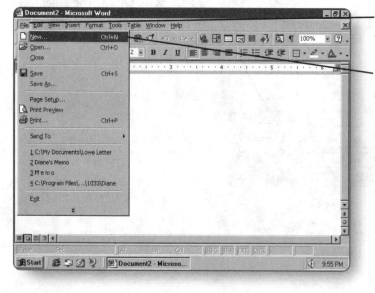

1. Click on **File**. The File menu will appear.

2. Click on **New**. A list of available templates will appear.

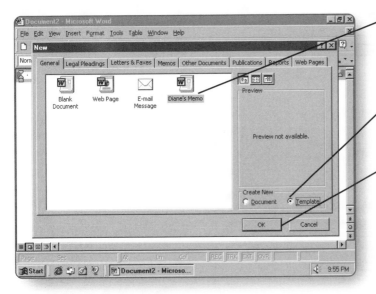

3. Click on the **template name** you want to modify. The template name will be highlighted.

4. Click on **Template**. The option will be selected.

5. Click on **OK**. An untitled template will appear with the text, graphics, formatting, and other attributes available in that template.

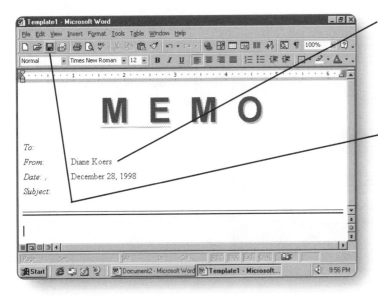

6. Add additional **text** or **edit** the document using methods you've already learned. The document will reflect the changes.

7. Click on **Save**. The Save As dialog box will open.

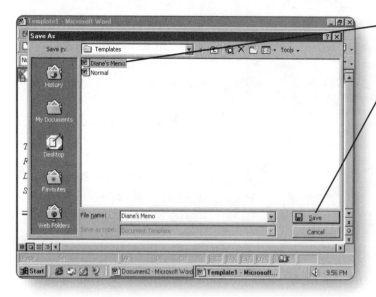

8. Click on the **name** of the original template. The template name will be highlighted.

9. Click on **Save**. A confirmation box will appear.

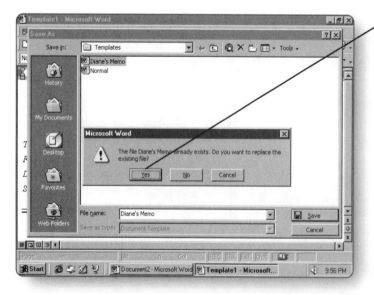

10. Click on **Yes**. The template will be saved and new documents based on the template will reflect any changes you made.

11. Click on **File**. The File menu will appear.

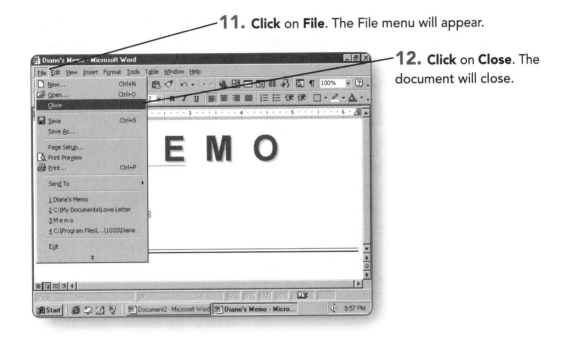

12. Click on **Close**. The document will close.

Deleting a Template

If you no longer need a customized template, you can easily delete it.

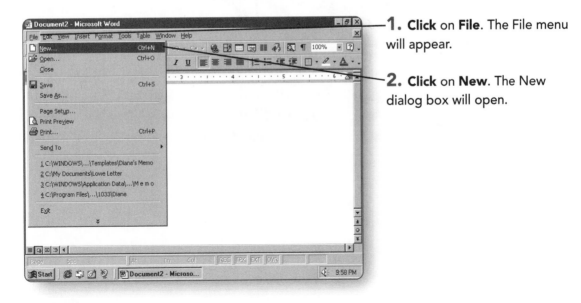

1. Click on **File**. The File menu will appear.

2. Click on **New**. The New dialog box will open.

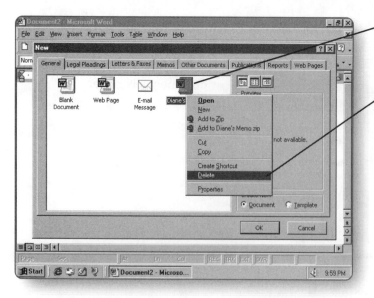

3. **Right-click** on the **template name** to be deleted. A shortcut menu will appear.

4. **Click** on **Delete**. A confirmation message will display.

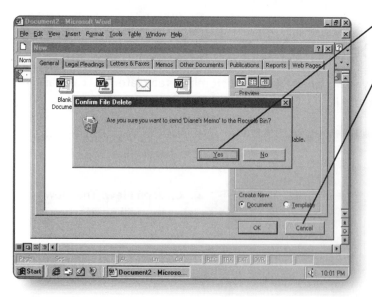

5. **Click** on **Yes**. The template will be deleted.

6. **Click** on **Cancel**. The New dialog box will close.

23

Adding Headers and Footers

Headers and footers are features used for placing information at the top or bottom of every page of a document. You can place any information in headers and footers: the author of the document, the date of last revision, or a company logo. When you start working with documents of more than one page, it's possible for the printed pages to get out of order or mixed up with another document. To easily identify which printouts belong to which document, it's a good idea to add headers and footers with dates and page numbers. In this chapter, you'll learn how to:

- Insert a header or footer
- Add page numbers and dates
- Align text in headers and footers
- Set up headers and footers to print differently on different pages

Inserting a Header or Footer

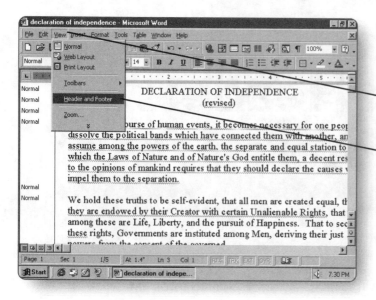

As you'd expect, a header prints at the top of every page, and a footer prints at the bottom.

1. Click on **View**. The View menu will appear.

2. Click on **Header and Footer**. The screen will change to Print Layout view, and the Header box will appear along with the Header and Footer toolbar.

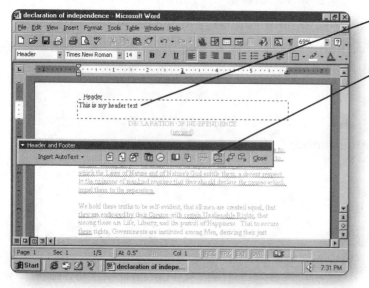

3. Type your **text**. Your text will appear in the Header box.

4. Click on the **Switch Between Header and Footer button.** The Footer box will appear.

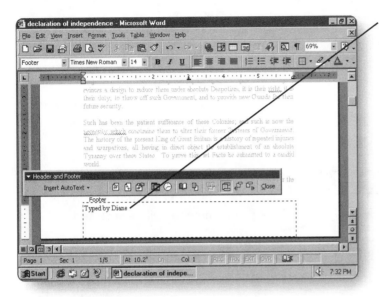

5. Type some **text**. The text will appear in the Footer text.

Adding Date, Time, or Page Number

When the Header or Footer box is open, you can add the date and/or time to either. This places a field for the current date or time; Word will insert the current date and time in that field based on the computer's clock and calendar settings when you print the document. The Insert Page Number feature places the correct page number on each page.

1. Type some **text**. The text will appear along the left margin.

2. Press the **Tab key**. The insertion point will jump to the center of the page.

3. Click on the **Insert Date button**. The current date will be inserted.

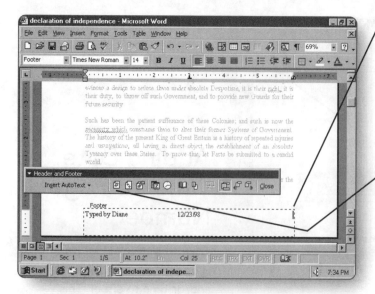

4. Press the **Tab key**. This will right-align the next text you insert.

When adding page numbering, Word will use a code. Don't just type a number in.

5. Click on the **Insert Page Number button**. The page number will be inserted.

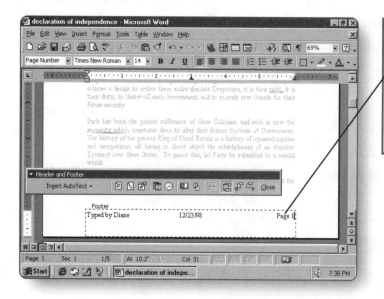

TIP

Optionally, precede the insertion of the page numbering with any desired text, such as "Page."

Arranging Headers and Footers on Different Pages

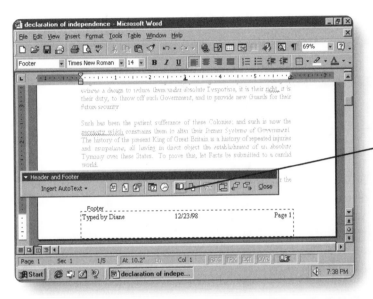

When the Header or Footer box is open, you can choose to have different headers and footers on odd or even pages, or a different header or footer on just the first page of the document.

1. Click on the **Page Setup button.** The Page Setup dialog box will open.

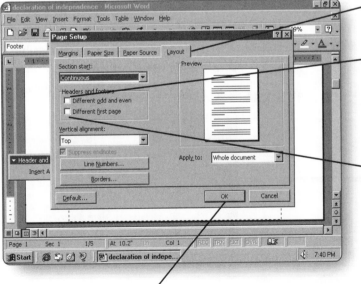

2. Click on the **Layout tab**. The layout tab will come to the front.

3. Click in the **Different odd and even check box** to have a different header or footer on odd and even pages. The option will be selected.

4. Click in the **Different first page check box** to allow the first page of the document to have a different or blank header or footer. The option will be selected.

5. Click on **OK.** The Page Setup dialog box will close.

TIP

Don't enter anything in the Header or Footer boxes for the first page if you don't want a header of footer on the first page of your document.

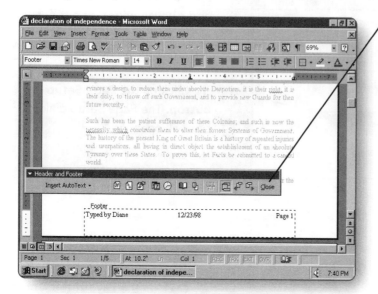

6. Click on **Close** on the Header and Footer toolbar. You will return to your document window.

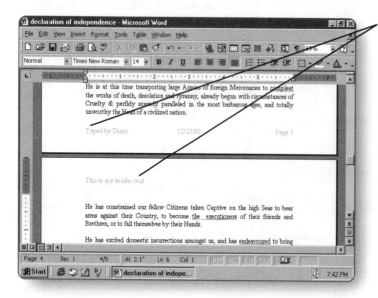

Headers and footers are visible only when you are using Print Layout view or Print Preview.

24

Working with Footnotes and Endnotes

Often reports present material that require notes set off from the regular text, for example, when you credit material from another source. You can use the Word Footnote or Endnote feature to add these explanatory or source notes to your document. In this chapter, you'll learn how to:

- Create and copy footnotes and endnotes
- Move and delete footnotes and endnotes
- Preview and convert footnotes and endnotes

Creating a Footnote or Endnote

To give credit where credit is due, you can use the Word Footnote or Endnote feature. Word places footnotes on the page where the note reference mark appears and places endnotes at the end of the document.

When creating a footnote, Word will automatically add a number or character to mark the reference as well as add a separating line. If you have both footnotes and endnotes in a document, Word will number them independently.

Footnotes and endnotes are easiest to create if you are working in Normal view.

1. Click on **View**. The View menu will appear.

2. Click on **Normal**. The document will display in Normal view.

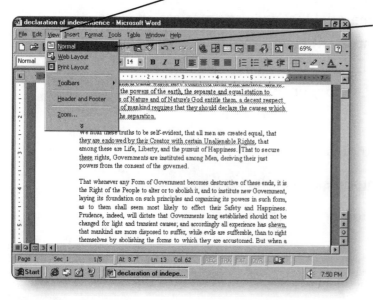

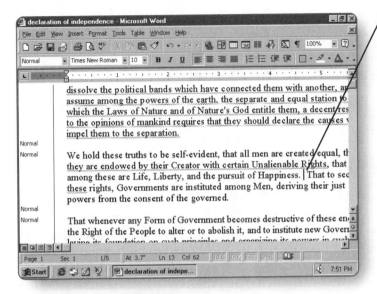

3. Click the **mouse pointer** where you want the note reference mark to appear. A blinking insertion point will appear.

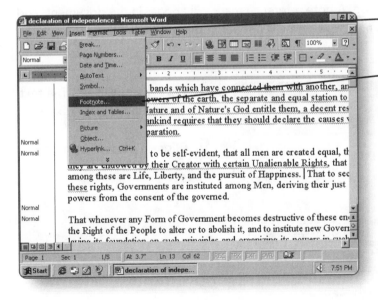

4. Click on **Insert**. The Insert menu will appear.

5. Click on **Footnote**. The Footnote and Endnote dialog box will open.

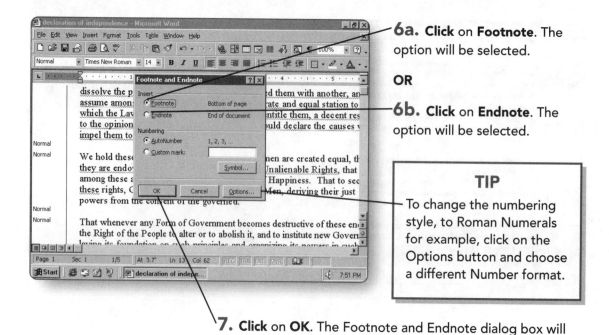

6a. **Click** on **Footnote**. The option will be selected.

OR

6b. **Click** on **Endnote**. The option will be selected.

TIP

To change the numbering style, to Roman Numerals for example, click on the Options button and choose a different Number format.

7. **Click** on **OK**. The Footnote and Endnote dialog box will close. A note reference mark will appear in the document, and a note text area will appear at the bottom of the page.

8. **Type** the **note text**. The text will appear in the note text area.

9. **Click** on **Close**. The note text area will close.

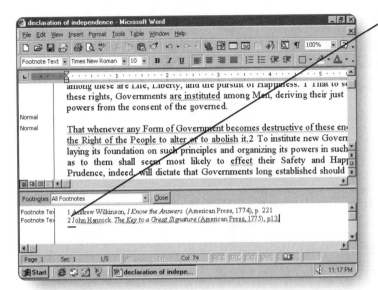

10. **Repeat steps 3 through 9** to add additional notes. Word will automatically assign the next number to each additional note.

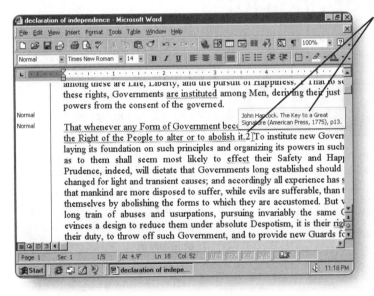

If you position the mouse pointer over the note reference mark in the body of the document, the note text will appear in a box similar to a ToolTip.

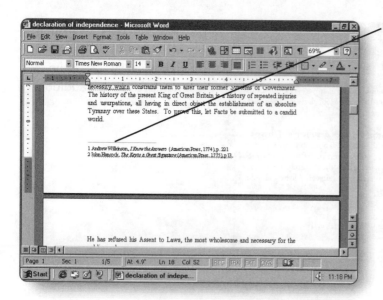

When looking at a note in Print Layout view you can see the separating line.

Copying Notes

Sometimes you will refer to a source more than once in a document. Fortunately, you don't have to retype the text for the footnote; you can copy and paste it into a new location. Word will renumber all the notes affected by the change.

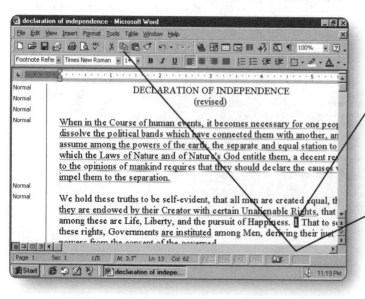

1. Select the **note reference mark** of the footnote or endnote that you plan to copy. The reference mark will be highlighted.

2. Click on the **Copy button**. The text will be copied to the Windows Clipboard.

3. Click the **mouse pointer** at the location for the duplicated note. A blinking insertion point will appear.

4. Click on the **Paste button**. The duplicate note will be placed in the document.

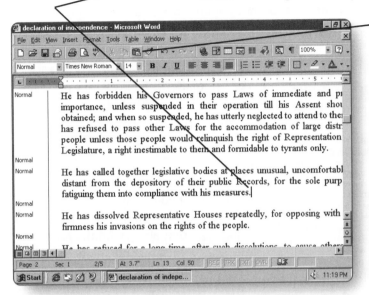

The note reference mark of the copied footnote or endnote will appear in the original and new location, and the footnote or endnote will appear in the footnote or endnote text area with the correct numbering.

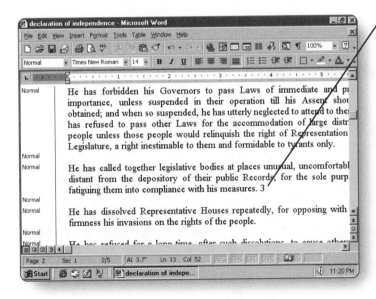

Moving Notes

You can move a footnote or endnote to a new location, and Word will renumber all of the notes affected by the move.

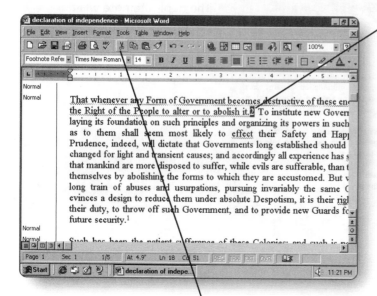

1. Select the **note reference mark** of the note that you plan to move. The reference mark will be highlighted.

TIP

If you want to move any surrounding document text along with the reference number, highlight it as well.

2. Click on the **Cut button**. The text will be copied to the Windows Clipboard and removed from the document.

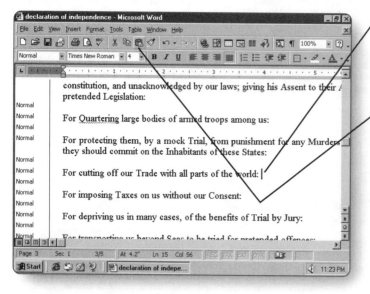

3. Click the **mouse pointer** at the new location for the note. A blinking insertion point will appear.

4. Click on the **Paste button**. The note will be placed in the new location in the document and renumbered if necessary.

Deleting a Footnote or Endnote

As you've already noticed, the role of the note reference mark in Word is important. You insert a footnote or endnote by indicating where to place the note reference mark, and then you type the footnote or endnote. You delete a footnote or endnote by deleting the note reference mark, not by deleting the footnote or endnote.

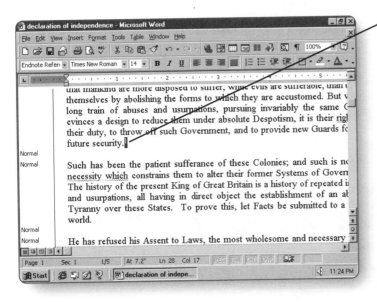

1. **Select** the **note reference mark** of the footnote or endnote that you plan to delete. The reference mark will be highlighted.

2. **Press** the **Delete key.** Word will delete the note reference mark and the footnote or endnote in the text area and then renumber all the notes affected by the deletion.

Converting a Footnote to an Endnote

What happens if you create footnotes throughout your report and then decide that you should have used endnotes? Word can convert footnotes to endnotes and endnotes to footnotes—saving you the headache of retyping each entry.

1. Click on **Insert**. The Insert menu will appear.

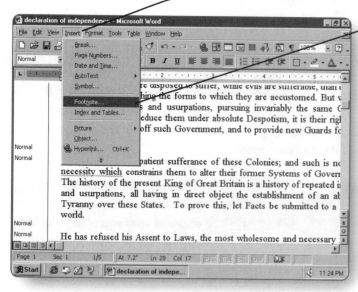

2. Click on **Footnote**. The Footnote and Endnote dialog box will open.

3. Click on **Options**. The Note Options dialog box will open.

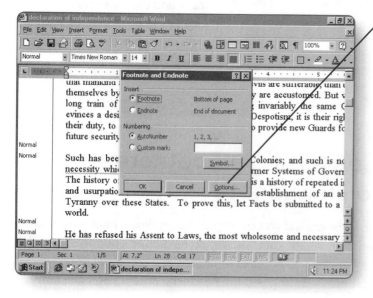

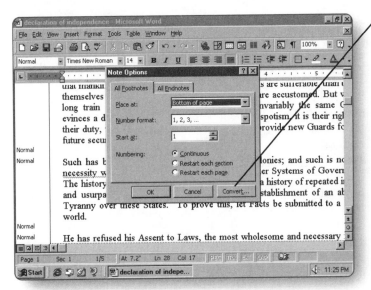

4. **Click** on **Convert**. The Convert Notes dialog box will open, with the option to convert the type of note you're using to the other type already selected.

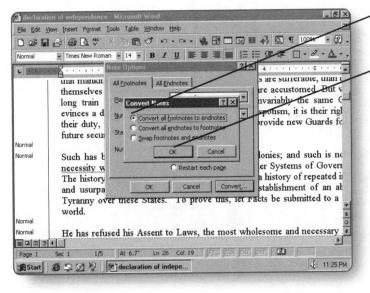

5. **Click** on an **option**. The option will be selected.

6. **Click** on **OK**. The Convert Notes dialog box will close, and the conversion will begin. The Note Options dialog box will open.

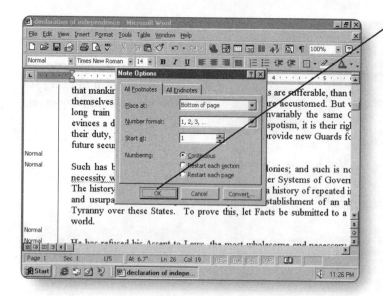

7. **Click** on **OK**. The Note Options dialog box will close. The Footnotes and Endnotes dialog box will open.

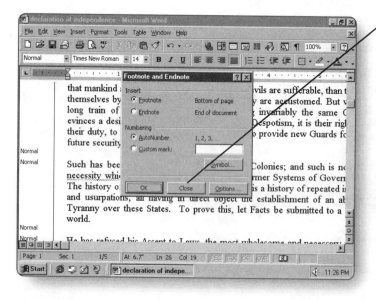

8. **Click** on **Close**. The Footnotes and Endnotes dialog box will close.

TIP

Be careful to click on Close and not on OK. Clicking on OK will result in Word inserting a new footnote or endnote.

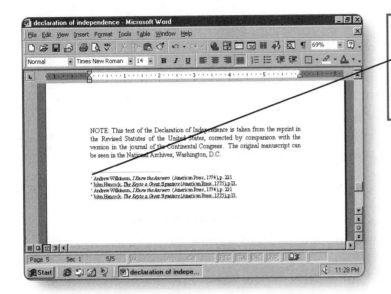

Part VI Review Questions

1. What types of elements are included in a style? *See "Working with Paragraph Styles" in Chapter 21*

2. What is the name of Word's default style? *See "Working with Word Styles" in Chapter 21*

3. If you delete a style, what happens to text that had that style applied to it? *See "Deleting a Style" in Chapter 21*

4. What does a template determine about a Word document? *See "Discovering Templates" in Chapter 22*

5. When applying a template to an open document, what is added to the current document? *See "Applying a Template" in Chapter 22*

6. Where does a header print? *See "Inserting a Header or Footer" in Chapter 23*

7. Where do Word's date and time fields get their information? *See "Adding Date, Time or Page Numbers" in Chapter 23*

8. What views can be used to see headers or footers? *See "Arranging Headers and Footers on Different Pages" in Chapter 23*

9. Where does Word place endnotes? *See "Creating a Footnote or Endnote" in Chapter 24*

10. What do you highlight to delete a footnote or endnote? *See "Deleting a Footnote or Endnote" in Chapter 24*

PART VII

Taking Word to the Web

25

Using a Wizard to Create Web Pages

Word 2000 makes creating a Web page almost as easy as creating a standard document. You can actually create Web pages in two different ways: you can use a wizard or template, or you can convert an existing Word document to Web page format—known as HTML *(HyperText Markup Language)*. Although the name sounds complicated, the process is very easy. In this chapter, you'll learn how to:

- Use the Web Page Wizard to create a Web page
- Insert links and graphics
- View your Web page
- Create a Web page from a Word document

Creating a Web Page

Studies have shown that Web surfers lose patience with Web pages that take longer than 20 seconds to load; therefore try to design your Web pages to load quickly. Large graphic images often slow the loading of a Web page.

Using the Web Page Wizard

Some people think that only a wizard can understand all the ins and outs of the World Wide Web. By using the Web Page Wizard you have the capacity to become a master Web page builder. Using the Web Page Wizard is the easiest way to create a Web page.

1. **Click** on **File**. The File menu will appear.

2. **Click** on **New**. The New dialog box will open.

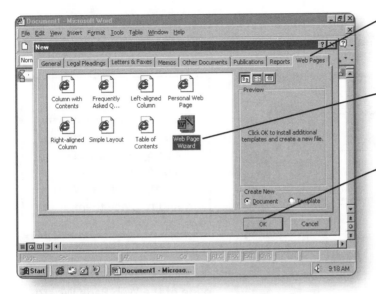

3. Click on the **Web Pages tab**. The Web Pages tab will come to the front.

4. Click on the **Web Page Wizard icon**. The icon will be highlighted.

5. Click on **OK**. The beginning screen of the Web Page Wizard will appear.

It may take a few moments the first time you use this feature. Windows may need to update the settings for Microsoft Office.

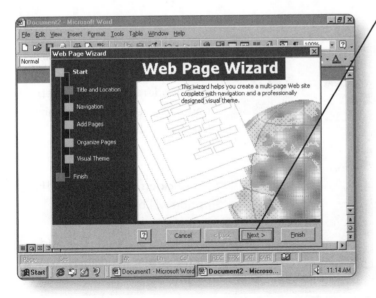

6. Click on **Next**. The next page of the wizard will display.

7. Type a **title** for the Web site. The text will appear in the Web site title: text box.

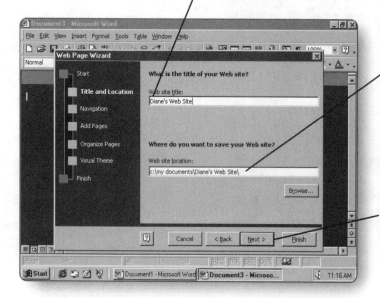

TIP

You can optionally specify a file location for your Web pages. Generally however, it's best just to leave them where Word is trying to place them.

8. Click on **Next**. The next page of the Web Page Wizard will appear.

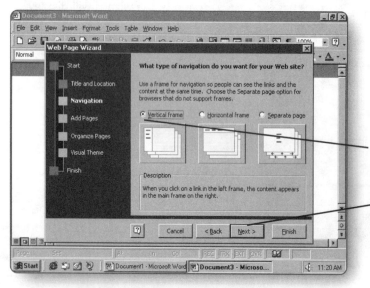

Next you'll need to specify a format of *frames*, which are independent boxes on a Web page. Frames help to organize links and other options on a page.

9. Click on a **frame style**. The option will be selected.

10. Click on **Next**. The Add Pages screen will display.

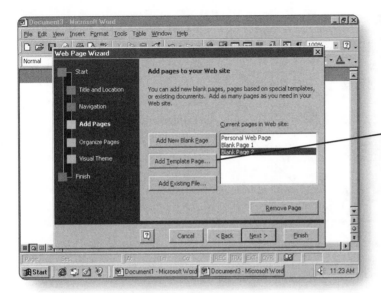

Now you'll need to decide what types of additional pages you'll want for your Web site. The easiest method is to use Word's predefined templates.

11. Click on **Add Template Page**. A dialog box displaying the different types of templates will open.

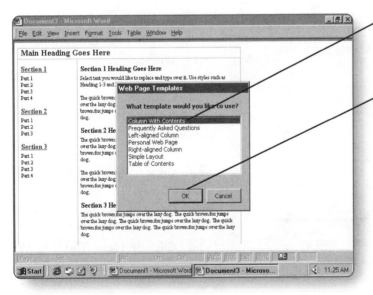

12. Click on an **option**. A sample of the selection will appear behind the dialog box.

13. Click on **OK**. The Web Page Wizard will reappear.

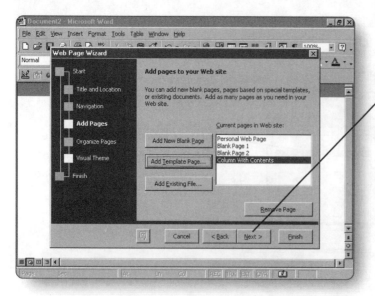

14. **Repeat steps 10 through 13** for each additional page you want to include.

15. **Click** on **Next**. The Organize Pages screen will display.

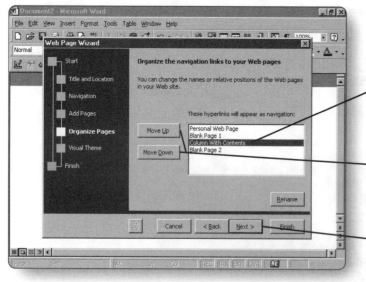

Here you can decide the order in which you want the various pages to appear.

16. **Click** on a page **description**. The description will be highlighted.

17. **Click** on **Move Up or Move Down**. The page order will be rearranged.

18. **Click** on **Next**. The Themes page will display.

Using Word Themes

Themes are a collection of background colors/patterns, bullet styles, line styles, heading styles, and font styles. When you select a theme, you make available, in your document, all the styles associated with the theme. Most people use themes when designing Web pages.

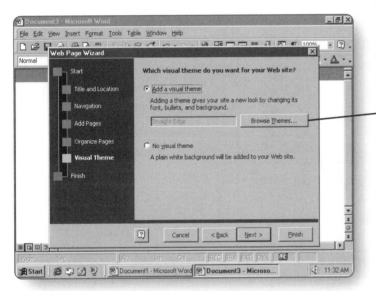

1. Click on **Browse Themes**. A list of available themes will display.

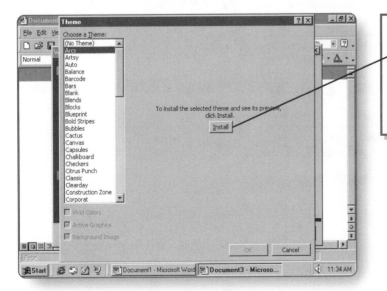

TIP

If you don't see a preview, you'll need to click on Install and insert your Word CD to install Themes.

2. Click on a **Theme**. A sample of the theme will display in the preview box.

3. Click on **OK**. The Theme dialog box will close and the Web Page Wizard will redisplay.

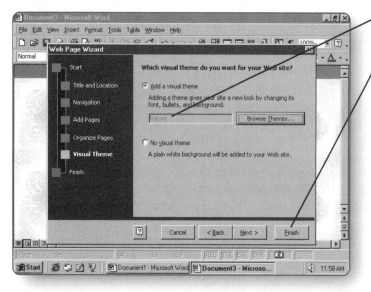

The name of the theme you selected will display.

4. Click on **Finish**. The Wizard will close.

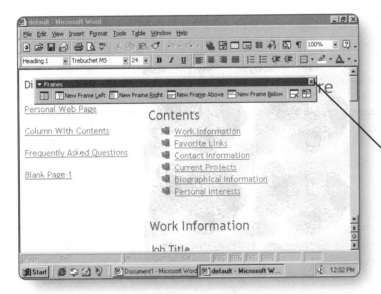

The individual pages will be saved and Word will display the opening (default) page as well as the Frames toolbar. You'll now be ready to edit the page with your information.

5. **Click** on the Frames toolbar **close box**. The Frames toolbar will close.

Editing a Web Page

Now that the Web Page Wizard has supplied a skeleton Web page, you'll want to make changes to it.

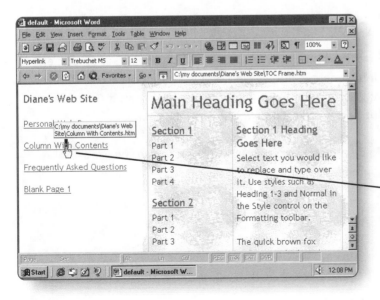

Typing Text

The Web Page Wizard supplies "dummy" text where you should supply real text. You change the text on a Web page document the same way that you change text in any Word document.

1. **Click** on a **page** to edit. The selected page will display in a different frame.

2. Select some **text**. The text will be highlighted.

3. Type the **replacement text**. The new text will replace the highlighted text.

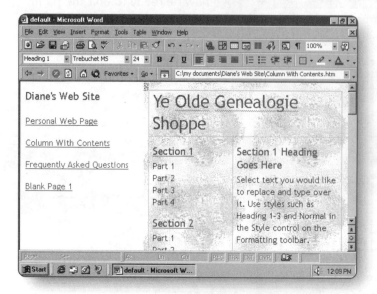

4. Repeat steps 2 and 3 for each portion of text to be modified. The text will appear on screen.

Adding Scrolling Text

Scrolling text on a Web page provides quite a dramatic effect. Unfortunately, not all Web browsers support scrolling text. Any surfer who happens to be using a browser that doesn't support scrolling text will see regular text.

To create scrolling text, you'll need to use the Web Tools toolbar.

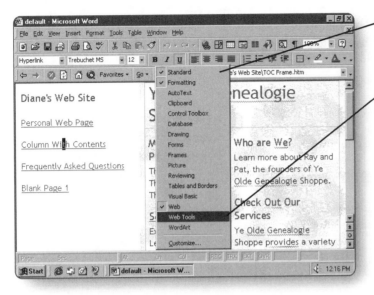

1. Right-click on any **toolbar** button. A shortcut menu will appear.

2. Click on **Web Tools**. The Web Tools toolbar will display.

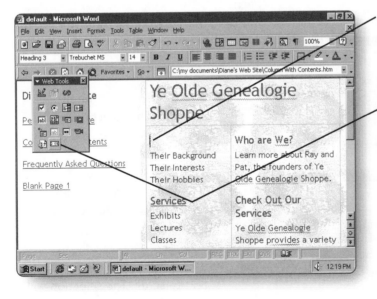

3. Click the **mouse pointer** at the location you want the scrolling text. The blinking insertion point will appear.

4. Click on the **Scrolling Text** tool from the Web Tools toolbar. The Scrolling Text dialog box will open.

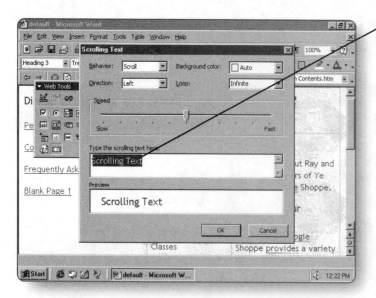

5. Select the words **Scrolling Text** in the Type the scrolling text here: text box. The text will be highlighted.

6. Type the **text** you want to appear. The new text will replace the original text.

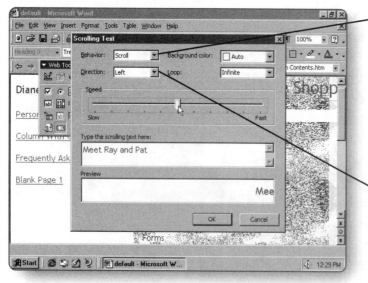

7. Click on the **Behavior: down arrow**. A list of choices will appear.

8. Click on a **method** of scrolling. The selection will appear in the Behavior: drop-down list box.

9. Click on **Direction: down arrow**. A list of choices will appear.

10. Click on a **direction** for the text to scroll. The selection will appear in the Direction: drop-down list box.

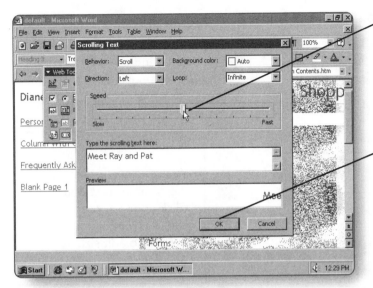

11. **Drag** the **speed knob** to the left or right. Dragging to the left will slow down the speed of the scrolling text, while dragging to the right will increase the speed.

12. **Click** on **OK**. The Scrolling Text dialog box will close and you will return to your Web page.

It may appear that the right column has disappeared. It hasn't, but because the box surrounding the scrolling text box is long, you can't see it. You'll probably need to resize the scrolling text box.

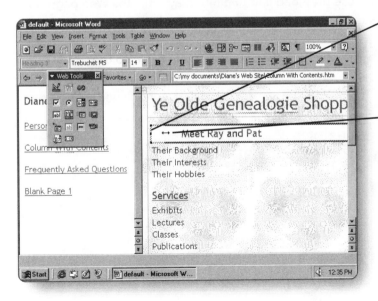

13. **Position** the **mouse pointer** over the left selection handle. The mouse pointer will turn to a double-headed arrow.

14. **Press the mouse button and drag** the **handle** to the right. A dotted line will indicate the new size.

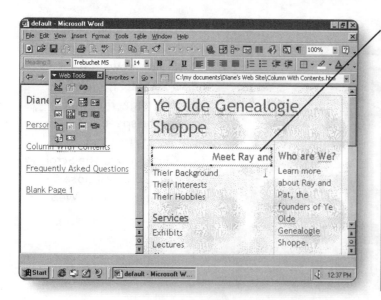

15. Release the **mouse button**. The text box will be resized, and when it's small enough, you'll be able to see the balance of your text.

> **TIP**
>
> You can now further edit the scrolling text object. Click on the appropriate choices from the Standard toolbar to edit size, font, or color.

Including a Background Sound

You can have a background sound play when someone views your Web page; background sounds don't slow Web browsers because they load and begin to play while the Web page is loading.

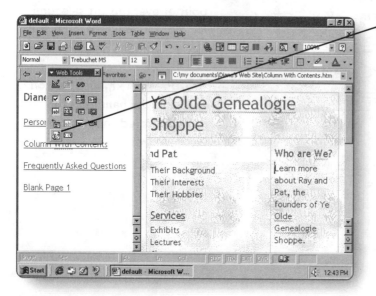

1. On the Web tools toolbar, **click** on the **Sound button**. The Background Sound dialog box will open.

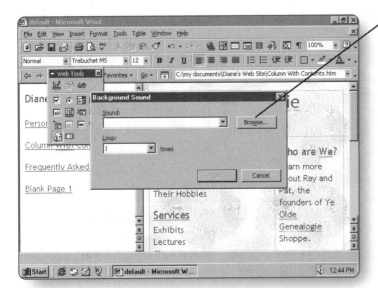

2. Click on **Browse**. A list of sounds available on your hard drive will display.

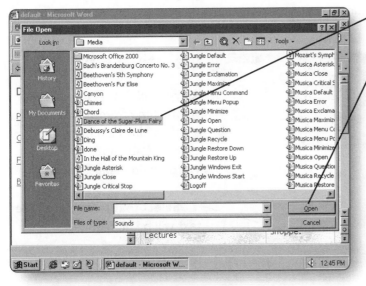

3. Click on a **sound**. The file name will be highlighted.

4. Click on **Open**. The Background Sound dialog box will reopen.

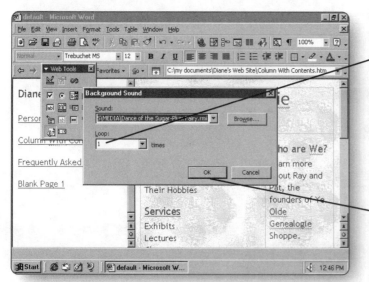

Changing the number in the Loop: drop-down list box determines the number of times the sound will play.

6. Click on **OK**. The sound will begin to play and will play all the way through once until it finishes.

In the future, the sound will play only when you open the Web page or, after you publish the page, when a Web surfer views your page.

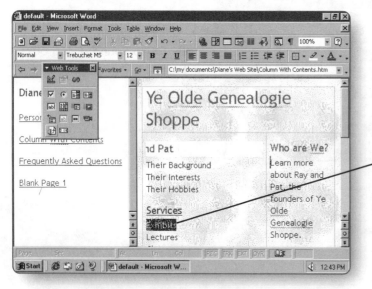

Inserting Links

A *hyperlink* is text that allows you to jump from one area to another. Links are frequently used in Web pages and in Word's help menus.

1. Select text to be a link. The text will be highlighted.

2. Click on **Insert**. The Insert menu will appear.

3. Click on **Hyperlink**. The Insert Hyperlink dialog box will open.

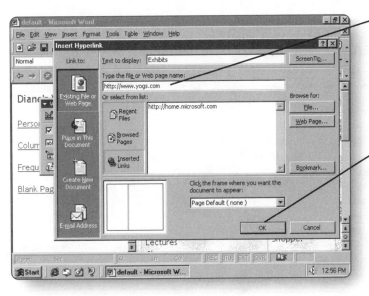

4. Type the **path** and **file name** of the Web page or document you want to link to your Web page. The name will display in the Type the file or Web page name: text box.

5. Click on **OK**. Word will create a link to the document.

Inserting a Picture

Web pages usually include some graphics to create visual interest. You can insert and edit a drawing or picture into a Web page by following the directions in Chapter 11, *"Communicating Your Ideas with Clip Art."*

Saving Your Web Pages

When you save a Web page that you create, you actually save several different files. Word saves each element of the Web page (graphic images, bullets, lines, and so on) separately using the path name you specified while using the Web Page Wizard. Keeping all the files for a Web page together becomes important when it's time to publish the Web page; you'll need to make sure then that you publish all the files.

1. **Click** on **File**. The File menu will appear.

2. **Click** on **Save As**. The Save As dialog box will open.

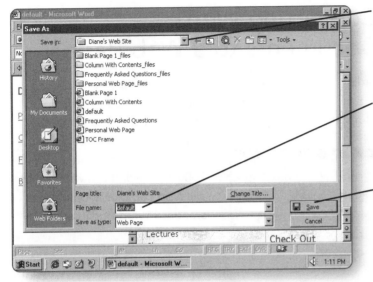

Notice that the default folder Word suggests is the one you identified in the Web Page Wizard.

You can leave the name "Default.htm" or you can change it to something you'll recognize.

3. Click on **Save**. The current page and all pages associated with the Web page will be saved.

Publishing Web Documents

You've created your Web documents; now the issue becomes how to make your Web pages accessible to your company's intranet or on the World Wide Web.

You'll need to save your Web pages and their related files (the graphics, lines, bullets, and so on) to a *Web folder*, which is a shortcut to a Web server. The Web server must support Web folders.

This varies between servers, so you'll need to check with your system administrator or Internet Service Provider.

Converting Word Documents to a Web Page

Earlier in this chapter, you learned how to use the Web Page Wizard to create a Web page. But suppose that you have information in a regular Word document that you would like to publish as a Web page. You don't need to re-create it. Word 2000 also includes a wizard that will help you convert multiple standard Word documents into Web pages.

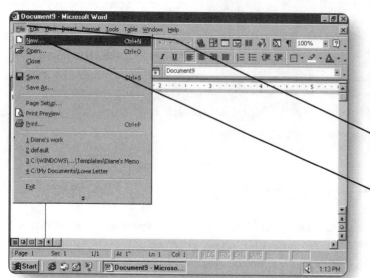

1. Click on **File**. The File menu will appear.

2. Click on **New**. The New dialog box will open.

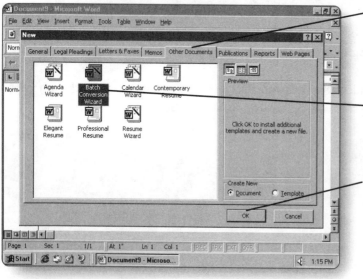

3. Click on the **Other Documents tab**. The Other Documents tab will come to the front.

4. Click on the **Batch Conversion Wizard**. The icon will be highlighted.

5. Click on **OK**. The Conversion Wizard will begin.

6. Click on **Next**. The From/To page will display.

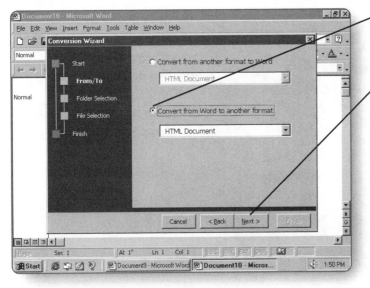

7. Click on **Convert from Word to another format**. The option will be selected.

8. Click on **Next**. The Folder selection page will display.

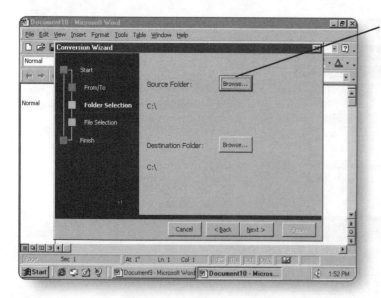

9. Click on the Source Folder: **Browse button**. The Browse for Folder dialog box will open.

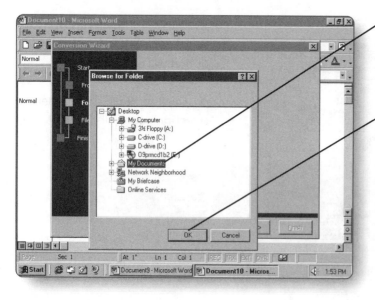

10. Click on the **folder** that contains the files you want to convert. The folder name will be highlighted.

11. Click on **OK**. The Folder Selection page will redisplay.

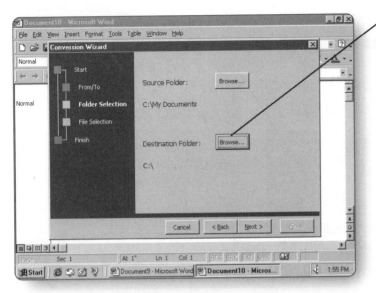

12. Click on the Destination Folder: **Browse button**. The Browse for Folder dialog box will open.

13. Click on the **folder** you want to contain the converted files. The folder name will be highlighted.

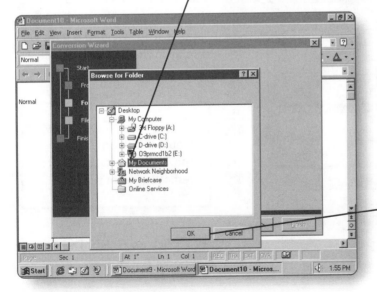

TIP

You can save the files to the same folder where they are originally stored because you won't be overwriting files, just adding another version.

14. Click on **OK**. The Folder Selection page will redisplay.

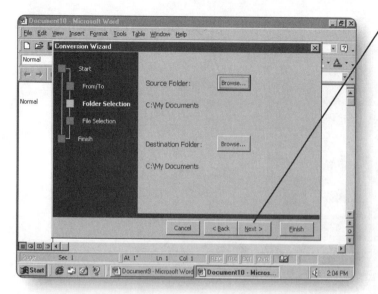

15. **Click** on **Next**. The File Selection page will display.

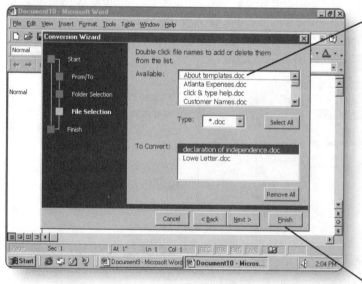

16. **Double-click** on each **file** you want to convert to an HTML document from the Available: list box. The selected names will display in the To Convert: list box.

> ## TIP
> Double-click on a file in the To Convert: list box to remove it from the list.

17. **Click** on **Finish**. The wizard will begin the conversion.

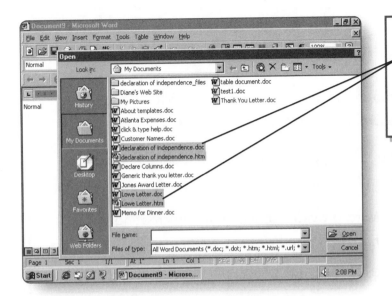

TIP

When you click on File, Open, you'll see .HTM files for each file you chose to convert.

Part VII Review Questions

1. What are the two different ways you can create a Web page? *See "Using a Wizard to Create Web Pages" in Chapter 25*

2. What is the format of a Web page called? *See "Using a Wizard to Create Web Pages" in Chapter 25*

3. What is the feature Word provides to assist you in creating Web Pages? *See "Using the Web Page Wizard" in Chapter 25*

4. What purpose do frames provide on a Web page? *See "Using the Web Page Wizard" in Chapter 25*

5. What are themes? *See "Using Word Themes" in Chapter 25*

6. What happens to scrolling text if a user's Web browser doesn't support scrolling text? *See "Adding Scrolling Text" in Chapter 25*

7. Do Web pages load slower if they have a background sound included? *See "Including a Background Sound" in Chapter 25*

8. What are two of the most common uses for a hyperlink? *See "Inserting Links" in Chapter 25*

9. What is the Batch Conversion Wizard used for? *See "Converting Word Documents to a Web Page" in Chapter 25*

10. What is the file name extension given to Web page documents? *See "Converting Word Documents to a Web Page" in Chapter 25*

PART VIII

Appendixes

A

Office 2000 Installation

Installing Office 2000 is typically very quick and easy. In this appendix, you'll learn how to:

- Install Office 2000 on your computer
- Choose which Office components you want to install
- Detect and repair problems
- Reinstall Office
- Add and remove components
- Uninstall Office 2000 completely
- Install content from other Office CDs

Installing the Software

The installation program for the Office 2000 programs is automatic. In most cases, you can simply follow the instructions onscreen.

> ## NOTE
> When you insert the Office 2000 CD for the first time, you may see a message that the installer has been updated, prompting you to restart your system. Do so, and when you return to Windows after restarting, remove the CD and reinsert it so that the Setup program starts up automatically again.

1. **Insert** the **Office 2000 CD-ROM** into your computer's CD-ROM drive. The Windows Installer will start and the Customer Information dialog box will open.

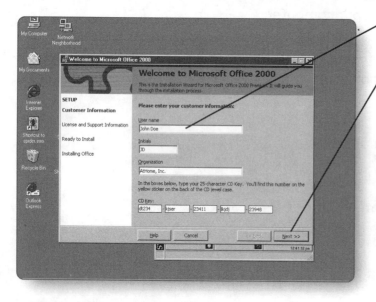

2. **Type** all of the **information** requested.

3. **Click** on **Next**. The End User License Agreement will appear.

> ## NOTE
> You'll find the CD Key number on a sticker on the back of the Office CD jewel case.

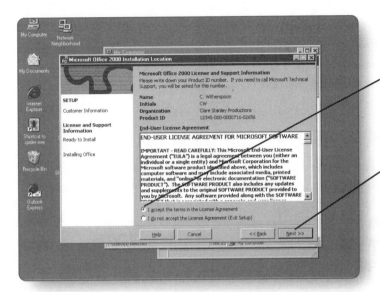

4. Read the **License Agreement**.

5. Click on the **I accept the terms in the License Agreement option button**. The option will be selected.

6. Click on **Next**. The Ready To Install dialog box will open.

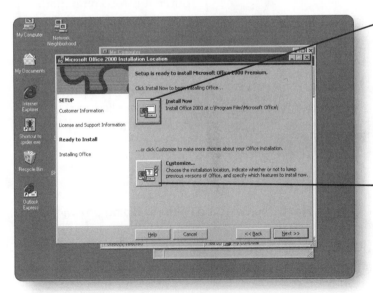

7a. Click on the **Install Now button.** Use this option to install Office on your computer with the default settings. This is the recommended installation for most users.

OR

7b. Click on the **Customize button**, if you want to choose which components to install or where to install them. The Installation Location dialog box will open. Then see the next section, "Choosing Components," for guidance.

8. Wait while the **Office software** installs on your computer. When the setup has completed, the Installer Information box will open.

9. **Click** on **Yes**. The Setup Wizard will restart your computer. After your computer has restarted, Windows will update your system settings and then finish the Office installation and configuration process.

Choosing Components

If you selected option 7b in the previous section, you have the choice of installing many different programs and components.

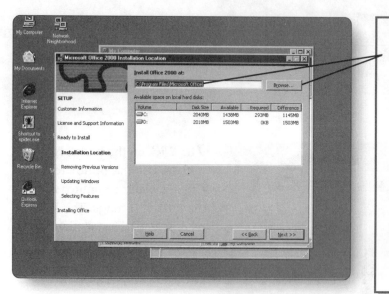

NOTE

For a custom installation, you have the option of placing Office in a different location on your computer. It is recommended that you use the default installation location. If you want to install Office in a different directory, type the directory path in the text box or click on the Browse button to select a directory.

1. **Click** on **Next**. The Selecting Features dialog box will open.

2. **Click** on a **plus sign (+)** to expand a list of features. The features listed under the category will appear.

3. **Click** on the **down arrow (▼)** to the right of the hard drive icon. A menu of available installation options for the feature will appear.

4. **Click** on the **button** next to the individual option, and choose a setting for that option:

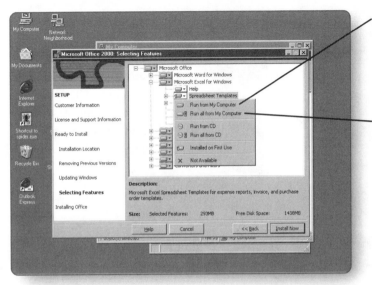

- **Run from My Computer**. The component will be fully installed, so that you will not need the Office CD in the CD-ROM drive to use it.

- **Run all from My Computer**. The selected component and all the components subordinate to it will be fully installed.

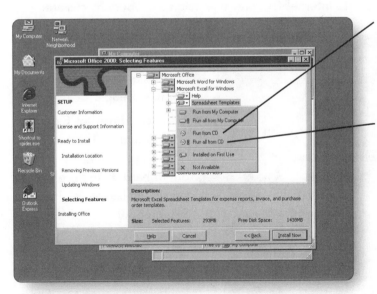

- **Run from CD**. The component will be installed, but you will need to have the Office CD in the CD-ROM drive to use it.

- **Run all from CD**. The selected component and all the components subordinate to it will need to have the Office CD in the CD-ROM drive to use it.

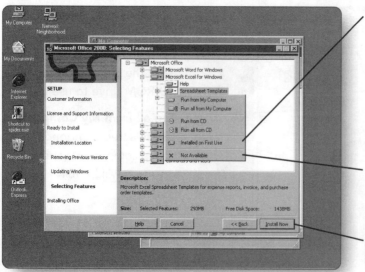

● **Installed on First Use**. The first time you try to activate the component, you will be prompted to insert the Office CD to fully install it. This is good for components that you are not sure whether you will need or not.

● **Not Available**. The component will not be installed at all.

5. Click on **Install Now**. The Installing dialog box will open.

In a Custom installation, you'll be asked whether you want to update Internet Explorer to version 5.0. Your choices are:

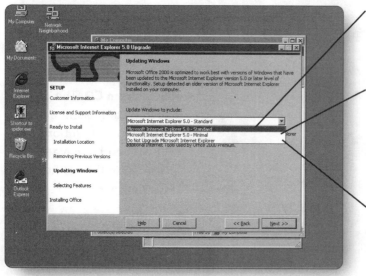

● **Microsoft Internet Explorer 5.0—Standard**. This is the default, and the right choice for most people.

● **Microsoft Internet Explorer 5.0—Minimal**. This is the right choice if you are running out of hard disk space but still would like to use Internet Explorer 5.0.

● **Do Not Upgrade Microsoft Internet Explorer**. Use this if you don't want Internet Explorer (for example, if you always use another browser such as Netscape Navigator, or if you have been directed by your system administrator not to install Internet Explorer 5).

Working with Maintenance Mode

Maintenance Mode is a feature of the Setup program. Whenever you run the Setup program again, after the initial installation, Maintenance Mode starts automatically. It enables you to add or remove features, repair your Office installation (for example, if files have become corrupted), and remove Office completely. There are several ways to rerun the Setup program (and thus enter Maintenance Mode):

- Reinsert the Office 2000 CD. The Setup program may start automatically.

- If the Setup program does not start automatically, double-click on the CD icon in the My Computer window.

- If double-clicking on the CD icon doesn't work, right-click on the CD icon and click on Open from the shortcut menu. Then double-click on the Setup.exe file in the list of files that appears.

- From the Control Panel in Windows, click on the Add/Remove Programs button. Then on the Install/Uninstall tab, click on Microsoft Office 2000 in the list, and finally, click on the Add/Remove button.

After entering Maintenance Mode, choose the button for the activity you want. Each option is briefly described in the following sections.

Repairing or Reinstalling Office

If an Office program is behaving strangely, or refuses to work, chances are good that a needed file has become corrupted.

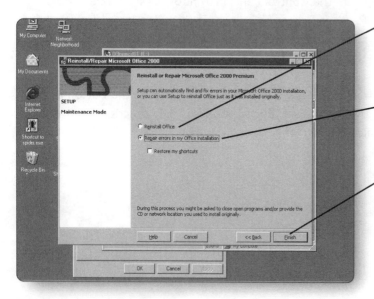

But which file? You have no way of knowing, so you can't fix the problem yourself.

If this happens, you can either repair Office or completely reinstall it. Both options are accessed from the Repair Office button in Maintenance Mode.

1. Click on the **Repair Office button** in Maintenance Mode.

2a. Click on **Reinstall Office** to repeat the last installation.

OR

2b. Click on Repair errors in my Office installation to simply fix what's already in place.

3. Click on **Finish**. The process will start.

> **TIP**
>
> You can also repair individual Office programs by opening the Help menu in each program and clicking on Detect and Repair. This works well if you are sure that one certain program is causing the problem, and it's quicker than asking the Setup program to check all of the installed programs.

Adding and Removing Components

Adding and removing components works just like selecting the components initially.

1. Click on the **Add or Remove Features button** in Maintenance Mode. The Update Features window will appear. This window works exactly the same as the window you saw in the "Choosing Components" section earlier in this appendix.

> **NOTE**
>
> Some features will attempt to automatically install themselves as you are working. If you have set a feature to be installed on first use, attempt to access that feature. You will be prompted to insert your Office 2000 CD, and the feature will be installed without further prompting.

Removing Office from Your PC

In the unlikely event that you should need to remove Office from your PC completely, click on Remove Office from the Maintenance Mode screen. Then follow the prompts to remove it from your system.

After removing Office, you will probably have a few remnants left behind that the Uninstall routine didn't catch. For example, there will probably still be a Microsoft Office folder in your Program Files folder or wherever you installed the program. You can delete that folder yourself.

CAUTION

If you plan to reinstall Office later, and you have created any custom templates, toolbars, or other items, you may want to leave the Microsoft Office folder alone, so that those items will be available to you after you reinstall.

Installing Content from Other Office CDs

Depending on the version of Office you bought, you may have more than one CD in your package. CD 1 contains all the basic Office components, such as Word, Outlook, PowerPoint, Excel, Access, and Internet Explorer. It may be the only CD you need to use.

The other CDs contain extra applications that come with the specific version of Office you purchased. They may include Publisher, FrontPage, a language pack, or a programmer and developer resource kit. Each of these discs has its own separate installation program.

The additional CDs should start their Setup programs automatically when you insert the disk in your drive. If not, browse the CD's content in My Computer or Windows Explorer and double-click on the Setup.exe file that you find on it.

B

Using Keyboard Shortcuts

You may have noticed the keyboard shortcuts listed on the right side of several of the menus. You can use these shortcuts to execute commands without using the mouse to activate menus. You may want to memorize these keyboard shortcuts. Not only will they speed your productivity, but they will also help decrease wrist strain caused by excessive mouse usage. In this appendix, you'll learn how to:

 Get up to speed with frequently used keyboard shortcuts

 Use keyboard combinations to edit text

Learning the Basic Shortcuts

Trying to memorize all these keyboard shortcuts isn't as hard as you may think. Windows applications all share the same keyboard combinations to execute common commands. Once you get accustomed to using some of these keyboard shortcuts in Word, try them out on some of the other Office programs.

Getting Help

You don't need to wade through menus to get some help using the program. Try these useful keyboard shortcuts.

To execute this command	Do this
Use Help	Press the F1 key
Use the What's This? Button	Press Shift+F1

Working with Documents

The following table shows you a few of the more common keyboard shortcuts that you may want to use when working with documents.

To execute this command	Do this
Create a new document	Press Ctrl+N
Open a different document	Press Ctrl+O
Switch between open documents	Press Ctrl+F6
Save a document	Press Ctrl+S
Print a document	Press Ctrl+P
Close a document	Press Ctrl+W

Working with Text

The easiest keyboard shortcuts to learn are those that manipulate text. Try your hand at selecting, editing, and formatting text using some of the commonly used text combinations.

Selecting Text

Before you can perform any editing and formatting task to the text in your document, you'll need to select the text. This table shows you how to use keyboard combinations to select text. Before you begin, you'll need to move the cursor to the beginning of the text that you want to select.

To execute this command	Do this
Highlight the character to the right of the cursor	Press Shift+Right Arrow
Highlight the character to the left	Press Shift+Left Arrow
Highlight an entire word	Press Ctrl+Shift+Right Arrow
Highlight an entire line	Press Shift+End
Highlight a paragraph	Press Ctrl+Shift+Down Arrow
Select an entire page	Press Ctrl+A
Go to a specific page	Press Ctrl+G

Editing Text

Once you have selected the text to which you want to make the editing changes, apply one of the combinations in the following table.

To execute this command	Do this
Delete the character to the left of the cursor	Press Backspace
Delete the character to the right	Press Delete
Delete the word to the left of the cursor	Press Ctrl+Backspace
Delete the word to the right	Press Ctrl+Delete
Delete selected text	Press Ctrl+X
Make a copy of selected text	Press Ctrl+C
Paste the copied text	Press Ctrl+V
Spell check a document	Press the F7 key
Find text in a document	Press Ctrl+F
Replace text in a document	Press Ctrl+H
Undo an action	Press Ctrl+Z
Redo an action	Press Ctrl+Y

Formatting Text

To make your text look good, you may want to change the font, font style, or one of the many standardized paragraph styles.

To execute this command	Do this
Change the font	Press Ctrl+Shift+F
Change the size of the font	Press Ctrl+Shift+P
Make selected text bold	Press Ctrl+B
Make selected text italic	Press Ctrl+I
Make selected text underlined	Press Ctrl+U
Make selected text double underlined	Press Ctrl+Shift+D
Remove character formatting	Press Ctrl+Spacebar
Single space a paragraph	Press Ctrl+1
Double space a paragraph	Press Ctrl+2
Set 1.5 line spacing	Press Ctrl+5
Center a paragraph	Press Ctrl+E
Left align a paragraph	Press Ctrl+L
Right align a paragraph	Press Ctrl+R
Justify a paragraph	Press Ctrl+J
Left indent a paragraph	Press Ctrl+M
Right indent a paragraph	Press Ctrl+Shift+M
Remove paragraph formatting	Press Ctrl+Q

Glossary

Alignment. The arrangement of text or an object in relation to a document's margins or the edges of a cell in a table. Alignment can be left, right, centered, or justified.

Applet. A small software program provided with Word for Windows that enables you to perform additional operations, such as WordArt, for enhanced text effects.

AutoCorrect. A feature of Word that automatically corrects common spelling mistakes (such as "teh" for "the").

AutoFormat. A Word feature used with tables. AutoFormat enables you to apply predefined sets of formatting to a table's text, rows, and columns.

AutoText. A feature of Word that enables you to save a set of text and insert it in your document by typing a word or phrase.

Bold. A style applied to text to make the font lines thicker.

Border. A visible line surrounding text or objects.

Break. An instruction embedded into a Word document that indicates a change, such as a Page Break, to start a new page.

Bullet. A symbol that precedes an item in a list. Bullets can be any shape found in a typeface, but most commonly, are solid black circles.

Cell. The area in which a row and column in a table intersect.

Chart. Also called Graph. A visual representation of numerical data.

Clip Art. A ready-made drawing that can be inserted in a Word document.

Clip Gallery. A collection of clip art, pictures, and sound files that comes with Microsoft Word.

Collect and Paste. A feature of Word that enables you to copy several selections to the Windows clipboard and paste them in a new location all at once.

Data form. A place where data, such as data used in a mail merge operation, is stored in individual records.

Data source. In a Word for Windows mail merge, the information that is used to replace field codes with personalized information, such as names and addresses.

Desktop. The main area of Windows where you can open and manage files and programs.

Dialog box. A window that appears during some procedures in Word that enables you to make settings by entering text, selecting things from lists, or checking boxes or buttons.

Drag and drop. A method of moving text or objects by clicking on an object with a mouse, dragging it to a new location, and releasing the mouse button to drop it into its new location.

Field. In a form letter, a field is a placeholder for corresponding data.

Fill. To place a color or line pattern in the interior of an object, such as a square or cell of a table.

Font. A design set of letters, symbols, and numbers.

Footer. Text entered in a footer placeholder, which is then automatically placed at the bottom of each document page.

Format. To add settings for font, font style, color, and line style to text or an object.

Format painter. A feature of Word that enables you to easily copy all formatting that's applied to one set of text to any other.

Go To. A feature of Word that enables you to enter a variety of criteria, such as page number or specific text, so that Word can place that location in your document on screen.

Gradient. A shading effect that moves from lighter to darker in such a way that it suggests a light source shining on the object containing the gradient.

Graph. Also called Chart. A graph is a visual representation of numerical data.

Gridlines. The lines dividing rows and columns in a table.

Handle. Small squares that appear when you select an object that enable you to resize it.

Header. Text entered in a header placeholder, which is then automatically placed at the top of each document page.

Highlight. A feature that places colored highlighting on screen for selected text.

Icon. A graphic representation used on toolbars to represent the various functions performed when those buttons are pressed with a mouse.

Indent. To set text away from a margin by a specific distance, as at the beginning of a paragraph.

Italic. A font style that applies a slanted effect to text.

Justify. One type of alignment that spreads letters on a line so that they are spaced out between the left and right margin.

Landscape. Orientation of a document so that, when printed, text runs from left to right along the longer edge of a piece of paper.

Legend. In a chart, a feature that defines the relationship of the graphic symbols to the data elements for the reader.

Line style. Effects using width, arrows, and dashes that can be applied to a line.

Mail merge. A procedure in which you use a form document, insert placeholders for types of data (called fields) and merge that document with specific data to produce personalized mailings.

Margin. A border that runs around the outside of a document page, in which nothing will print.

Object. Any graphic, drawing, or other multimedia file placed within a Word document that can be selected and formatted.

Office Assistant. A feature of Word 2000 that enables you to enter questions in natural English language sentences.

Orientation. A setting that designates whether a document will print with text running along the long or short side of a piece of paper.

Outline. A hierarchy of lines of text that suggests major and minor ideas.

Page break. An instruction that can be embedded into a Word document to instruct Word to move to a new page at that point.

Page Setup. The collection of settings that relate to how the pages of your document are set up, including margins, orientation, and the size of paper on which each page will print.

Paste. To place text or an object on the Windows clipboard in a document.

Pattern. An arrangement of dots or lines that can be used to fill the center of an object.

Portrait. An orientation that places text from left to right along the shorter side of a piece of paper.

Print Layout. A view in Word that is commonly used for arranging objects on a page and drawing.

Print Preview. A Word feature that enables you to see a preview of how your printed document will look on screen before you print it.

Protect. To make settings so that only someone with the correct password can modify a Word document.

Redo. To restore an action you have undone using the Undo command.

Right aligned. Text that is lined up with the right side of a tab setting or document margin, as with a row of numbers in a column.

Rotate. To move an object along a 360 degree path.

Ruler. An on-screen feature provided to help you place text and objects accurately on a page.

Scroll bar. A mechanism used with a mouse for navigating around a document horizontally or vertically.

Selection bar. An invisible bar along the left side of a document. When you place your mouse cursor in the bar, it can be used to select a single line or multiple lines of text.

Shading. A color that fills an object.

Shadow. A drawing effect that appears to place a shadow alongside an object.

Sort. To arrange data alphanumerically in either ascending (A-Z) or descending (Z-A) order.

Spelling checker. A feature of Word that checks the spelling of words in your document against a dictionary and flags possible errors for correction.

Status Bar. An area at the bottom of Word for Windows that provides information about the document, such as what page, line, and column your cursor is currently resting in.

Style. A predefined set of formats that you can apply to text all at once.

Symbol. A typeface that uses graphics such as circles, percentage signs, or smiling faces in place of letters and numbers.

Tab. A setting that can be placed along the width of a line of text that enables you to quickly jump your cursor to that setting.

Table. A collection of columns and rows, forming cells at their intersection, to organize sets of data.

Template. A predefined collection of formatting and style settings on which you can base a new document.

Text box. A floating text object that is created using the Word drawing toolbar; text can be entered into this object, which can be moved and resized, just like graphic objects.

Text wrap. This feature forces newly entered text to wrap to the next line when the insertion point reaches the right margin.

Tool tip. A Word Help feature that displays the name of a tool in a small box when you move your cursor over the tool.

Undo. To reverse the last action performed.

Uppercase. A capital letter.

View. In software, various displays of documents or information that enable you to perform different tasks or see different perspectives on information; for example, the Outline view in Word.

Wizard. A feature that walks you through certain procedures, producing something, such as a table, letter, or chart, based on answers you give to questions and selections made in Wizard dialog boxes.

WordArt. An applet included with Word used for adding special effects to text, such as curving the text.

Word count. A tally of the number of words in a document.

Wrap. See Text Wrap.

Zoom. To modify view settings so that what you are seeing on your screen is a percentage (larger or smaller) of a document page's actual size.

Index

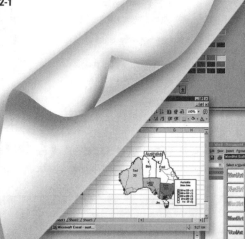